# The Evolution of Data Protection Laws in China, Japan, and Korea

Hiroshi Miyashita • Nohyoung Park
Xiangshun Ding
Editors

# The Evolution of Data Protection Laws in China, Japan, and Korea

Springer

*Editors*
Hiroshi Miyashita
Faculty of Policy Studies
Chuo University
Tokyo, Japan

Nohyoung Park
School of Law
Korea University
Seoul, Korea (Republic of)

Xiangshun Ding
School of Law
Beijing Foreign Studies University
Beijing, China

ISBN 978-981-95-8608-0 ISBN 978-981-95-8609-7 (eBook)
https://doi.org/10.1007/978-981-95-8609-7



This Springer imprint is published by the registered company Springer Nature Singapore Pte Ltd.
The registered company address is: 152 Beach Road, #21-01/04 Gateway East, Singapore 189721, Singapore

# Introduction

## Overlapping Consensus Findings in China, Japan, and Korea

The reason for studying data protection laws in China, Japan, and Korea lies not only in their geographic proximity and economic ties, but also in the fact that these three countries are emerging technological drivers attracting global attention. China in AI, 5G/6G, and EVs; Japan in edge AI, smart mobility, and satellite data; and Korea in semiconductors, humanoid robotics, and biotechnology. World Bank's 'Population' and 'GDP' statistics in 2024 note that these countries represent approximately 20% of the world's population (China accounting for about 1.4 billion people, Japan 125 million, and Korea 52 million) and nearly a quarter of global GDP, totaling around 25 trillion USD in nominal terms. According to the CAICT, Grand View Research on Artificial Intelligence Market Size, Share & Trends Analysis Report by Solution, by Technology 2025–2030, these three countries collectively command roughly 40–45% of the global AI market share, which is equivalent to the US AI market. Collectively, China, Japan, and Korea are at the forefront of digital transformation, making their approaches to digital regulation unavoidable reference points for stakeholders around the world.

Relations in China, Japan, and Korea have largely been understood through the lens of economic ties, with commercial interests often taking precedence. However, if the three countries are to deepen their economic cooperation in the future, it will be necessary to overcome legal differences. Even where their legal traditions and systems remain distinct, a certain degree of mutual understanding and interoperability will increasingly be required.

A widely held assumption suggests that Japan and Korea, having secured EU adequacy decisions, adhere to a Western-style framework, while China pursues a distinctive model that privileges state surveillance over individual privacy. As a broad sketch of the geopolitics surrounding data, this characterization is not entirely misplaced. This book also includes a legal analysis of the geopolitical issues surrounding data flows in China, Japan, and Korea, drawing on cases such as DeepSeek; however, it does not frame these issues as political controversies, but rather examines them from a purely legal or regulatory perspective. The differences among these three jurisdictions may lie less in the formal structure of their legal frameworks than in the manner of their implementation and enforcement, which in turn reflect distinct political contexts and social norms.

Yet, a careful examination of particular topics demonstrates that the assumption does not hold in every instance. As this book illustrates, the dualism of national security and individual rights is more nuanced: court decisions imposing certain restrictions on the so-called 'facial recognition heaven,' alongside a relatively stringent approach to harms arising from personal data processing when AI services are offered to the public. Even with respect to data transfers, while a security assessment is required, China simultaneously demonstrates a commitment to the deep integration of its digital economy with the international market. These observations may reveal parallels with the Japanese and Korean models, suggesting that much of China's exceptionalism seems to be a difference of degree except where issues become overtly politicized.

To invite readers to consider carefully whether and in what respects the Chinese model differs from those of Japan and Korea, and whether meaningful divergences also arise among all three jurisdictions, the book highlights common themes while exploring issues specific to each country. As a legal work authored by scholars of law, matters of geopolitics lie beyond its remit. This book consists of four parts: (1) overview of the legal regime on data protection, (2) data protection in the context of artificial intelligence, (3) biometric data, and (4) data transfer issues.

## Overview of This Book

Theme one explains a comparative analysis of the legal frameworks governing data privacy in the three countries (personal data, rights, duties, supervisory authority), supplemented by discussion of landmark judicial decisions including relationship between privacy and personal data. While each chapter addresses the distinct legal substance of its respective jurisdiction, they collectively identify converging regulatory trajectories and shared challenges. Du and Ding provide an extensive doctrinal analysis of China's rapidly maturing data governance frameworks. It focuses on the three central laws: the Cybersecurity Law (CSL), the Data Security Law (DSL), and the Personal Information Protection Law (PIPL). They demonstrate a structured exposition of how the CSL–DSL–PIPL 'Troika' interacts, highlighting the coherence of China's top-down legislative architecture. Noro outlines the history of the Act on the Protection of Personal Information (APPI), the process by which the public and private sector regimes were integrated, and the development of the right to privacy in Japan. He also explains that judicial practice treats the right to privacy as distinct from the APPI, giving it a unique position within Japan's data privacy architecture. Ko, Lee, and Kim examine the Korean Personal Information Protection Act (PIPA), highlighting the scope of personal information and the concept of pseudonymised information. A series of amendments to the PIPA have strengthened data-subject rights and expanded its extraterritorial application.

Theme Two deals with the regulation of biometric data across the three jurisdictions. While biometric data is commonly used for identity authentication, its secondary uses pose significant risks to privacy and individual autonomy. Each chapter examines the relevant legal frameworks and case-law governing biometric data, highlighting the implications of its sensitivity within the context of each jurisdiction's legal culture. Ma introduced some judicial cases on biometric data in China, including the case where the court ordered the deletion of the plaintiff's facial and fingerprint information. According to his analysis, China adopts a multilayered approach that combines comprehensive legislation with industry standards, judicial interpretations, and guiding cases to address specific scenarios, resulting in a diverse yet internally coherent mechanism for protecting personal biometric data. Miyashita examines the 'neuroprivacy', focusing on privacy concerns related to neurotechnology such as brain–computer interfaces (BCIs) in Japan. He suggests that neuroprivacy requires culturally contextualized legal safeguards and a rights-based approach encompassing cognitive liberty, bodily integrity, and mental autonomy. Chung analyzes how Korea's rigid consent and data-protection rules hinder the effective secondary use of biodata for research and argues that a dynamic consent model, using digital interfaces to allow ongoing, flexible, and transparent consent, offers a viable solution. He concludes that legal reforms are necessary to relax written-consent requirements, permit flexible modification of consent, and streamline oversight so that dynamic consent can function in practice.

Theme Three explores the evolving challenges that artificial intelligence (AI) technologies pose to data protection law. As AI systems increasingly rely on vast amounts of personal data, their deployment raises complex legal questions surrounding the existing data protection principles. This section introduces the emerging AI-related regulatory frameworks in China, Japan, and Korea, examining how these jurisdictions are responding to the interplay between AI innovation and individual data privacy. Through concrete case studies, the chapters analyze how existing data protection laws are being interpreted or adapted in the context of AI applications such as facial recognition, automated decision-making, and algorithmic profiling. China's AI policies, together with its data protection law and Civil Code jurisprudence, drawing on judicial cases concerning automated decision-making (ADM) and facial recognition technology (FRT). She concludes that China has taken a relatively stringent approach to addressing harms arising from personal data processing when AI services are offered to the public, while maintaining a more permissive stance toward the regulation of AI model training. Itakura contributes to the interaction between artificial intelligence and data protection law from a Japanese perspective, focusing on how existing legal frameworks such as the APPI address issues of personal data use, learning, and downstream deployment. This chapter argues that Japan's approach emphasizes flexibility, ex post governance, and innovation-friendly interpretation, reflecting both legal structure and policy choices distinct from the EU's rights-centered regulatory model. Park observes the "dual-track" approach in South Korea, balancing the promotion of industry under the AI Basic Act with the protection of individual rights under the Personal Information Protection Act (PIPA). His case study of Deepseek under PIPA demonstrates the proactive enforcement capacity of the Personal Information Protection

Commission (PIPC), including its reach over foreign operators, particularly regarding cross-border data transfers and transparency obligations.

Theme Four addresses the legal complexities surrounding cross-border data transfers. Data transfer is one of the most challenging aspects of data protection law, involving a delicate balance between facilitating international commerce and safeguarding personal information. The chapters in this section analyze the legal frameworks governing data transfers in China, Japan, and Korea, including mechanisms such as adequacy decisions, standard contractual clauses, and data localization requirements. Case studies illustrate how each jurisdiction navigates these issues in practice, shedding light on compliance challenges, enforcement trends, and regional responses to global standards such as the GDPR. Meng notes China has developed a comprehensive legal framework for cross-border data transfer, which is anchored by the Cybersecurity Law, Data Security Law, and Personal Information Protection Law, that balances openness with security, facilitates data flow, and safeguards national cyberspace and personal information rights. This system, reinforced by coordinated governance, streamlined compliance mechanisms, and active international engagement, aims to reduce compliance costs, promote digital trade, and integrate China's digital economy with global markets. Takahashi examines the key issues arising from cross-border data transfers in direct tax matters between the EU and Japan, where the automatic exchange of large volumes of personal data plays a central role in combating tax avoidance and evasion. While such data transfers can enhance the detection of high-risk cases, they also raise concerns about potential violations of taxpayers' rights to data protection. In Jeon's article, the 2023 amendments to Korea's PIPA shift cross-border data transfers from a consent-only model to a multi-pillar, risk-based framework, clarifying extraterritorial application and differentiating third-party provision from outsourcing. While the reforms enhance global interoperability and enforcement, gaps remain, notably the lack of SCC-like safeguards and a clear hierarchy among transfer bases.

## Future Ahead

Legal scholarship requires rigor and composure, along with generosity and adaptability. Our ability to sense each other fostered a commitment to respecting different legal cultures while learning from one another and gradually building overlapping consensus. The journey of this book started in 2012 when Miyashita and Ding met at Harvard Law School where they conducted research in comparative law as visiting scholars for the East Asian Legal Studies. Miyashita continued this exchange by giving lectures on privacy-related issues at Renmin University of China, while Ding delivered similar lectures at Chuo University. In 2017, the Cybersecurity Symposium held at Korean University became a turning point that broadened the venues and scope of our academic collaboration. Park, who also conducted research at Harvard Law School, further expanded the analytical horizon of privacy studies, encouraging us to consider these issues from a wider perspective. Park also gave lectures at

Chuo University, contributing to the steady deepening of legal exchanges among China, Japan, and Korea.

Against this background, a trilateral legal symposium among China, Japan, and Korea was held at Korean University in December 2023. At this symposium, early-career scholars from the three countries presented on legal challenges commonly shared in cyberspace. In August 2025, at the academic session of the LAWASIA Data Protection Workshop hosted by Chuo University, the outlines of each chapter of this volume were presented, allowing us to examine common issues across the three jurisdictions with the kind support of Dr. Sunil D.B. Abeyaratne, Professor Tatsuya Kitai, and Professor Nobuyuki Sato in bringing together the authors at the LAWASIA workshop. This book represents the culmination of these collaborative efforts with the funds from Chuo University Grant for Special Research "Comparative Study of Personal Data Protection Laws in Japan, China, and Korea."

There are sometimes sensitive political issues among China, Japan, and Korea. However, in our discipline as legal scholars, we are expected to refrain from politicizing contentious questions and instead to analyze them rigorously from a legal or regulatory perspective. We have continued future-oriented academic exchanges that respect each other's legal cultures, seek overlapping consensus, and foster the development of young researchers. While examining different legal systems to identify their differences is relatively straightforward, discerning the underlying intellectual connections through which universal truths are pursued presents a more rewarding challenge. To address this challenge, we believe that the neighboring countries of East Asia—China, Japan, and Korea—will continue to provide an important forum for academic exchange in the years to come. It is our hope that this book will serve as a starting point for such efforts.

Tokyo, Japan — Hiroshi Miyashita
Seoul, Republic of Korea — Nohyoung Park
Beijing, China — Xiangshun Ding

# Contents

# About the Editors

**Hiroshi Miyashita** is Professor of Law, Faculty of Policy Studies, at Chuo University. He specializes in Constitutional Law and Information Law.

Prior to this, he has served for the Office of Personal Information Protection, Quality-of-Life Policy Bureau, in the Cabinet Office. He received his LL.D. from Hitotsubashi University and has conducted research on data privacy as a visiting scholar at Harvard Law School, Brussels Privacy Hub, Vrije Universiteit Brussel, CRIDS (Centre de Recherche Information, Droit et Société), University of Namur, and Georg-August-Universität Göttingen. He serves as Vice-Chair of LAWASIA's Communications, Technology & Data Protection Committee.

He has been recognized with several academic awards for his contributions to the field of data protection and constitutional law, including the Telecommunications Advancement Foundation's Telecom Awards for Humanity and Social Science and KDDI's Nextcom Article Awards. He published six single-authored books on data privacy in Japanese and over 100 articles.

**Nohyoung Park** is Professor Emeritus at Korea University School of Law, where he had served as a faculty member since September 1990. Originally specializing in international economic law with a focus on the WTO, he has broadened his academic interests to include cybersecurity and data privacy, negotiation and mediation, and digital trade and AI.

He served as Director of the Cyber Law Centre at Korea University, and now serves as President of the International Cyber Law Studies in Korea and Chairman of the Korea International Mediation Centre (KIMC). He has advised Korean governments and industries on various international legal matters, including participation in the negotiations of the Korea–Chile Free Trade Agreement, the first FTA of Korea, and attendance at the fourth and fifth UNGGEs on information security between 2014 and 2017.

Professor Park received his LL.B. (1981) and LL.M. (1983) from Korea University, an LL.M. from Harvard Law School (1985), and a Ph.D. in International Law from the University of Cambridge (1990). He was awarded an honorary doctorate in law by Far Eastern Federal University in Vladivostok, Russia, in October 2018.

**Xiangshun Ding** is Dean, School of Law, Beijing Foreign Studies University.

He obtained S.J.D., Robert H. Mckinney School of Law, Indiana University (2019), LL.M., Indiana University (2006), Ph.D. in Law, Law School, Renmin University of China (2000), LL.M., Law School, Ji Lin University (1994), and LL.B., Law School, Ji Lin University (1992).

Professor Ding served as Vice President of Comparative Law Society of China Law Society; Vice President of Comparative Law Society of Beijing Law Society; Vice President of Beijing Law Society of the Belt and Road. Before he moved to BFSU, he served as Vice Director of Legal Culture Research Center, Renmin University of China; Vice President of American Law Institute, Renmin University of China; Vice President of Legal Profession Institute, Renmin University of China; and President of Asian Law Research Center, Renmin University of China.

# Part I
# Data Protection Laws in East Asia

# Chapter 1
# The Legal System Governing Data Protection in China

**Jialu Du and Xiangshun Ding**

## 1.1 Emerging Data Concepts and Data Privacy Needs

China's legal system for data governance is not a simple collection of rules, but a carefully constructed and refined structure. In order to systematically elucidate this system, this chapter will follow a macro-to-specific analytical path: first, it will define the basic concept of 'data'; then, it will analyze data in two core dimensions. The first dimension is the classification system centered on national security and public interest, exploring from the top-level design of data classification to its specific identification practices. The second dimension is the protection framework centered on individual rights, which analyzes the dichotomy between 'privacy' and 'personal information related rights'.

### *1.1.1 The Concept and Legal Definition of Data*

Broadly speaking, data is the carrier of information, and digital is the way of data transmission and processing.[1] It exists in digital form, generates value-added information, and can be used to optimize targeted decision-making.[2] In terms of legisla-

[1] Shi 2023, p. 23.
[2] Xu and Yang 2024, p. 116.

J. Du
Renmin University of China, Beijing, China
e-mail: dujialu@ruc.edu.cn

X. Ding (✉)
Beijing Foreign Studies University, Beijing, China



H. Miyashita et al. (eds.), *The Evolution of Data Protection Laws in China, Japan, and Korea*, https://doi.org/10.1007/978-981-95-8609-7_1

tion, the starting point for data governance in China is the definition of the core concept of 'data' in the Data Security Law (DSL). Article 3 of the Law states that 'data, as referred to in this Law, means any record of information by electronic or other means'.[3] This definition is notably broad and is intended to create an all-encompassing legal basis. Firstly, it explicitly extends the scope of data processing activities to all industries, whether emerging digital industries or the traditional real economy, as long as it involves the recording of information, will be included in the regulatory field of vision. Secondly, the expression 'electronic or other means' ensures that the application of the law is not limited to digital information, but also covers traditional information carriers such as paper documents. This forward-looking and broad definition makes the DSL provide a fundamental conceptual support and logical starting point for subsequent data governance laws and regulations.

### *1.1.2 The First Dimension: Classification Centered on National Security and Public Interests*

After delineating the broad scope of data, China's data legal system unfolds along its first core dimension, i.e., macro-risk assessment and categorization and classification of data with national security and public interest as the benchmark. This dimension has strong national governance overtones, and its core objective is to identify and protect data assets of great value to the state and society, thus building a security line of defense for the digital frontier.

#### 1.1.2.1 Top-level Design: The Division of General Data, Key Data and Core Data

Based on the broad definition of the concept of 'data', Article 21 of the DSL establishes a data classification and protection system, which requires the state to classify and protect data according to its importance in economic and social development, as well as the degree of harm it will cause to national security, public interests or the legitimate rights and interests of individuals in the event of its tampering, destruction, leakage, or unlawful access or use, organizations' legitimate rights and interests. This system divides data into at least three layers: data, key data and core data.[4]

This risk-based hierarchical division provides a guiding idea for the subsequent establishment of a legal system for data governance, with different levels of data corresponding to different protection measures and compliance obligations. Data

---

[3] Data Security Law of the People's Republic of China (中华人民共和国数据安全法) Chapter 1 Article 3.

[4] Ibid.

are encouraged to flow freely to unlock economic value on the premise of meeting basic security requirements; key data are subject to key protection, and their handling (especially outbound) is subject to strict regulatory procedures; and core data, which are related to national security, the lifeblood of the national economy, vital livelihoods, and significant public interests, are subject to the most stringent management system. This top-level design of hierarchical classification reflects the precision and differentiation of regulation, aiming to focus limited regulatory resources on high-risk areas, thus seeking a balance between safeguarding security and promoting data utilization.

#### 1.1.2.2 Practical Focus: Data Identification Principles and Industry Implementation

China has adopted a combination of 'top-level design + industry practice' to implement data identification: the national level formulates general guidelines, while each industry authority is responsible for formulating specific catalogs in its own field.

According to the guidelines issued by the National Cybersecurity Standardization Technical Committee, the core idea of data classification is to classify data according to industry domains and then business attributes.[5] The guideline establishes several core principles for data classification and grading, including: scientific and practical principle, clear boundary principle, high level and strict manner principle, point and surface combination principle and dynamic updating principle, which provides specific operational guidance for identifying and classifying data in practice. Together, these principles constitute a guiding framework aimed at achieving accurate identification, avoiding 'one-size-fits-all' and striking a balance between security and development. The guide not only provides principles, but also lists specific factors that should be considered when classifying and categorizing data, such as whether it reflects national strategic reserves and whether it supports the operation of critical infrastructure.

Taking the securities industry as an example, the Data security risk prevention and control for securities and futures industry—Guidelines of data classification (GB/T 42775-2023) provides a data classification and grading template based on factors such as customer volume and transaction scale, while also considering issues such as data aggregation and timeliness. This industry-specific directory offers enterprises clear and actionable compliance guidelines, significantly reducing the uncertainty of data identification results. Other critical industries such as healthcare are also referencing national guidelines to gradually establish key data directories for their respective fields, gradually forming a dynamic identification system that combines top-down guidance with bottom-up practices.

---

[5] GB/T 43697–2024 Data Security Technology — Rules for Data Classification and Grading (数据安全技术 数据分类分级规则).

### *1.1.3 Second Dimension: Individual Rights-centered Classification*

If the classification centered on national security constitutes the macro framework of China's data governance, its second dimension enters the micro, focusing on each individual and constructing a set of fine-grained protection system based on individual rights. This dimension recognizes that data is not only a factor of production, but also an extension of personality rights, and is centered on balancing an individual's right to control his or her own information with the digital economy's need to utilize data.

#### 1.1.3.1 Dualistic Structure of Civil Rights: Privacy and Personal Information Related Rights and Interests

China has built an elaborate dualistic structure of protection at the civil rights level, i.e., the Civil Code of the PRC makes a clear distinction between the 'right to privacy' and the 'protection of personal information'. Book IV of the Civil Code of the PRC, entitled 'Personality Rights', provides for the definition of the scope of the right to privacy and the protection of personal information, the requirements for the protection of personal information, the subject of responsibility and the rights and obligations of the relative natural persons in the form of a special chapter.[6] The juxtaposition of the right to privacy and the protection of personal information in the Civil Code demonstrates the close relationship between the two. The right to privacy is traditionally understood as a passive defense right, the core of which lies in maintaining the peace and quiet of one's life and private space, private activities, and private information from intrusion and disclosure, and focuses more on the protection of human dignity. In contrast, 'protection of personal information' are shaped as a more proactive right of control, which recognizes the social and economic value of personal information in the era of the digital economy, and grants individuals a series of dominant rights over how their information is collected, used, processed, and transmitted, reflecting the principle of autonomy of private law.[7] This dualistic structure reflects the legislator's insight into the evolution of the connotation of individual rights in the data era: it seeks not only to protect individuals from intrusion in the traditional sense (the right to privacy), but also to grant individuals the right to make autonomous decisions in information processing activities (protection of personal information). This design goes beyond the one-dimensionality of the traditional western view of privacy as a right to be free from interference and provides a more flexible and modern way forward to deal with the commoditization and exploitation of personal data.

[6] Civil Code of the People's Republic of China (中华人民共和国民法典) Book IV Chap 6.

[7] Wang 2013, p. 62; Zhang 2015, p. 38.

#### 1.1.3.2 Dual Protection of High-Risk Information: Private Personal Information and Sensitive Personal Information

At the intersection of the right to privacy and the protection of personal information, there are two key concepts: 'private personal information' and 'sensitive personal information'. Article 1034, paragraph 3, of the Civil Code of the PRC clarifies that private personal information is a subset of personal information, but because of its highly private nature, it is also subject to enhanced protection under the rules on privacy.

This normative relationship has specific procedural consequences in judicial practice. For example, in the case of infringement of private personal information, the availability of privacy protections allows the infringed person to apply for a personality rights injunction under the Civil Code, a powerful ex ante remedy. In contrast, the remedies for infringement of non-private personal information are more likely to be civil damages after the fact, as well as administrative penalties imposed by the regulator under the Personal Information Protection Law (PIPL). On the other hand, the PIPL introduces the concept of 'sensitive personal information', which refers to personal information that, if leaked or illegally used, could easily lead to the infringement of a natural person's personal dignity or jeopardize the safety of his or her person or property, such as biometrics, religious beliefs, medical and health care, and so on.[8] The handling of sensitive personal information is subject to more stringent conditions, in particular the need to obtain the individual's 'separate consent'. Together, these two concepts form a double protection network for high-risk personal information, reflecting the law's refined idea of differentiating the intensity of protection for information of different risk levels.

#### 1.1.3.3 Compliance Boundaries for Data Utilization

For data-driven industries, the legal status of 'anonymization' and 'de-identification' is crucial, as it directly determines the compliance boundary of data utilization. Article 4 of the PIPL explicitly states that the scope of 'personal information' it protects 'does not include anonymized information'. Article 73 of the Law further defines 'anonymization' as 'the process by which personal information is processed in such a way that it cannot identify a specific natural person and cannot be recovered'. This means that once data has been completely and irretrievably anonymized, it is no longer personal information, and its subsequent processing is no longer regulated by the PIPL. This creates an important safe harbor for the development and utilization of data, especially in scenarios such as big data analysis and artificial intelligence model training.

[8] Personal Information Protection Law of the People's Republic of China (中华人民共和国个人信息保护法) Chapter 2 Section 2.

In contrast, 'de-identification' refers to the process of technically processing personal information so that it is impossible to identify a specific natural person without the aid of additional information. The key difference is that the possibility of re-identification of the de-identified data still exists. Therefore, de-identified information still falls within the scope of personal information, and its processing activities are still subject to the provisions of the PIPL, although in some scenarios their compliance burden may be relatively low. This fine distinction in the law is a concrete embodiment of the core legislative objective of balancing data protection and rational utilization, and it provides a clear path guide for enterprises to explore the value of data while ensuring compliance.

## 1.2 Constructing Order in the Digital Era: China's Data Governance Legislative System

The purpose of this chapter is to analyze the three pillars of China's data legal framework—the Cybersecurity Law (CSL), the Data Security Law (DSL), and the Personal Information Protection Law (PIPL)—often referred to as the 'Troika' in the industry. In order to systematically present this complex regulatory system, this chapter will first chronologically sort out the unique focus and core mechanism of each of the Troika, and explore how they interact with each other to build up a complete picture of the legal framework; and then further analyze the supporting normative system consisting of administrative regulations, departmental rules, and national standards. This chapter will then further analyze the supporting normative system consisting of administrative regulations, departmental rules, national standards, etc. From the three dimensions of conceptual refinement, scenario regulation and compliance process, this chapter explores how these subordinate laws transform the principle-based provisions of the top-level laws into concrete and actionable compliance obligations.

### *1.2.1 First Legislative Pillar: Cybersecurity Law (2017)*

The CSL, which came into force in 2017, is a groundbreaking piece of legislation in the field of data governance in China. It was introduced not only in response to the growing cybersecurity threats, but also as a major step to implement the country's overall security concept and safeguard the vital interests of the general public. Following the State Security Law of the PRC, the law once again reaffirms the principle of cyberspace sovereignty at the national legal level, extending national sovereignty from the three-dimensional space of land, sea and air to the fourth dimension of the 'cyber', and laying a fundamental institutional and theoretical foundation for the entire subsequent data legal system.

#### 1.2.1.1 Core System: Cyber Security Level Protection and Critical Information Infrastructure Protection

The CSL develops four aspects, namely, cyber security support and promotion, network operation security, network information security, and monitoring, early warning and emergency response.[9] The core system mainly includes two levels: the first is the cyber security level protection system. Article 21 of the CSL requires all network operators to classify their networks into different security protection levels according to the importance of the network in national security, social order, public interests and the legitimate rights and interests of citizens, legal persons and other organizations, as well as the degree of harm that may be caused in the event of sabotage, loss of functionality, or data leakage, and to fulfill the corresponding security protection obligations. These obligations include formulating an internal security management system, adopting technical measures against viruses and network attacks, and retaining network logs for no less than six months. Next is the critical information infrastructure security protection system. Article 31 of the CSL defines critical information infrastructure as important network facilities and information systems in important industries and fields such as public communications and information services, energy, transportation, water conservancy, finance, etc. that may seriously jeopardize national security, the people's livelihood and the public interest in the event of damage, loss of functionality or data leakage. For Critical Information Infrastructure operators, the law imposes stricter protection obligations than those for general network operators, such as setting up specialized security management agencies, conducting security background checks on the persons in charge and key position holders, and carrying out disaster-tolerant backups of important systems and databases.[10]

#### 1.2.1.2 Early Exploration and Founding Role in Data Protection

Although the legislative focus of the CSL is on the security of the 'cyber' itself, it has provided an important early exploration and institutional foundation for China's data protection legislation. In Chap. 4 of the CSL, 'Network Information Security', the Law systematically puts forward the requirements for the protection of personal information for the first time at the legal level. Article 41 of the Law establishes that the collection and use of personal information shall follow the principles of 'lawful, legitimate and necessary', and requires that the rules for collection and use be made public, and that the purpose, manner, and scope of collection be made clear, and that the consent of the person from whom the information is to be collected be obtained.

[9] Cybersecurity Law of the People's Republic of China (中华人民共和国网络安全法).

[10] Guiding Opinions on Implementing the Network Security Level Protection System and the Security Protection System for Critical Information Infrastructure (贯彻落实网络安全等级保护制度和关键信息基础设施安全保护制度的指导意见) (2020) <http://www.mps.gov.cn/n6557558/c7369310/content.html> accessed 28 November 2025.

This laid the foundation for the core principle of 'notice & consent' in the PIPL. In addition, Article 37 of the CSL embodies for the first time the two core requirements of data localization and outbound data security assessment, which became the source of China's subsequent construction of a regulatory regime for the cross-border flow of complex data. It can be said that the CSL has built the skeleton of China's data governance, and the core systems and principles it establishes paved the way for the birth of the DSL and the PIPL.

## *1.2.2 Second Legislative Pillar: Data Security Law (2021)*

If the CSL focuses on the 'pipes' that carry data, the DSL will shift its focus to the 'water' flowing in the pipes—the data itself. For the first time, the DSL brings all 'data processing activities' and their security protection into the scope of the law, realizing full coverage of online and offline data activities in all industries. The law establishes several core systems for data governance in China, including a risk-based data classification and grading system, a national-level data security review system, and a risk assessment, monitoring and warning system for data processors. Together, these systems point to one core objective: to set up a full-process security management obligation for all data processors throughout the data lifecycle.[11]

### 1.2.2.1 Core Obligations: Full Process Security Management Obligations for Data Processors

The DSL extends the scope of regulation from 'network operators' under the CSL to all 'data processors'. According to Articles 27 and 30 of the DSL, the core obligations that data processors must fulfill include: establishing and improving a full-process data security management system, organizing and carrying out data security education and training, and adopting corresponding technical measures and other necessary measures to safeguard data security. For processors handling key data, they are additionally required to fulfill more stringent obligations, namely, to specify the person in charge of data security and the management organization, and to conduct regular risk assessments of their data processing activities and submit risk assessment reports to the relevant competent authorities. These provisions build a closed-loop management system covering ex ante prevention, ex post control and ex post accountability.

[11] Data Security Law of the People's Republic of China (中华人民共和国数据安全法) Chapter 3.

#### 1.2.2.2 Dual Goals of Data Security and Development

Another legislative purpose of the DSL lies in its clearly stated dual objectives. Article 1 of the Law begins by stating that its legislative purpose is not only to 'regulate data processing activities and safeguard data security', but also to 'promote the development and utilization of data'. Article 13 further emphasizes that 'the State shall integrate development and security, and insist that equal importance be given to safeguarding data security and promoting the development and utilization of data'. This principle of 'equal emphasis on both security and development' runs through the entire law, indicating that legislators are keenly aware that data are not only assets and carriers of rights that need to be protected, but also key factors of production that drive the development of the digital economy. Therefore, the purpose of regulation is not to restrict the flow of data, but to promote the free flow of data in an orderly manner in accordance with the law on the premise of safeguarding security. This dual objective provides a legal basis and policy guidance for the subsequent dynamic adjustment of regulatory policies, especially the shift from stringent regulation to facilitation in areas such as cross-border data flows.

### *1.2.3 Third Legislative Pillar: Personal Information Protection Law (2021)*

The PIPL, which will come into effect in 2021 along with the DSL, is the third pillar of China's data protection system. While the CSL protects the 'pipeline' and the DSL regulates the 'flowing water', the PIPL focuses on the 'reflection' of each individual in the flowing water. It shifts the focus to the protection of individual rights, and is China's first comprehensive and specialized law in the field of personal information protection. The law is institutionalized through two core mechanisms: first, it establishes a behavioral boundary for data processors based on 'notice & consent', and imposes stricter procedural requirements for high-risk activities, such as 'individual consent'; and second, it gives individual subjects a set of rights and responsibilities based on the concept of information self-determination, which is the key to the protection of personal information.[12]

#### 1.2.3.1 Core Rule: 'Notice & Consent' Rule

The PIPL establishes a comprehensive set of behavioral norms for data processors, which begins with a series of basic principles that run through personal information processing activities, including the principles of lawfulness, legitimacy, necessity,

---

[12] Personal Information Protection Law of the People's Republic of China (中华人民共和国个人信息保护法) Chapter 2 Section 1 Article 17 and Chapter 4.

and good faith, clarity and relevance, minimization, openness and transparency, completeness and accuracy, and safety and security. Guided by these principles, the PIPL further establishes rules for the handling of personal information based on 'notice & consent'. That is, the primary basis of legality for the processing of personal information is 'obtaining the consent of the individual', and such consent must be given voluntarily and explicitly by the individual on the premise that he or she is fully informed. For high-risk data processing activities, Articles 14, 23, 25, 26, 29 and 39 of the PIPL introduce the more stringent procedural requirement of individual consent. When a processor is required to perform acts such as sharing personal information, disclosing personal information, processing sensitive personal information, or providing personal information outside the country, consent may not be obtained through blanket authorization, but rather separate authorization must be obtained from the individual individually and explicitly for each of these specific matters. At the same time, recognizing the complexity of the reality, the PIPL provides for exceptions to the requirement of obtaining an individual's consent for the processing of personal information in specific cases, such as the performance of a contract, the fulfillment of a legal obligation, or the response to a public health incident, preserving the necessary space for the normal functioning of the social economy.

#### 1.2.3.2 System of Rights for Subjects of Personal Information

In contrast to the strict obligations imposed on data processors, another major feature of the PIPL is that it establishes a comprehensive system of information rights for individuals at to ensure their control over their own information, including the internationally recognized rights to information, decision-making (including the withdrawal of consent), access to copying, rectification and supplementation, and deletion, etc.

Among the many rights, two have attracted much attention because of their profound impact on business models. The first is the right to explain and reject automated decision making behaviors such as big data discriminatory pricing. Article 24 of the PIPL stipulates that when automated decision making has a significant impact on the rights and interests of an individual, the individual has the right to request an explanation from the processor and the right to refuse to make a decision solely through automated decision making. At the same time, when commercial marketing is carried out through automated decision making, individuals must be provided with options that are not specific to their personal characteristics or an easy way to refuse. The second is the right to consult and duplicate of personal information aimed at breaking the monopoly of data. This right grants individuals the ability to request the transfer of their personal information from one platform to another platform of their designation, subject to prescribed conditions. The objective of establishing this right is to break down the data silos of large Internet platforms by facilitating the free flow of data, thereby enhancing market competition and safeguarding users' autonomy of choice. Although the right is still in its infancy in practice, relevant national standards (e.g., Information Security Technology Personal Information Transfer Requirements Based on Individual Requests (Draft for Public Comments)) are already being developed.[13]

### *1.2.4 Supporting Norms: Deepening and Landing of Legal Provisions*

While the CSL, the DSL, and the PIPL have established a macro legal framework for data governance in China, what puts these principles into practice is a rapidly evolving and increasingly elaborate system of supporting norms consisting of administrative regulations, departmental rules, and national standards. This system embodies China's philosophy of 'prudence, inclusiveness, and co-construction' in the field of digital governance, and responds positively to technological developments and social hotspots. In this section, the core components of this supporting normative system will be sorted out and introduced from three main functional dimensions: conceptual refinement, scenario regulation and compliance process.

First, an important function of the subordinate law is to transform the principle-based concepts in the top-level law into concrete, enforceable standards, thus providing a clear jurisprudential basis for data governance efforts. This is reflected in the implementation of the data classification and grading system. For example, in order to implement the principle provisions of the DSL, the National Cybersecurity Standardization Technical Committee issued GB/T 43697-2024 Data security technology—Rules for data classification and grading,[14] which covers important contents such as data classification and grading, identification of key data and national core data, and helps enterprises to carry out the business of data classification and grading and identification of key data.

Secondly, the supporting specification system can quickly respond to technological development and social hotspots, and accurately regulate specific scenarios and emerging technologies. In the face of the rapid development of generative AI, the Cyberspace Administration of China (CAC), in conjunction with seven departments, quickly issued the Interim Measures for the Administration of Generative Artificial Intelligence Services,[15] which, together with the Measures for Scientific

---

[13] Notice on National Standard 'Information Security Technology: Personal Information Transfer Requirements Based on Individual Requests' (Exposure Draft) (关于国家标准<信息安全技术基于个人请求的个人信息转移要求>征求意见稿征求意见的通知) (2024) <https://www.tc260.org.cn/front/bzzqyjDetail.html?id=20240403144959&norm_id=20231220162250&recode_id=54528> accessed 28 November 2025.

[14] Data Security Techniques Data Classification and Hierarchy Rules (数据安全技术 数据分类分级规则) (2024) <https://openstd.samr.gov.cn/bzgk/gb/newGbInfo?hcno=F0C385EDC38CBF277AEC021F23126ADE> accessed 28 November 2025.

[15] Interim Measures for the Administration of Generative Artificial Intelligence Services (生成式人工智能服务管理暂行办法) (2023) <https://www.gov.cn/zhengce/zhengceku/202307/con-

and Technological Ethics Review (for Trial Implementation),[16] jointly constructed a preliminary framework for the regulation and governance of generative AI in China.

Finally, legal obligations are transformed into internally enforceable procedures for enterprises. This function is embodied in both the ex-ante prevention and ex-post response aspects of compliance. In order to promote the compliance auditing obligations set out in Article 54 of the PIPL, the CAC has issued the Measures for the Administration of Compliance Audits of Personal Information Protection,[17] which provides guidelines for enterprises to establish a regularized internal handling and supervision mechanism. In order to standardize the handling of cybersecurity incidents, the CAC issued the Measures for the Administration of Cybersecurity Incident Reporting (Draft for Public Comments), which provides detailed provisions on the process, content and timeline of reporting. Among them, for larger security incidents involving key data or leakage of personal information of more than 1 million people, a strict time limit of 'within one hour' is proposed, aiming to force enterprises to establish an efficient emergency response system.[18]

## 1.3 Supervisory System and Supervisory Authorities

China has long developed the wisdom and experience of 'co-construction, co-governance and sharing' in its social governance practice, which presents a pattern of supervision and governance of a 'social governance community'.[19] In this chapter, we will first analyze the regulatory structure at the central level, and sort out the governance model with the Cyberspace Administration of China (CAC) as the core, and the collaboration of public security, industry information and market supervision departments, and analyze the new changes after the establishment of the National Data Bureau (NDB); then we will explain the vertical regulatory role played by the competent authorities of various industries, and discuss how industry associations, consumer organizations and other social forces can be involved in the process, so as to build a community of social governance together.

tent_6891752.htm> accessed 28 November 2025.

[16] Measures for Scientific and Technological Ethics Review (for Trial Implementation) (科技伦理审查办法(试行)) (2023) <https://www.most.gov.cn/xxgk/xinxifenlei/fdzdgknr/fgzc/gfxwj/gfxwj2023/202310/t20231008_188309.html> accessed 28 November 2025.

[17] Measures for the Administration of Compliance Audits of Personal Information Protection (个人信息保护合规审计管理办法) (2025) <https://www.cac.gov.cn/2025-02/14/c_1741233507681519.htm> accessed 28 November 2025.

[18] Notice of the National Internet Information Office on <Administration of Cybersecurity Incident Reporting (Draft for Public Comments)> Public Consultation (国家互联网信息办公室关于<网络安全事件报告管理办法(征求意见稿)>公开征求意见的通知) (2023) <https://www.cac.gov.cn/2023-12/08/c_1703609634347501.htm> accessed 28 November 2025.

[19] Zhang 2020, p. 3.

## 1.3.1 *Regulatory Authorities at the Central Level*

China's data protection regulatory structure at the central level is characterized by a de facto core coordinator, the CAC, and other key departments that form a governance network with both division of labor and the need for synergy.

### 1.3.1.1 Core of Coordination: Cyberspace Administration of China

The CAC is the central department of China's data governance system. Article 8 of the CSL, Article 6 of the DSL, and Article 60 of the PIPL all explicitly give it the highest authority to 'coordinate and harmonize'. Its powers cover the entire chain from macro-rulemaking to specific law enforcement approvals, including taking the lead in formulating key documents such as data exit security assessment methods, coordinating the regulatory work of various departments, being directly responsible for approving major matters such as cybersecurity reviews, and leading or coordinating major law enforcement activities against platforms such as Didi. This positioning of coordination and harmonization has enabled it to play the role of a super regulator in practice, ensuring the consistency and authority of the state's policies on the core topic of data security.

### 1.3.1.2 Major Coordinating Departments: Public Security, Industry and Market Supervision

Under the coordination of the CAC, several other key departments have formed a coordinated governance pattern based on their statutory responsibilities.

The Ministry of Industry and Information Technology (MIIT), as the competent authority for the industrial and telecommunication sectors, is particularly active in data protection enforcement. Its regulatory focus is on the protection of personal information in mobile internet apps, and it has become an important force in promoting the implementation of compliance obligations in the consumer internet sector through regularized special governance actions, and the notification and removal of apps with problems such as over-scope collection and frequent claiming of rights.

The State Administration for Market Regulation, on the other hand, mainly cuts into data governance from two dimensions: consumer protection and antitrust. It is responsible for reviewing unfair form clauses in privacy policies, and also pays high attention to whether platform-based companies use the data advantages they hold to implement behaviors that exclude or restrict competition, making it a key regulator at the intersection of data compliance and competition compliance.

The Ministry of Public Security's responsibilities focus primarily on cybersecurity enforcement and crime fighting. The public security authorities are the key supervisors of the cybersecurity level protection system and are responsible for criminal investigations of cybercrime activities such as stealing, illegally obtaining or selling personal information, and are the enforcers of the criminal punishment aspect of the data security legal liability system.

The formation of the NDB in 2023 was a major institutional reform in the field of data governance in China.[20] Its responsibilities are clearly defined as ‘responsible for coordinating and promoting the construction of a data foundation system, and coordinating the integration, sharing, development and utilization of data resources’. The establishment of the NDB reflects the legislative principle of equal emphasis on security and development in the institutional setting, strategically separating the two functions of ‘development’ and ‘security’. The NDB will play the role of ‘facilitator’ and focus on ‘using data well’, while the CAC will continue to focus on ‘managing data well’. This division of responsibilities aims to resolve the inherent contradiction of a single organization acting as both ‘referee’ and ‘athlete’, and lays a more reasonable institutional foundation for the long-term development of data governance in China.

### *1.3.2 Vertical Regulation and Social Complementation: Specialized Division of Labor and Multi-dimensional Co-Governance*

Below the central level is a network of industry authorities and social organizations.

Article 6 of the DSL explicitly stipulates that each industry authority assumes responsibility for data security regulation in its own field, forming a chain of vertical regulation. These authorities have a better understanding of the business characteristics and specific risks in their field and are able to formulate more targeted regulatory rules. For example, the State Administration of Financial Supervision and Administration is responsible for supervising the data governance of financial institutions, the National Health Commission is responsible for managing medical and healthcare data, while the Ministry of Science and Technology assumes the responsibility of approving and filing and managing data such as human genetic resources.

In addition to government regulation, social organizations and industry associations, represented by the China Consumers Association and the Internet Society of China, have formed a useful complement to official regulation by issuing APP compliance assessment reports, formulating industry self-regulatory conventions, and accepting complaints from users to create public opinion supervisory pressure on enterprises and promote best practices in data protection.

[20]The Establishment of the NDB is Timely and Far-reaching (国家数据局成立恰逢其时意义深远) (2023) <https://www.ndrc.gov.cn/wsdwhfz/202311/t20231107_1361831.html> accessed 28 November 2025.

To summarize, China's data protection supervision system presents a complex structure and a pattern of 'multiple governance' with many participants. Its advantage lies in the fact that it realizes wide coverage of data processing activities and in-depth supervision of key areas through a three-dimensional network of central coordination, departmental coordination, vertical supervision of industries, and complementary supervision by society. However, there are also challenges with this system. Multiple departments share enforcement powers, which in practice may bring about problems such as cross-functionality, inconsistent enforcement standards, and increased coordination costs.

## 1.4 Regulatory Trajectory and Landmark Administrative and Judicial Decisions

This chapter will shift from the theoretical discussions in the previous chapters to real-world practices, and through analyzing landmark case decisions, it will reveal the logic of the application of China's data protection laws in the real world, and the focus of law enforcement. To achieve this goal, this chapter selects three cases that represent three key areas of data governance in China: the '*Didi case*' demonstrates the state's will to enforce the law in the field of data security and the impenetrable red line of national security; the '*Xiaowangshen case*' signifies the judicial system's understanding of the property rights of data as a commercial asset; and the '*AI Companion case*' heralds the extension and application of personality rights in the era of AI.

### *1.4.1 The* 'Didi Case' *and the Red Line of National Security*

The '*Didi case*' began in July 2021, when the CAC implemented a cybersecurity review of Didi in accordance with the National Security Law (NSL) and the CSL in order to prevent national data security risks. After a year-long in-depth investigation, the regulator confirmed that Didi had a total of 16 illegal facts, and that its data processing activities had seriously violated the provisions of the CSL, the DSL, and the PIPL. There are many illegal facts disclosed by the authorities. Considering the severity, duration, and scope of the misconduct, the CAC in July 2022 imposed an administrative fine of 8.026 billion yuan on Didi and an additional 1 million yuan each on its chairman Cheng Wei and president Liu Qing.[21]

---

[21] Decision of the Cyberspace Administration of China on Administrative Penalties Related to Cybersecurity Review against Didi Global Co., Ltd. (国家互联网信息办公室对滴滴全球股份有限公司依法作出网络安全审查相关行政处罚的决定) (2022) <https://www.cac.gov.cn/2022-07/21/c_1660021534306352.htm> accessed 28 November 2025.

The *Didi case* resulted in the largest fine ever imposed for data compliance in China and underscored the primacy of national security in data governance. The CAC found that Didi's data processing activities 'seriously affected national security,' and withheld case details for security reasons. The decision made clear that companies operating critical information infrastructure and handling vast amounts of sensitive data engage not only in commercial activity but also in matters of national security and public interest.

This case marked the first comprehensive application of China's three key data laws—CSL, DSL, PIPL—demonstrating their coordinated enforcement. It illustrated how cybersecurity review, data processing obligations, and personal information protection operate synergistically under a unified regulatory framework.

Moreover, the personal fines imposed on Didi's founder and executives reflected the PIPL's 'double penalty' mechanism. By holding senior management personally liable for decisions that led to violations, the ruling signaled a shift from corporate-only accountability to individual responsibility at the executive level, heightening the deterrent effect of data compliance enforcement.

### *1.4.2 The* 'Xiaowangshen Case' *and the Exploration of Data Resource Property Rights*

In June 2025, the Nanjing Intermediate People's Court issued the first-instance judgment in the 'Xiaowangshen' software infringement case, recognized as China's first 'data resources rule of law' case since the implementation of the DSL. The dispute centered on protecting the commercial value of data products created through substantial investment by platform enterprises. The plaintiff, Taobao, developed an intelligent analytics tool called Business Counsel, which lawfully processed and analyzed massive transaction data from the Taobao and Tmall platforms to generate derivative data of high commercial value. The defendant, Amoy Digital, created a parasitic software named Xiaowangshen that illegally infiltrated and reverse-engineered Business Counsel to extract its core business data. It also used web crawlers to capture platform data on a large scale and sold API interfaces for profit. The court found that the defendant's actions constituted unfair competition, ordered it to cease the infringement, and awarded Taobao over 30 million yuan in damages and expenses.[22]

The question of data ownership remains unresolved and highly debated. Rather than addressing this theoretical issue directly, the court adopted a pragmatic approach by granting different legal protections based on the nature of the data involved.

---

[22] *Taobao (China) Software Co., Ltd* (淘宝(中国)软件有限公司)*, etc. v Taoshu Technology (Beijing) Co., Ltd.* (淘数科技(北京)有限公司), etc. [2023] Nanjing Intermediate People's Court Decision Civil 01-4082 (*苏01民初4082号).*

For non-public business data, the court applied the trade secret provisions under the Anti-Unfair Competition Law. It followed the three elements of 'secrecy, value, and confidentiality measures,' finding that undisclosed transaction data—such as real sales figures and industry summaries—had significant commercial value. Because the plaintiff implemented measures like encryption, firewalls, and data desensitization, these datasets qualified as trade secrets in the legal sense. The defendant's act of 'index key restoration' therefore constituted a direct infringement of the plaintiff's trade secrets.

For publicly available data, the court took an innovative stance by recognizing the platform's data rights and interests. It rejected the view that publicly accessible product names or prices were mere 'public goods' open to free use. Instead, the court reasoned that the platform had independent competitive interests in these large-scale, structured datasets, emphasizing three dimensions: lawful access, substantial investment, and competitive value. The plaintiff had obtained user authorization to process the data, incurred substantial costs in managing, maintaining, and supervising it, and transformed it into a core business asset capable of generating direct economic benefits.

Accordingly, even though the data originated from public sources, the resulting data products—formed through the platform's intellectual, financial, and labor input—deserved legal protection. The '*Xiaowangshen case*' thus represents a substantive judicial acknowledgment of data assets as protectable commercial property.

### *1.4.3 The* **'AI Companion Case'** *and the Protection of Personal Rights in the Digital Age*

The '*AI Companion Case*' concerns the protection of personal likeness and personality rights in the digital age. The defendant technology company operated software that allowed users to create 'AI companions'. Many users modeled these companions after a well-known public figure, Mr. He, uploading his real photos and personal information. Rather than acting as a neutral platform, the company actively participated in generating and promoting these AI avatars. It categorized and recommended the AI version of 'He', encouraged users to upload more materials to train the model, and created an interactive simulation resembling Mr. He's real persona. The Beijing Internet Court ruled that the company's conduct systematically infringed upon Mr. He's personality rights and ordered it to issue a public apology and compensate him for both moral and economic damages.[23]

The court rejected the defendant's claim that the infringing content was merely 'user-generated'. It found that although users uploaded the initial images, the company aggregated, categorized, and promoted them through its algorithms, thereby

[23] *He* (何某) *v Shanghai ZiX Artificial Intelligence Technology Co., Ltd.* (上海自某人工智能科技有限公司) [2020] Beijing Internet Court Decision Civil 0491-9526 (京*0491*民初*9526*号).

acting as a network content provider rather than a neutral platform. Consequently, it could not invoke the 'notice and delete' safe harbor and bore direct liability for the unauthorized commercial use of Mr. He's name and likeness, which infringed his specific personality rights.

More importantly, the court extended protection to human dignity and personal freedom under Article 990 of Book IV of the Civil Code, which safeguards other personality interests based on these fundamental values. It held that the company's algorithmic integration of Mr. He's name, portrait, and personality traits to create a publicly recognizable 'virtual image of He' amounted to a commercial exploitation of his overall personality. The software's features—allowing users to simulate intimate interactions with this virtual figure—placed Mr. He's digital likeness in situations that could degrade and objectify him, constituting a direct infringement of his human dignity. Thus, the misuse of a digital persona closely associated with a real individual was deemed equivalent to violating that person's personality rights.

## 1.5 Balancing Personal Data Protection and the Development of China's Digital Economy

After systematically sorting out the legal framework, regulatory system and judicial practice of data protection in China, this chapter aims to build on the previous chapters to explore the three core themes of data governance in China. First, at the level of national strategy, it discusses the game between the security concept represented by data sovereignty and the development concept represented by promoting the orderly flow of data; second, at the level of market competition, it analyzes how to deeply integrate data governance with the rules of competition in order to reshape the healthy competitive order of the digital market; and lastly, at the level of the individual dimension, it traces how the law and the judicial practice can jointly promote the individual's right to move from a formal state to a substantial one, advancing toward the broader vision of digital human rights.

### *1.5.1 National Strategy: The Game of Security and Development*

'Data sovereignty' is inextricably linked to 'cyberspace sovereignty', which asserts a state's jurisdiction over data generated, collected, and processed within its borders. According to this theory, in the digital age, data has become a fundamental strategic resource of the State, directly related to national security, economic development and social stability. Therefore, the State has the right and the need to regulate the cross-border flow of data and establish data localization storage requirements and an outbound security assessment system to prevent external risks and safeguard the core interests of the State.[24] Against the backdrop of increasing geopolitical competition, data sovereignty is not just a mere legal concept, but has become a strategic tool for China to deal with external pressures. It aims to ensure China's autonomy in the digital space, prevent key data resources from being subject to others, and serve as a starting point for participating in and shaping the rules of global digital governance.

However, after the strict implementation of early regulations such as the Measures for Data Export Security Assessment,[25] its high compliance costs and hindering effects on normal international economic and trade activities have gradually emerged, causing widespread concerns among market players.[26] In the face of these economic pressures, and in order to maintain the macro-policy objectives of opening up and attracting foreign investment, the regulators have made significant adjustments. In 2024, the introduction of the Provisions for Promoting and Regulating the Cross-Border Flow of Data demonstrates China's commitment to a dynamic balance between 'security' and 'development'. The new regulation significantly relaxes restrictions on the exit of medium-risk and low-risk data by creating exemption scenarios and significantly raising the regulatory threshold.[27] China's 'data sovereignty' is not about cutting off data links with the world, but rather about leaving enough space to promote the development of the digital economy and international cooperation while ensuring that core data and national security are not threatened.

### *1.5.2 Market Competition: Data Protection and Platform Anti-Monopoly*

Data protection and anti-monopoly are the core issues of market regulation in the digital era, because in the digital economy, the control of data is often the root cause of market dominance and unfair competition.The 2017 Anti-Unfair Competition Law set up a 'special article on the Internet' for the first time. However, there is a great diversity of unfair competition behaviors on the Internet. The Anti-Unfair Competition Law (Amendment), which was amended and passed on June 27, 2025, responds to the typical problems of unfair competition on the Internet that have been

[24] Qi and Pan 2015, p. 64; Zhang and Xu 2016, p. 139; He 2022, p. 74.

[25] Measures for Data Export Security Assessment (数据出境安全评估办法) (2022) <https://www.moj.gov.cn/pub/sfbgw/flfggz/flfggzbmgz/202305/t20230509_478370.html> accessed 28 November 2025.

[26] Ye and Yan 2024, p. 57.

[27] Provisions for Promoting and Regulating the Cross-Border Flow of Data (促进和规范数据跨境流动规定) (2024) <https://www.gov.cn/gongbao/2024/issue_11366/202405/content_6954192.html> accessed 28 November 2025.

exposed over the past few years in practice.[28] It also reflects China's current clear attitude towards the governance of 'race-to-the-bottom' competition, marking the beginning of China's digital competition regulation. It also reflects China's current clear attitude towards 'race-to-the-bottom' competition governance, marking a new stage of maturity and refinement in China's digital competition regulation.

First, for the first time, the Amendment explicitly prohibits the illegal acquisition of data at the legal level. The new Article 13, in essence, fixes in the form of a statutory law the governance tendency established in judicial decisions such as the '*Xiaowangshen Case*' to protect data products formed at great cost to enterprises. Secondly, the Amendment systematically strengthens the responsibilities of platform operators, positioning them as the 'gatekeepers' and 'governors' of the platform ecosystem. Articles 14 and 21 require platforms to curb 'internal' vicious competition, establishing at the legal level the active management responsibility of platforms for fair competition within the platform and maintaining a healthy competitive ecosystem within the platform. Finally, the revised version adds a new Article 15 to regulate the abuse of relative superiority, greatly expanding the scope of application of the Anti-Unfair Competition Law and providing a powerful tool to regulate large technology platforms that use their data and technological advantages to engage in unfair transactions with small and medium-sized enterprises within their ecosystems.

### *1.5.3 Individual Dimension: From Information Self-determination to Digital Human Rights*

Within the tripartite structure of 'state-market-individual', the protection of the individual dimension has been a key focus of legal attention in recent years. This is not only reflected in the legislative empowerment represented by the PIPL, but also in the extended protection of individual rights in judicial practice, ultimately pointing toward the broader policy vision of digital human rights.

Meanwhile, the protection of the individual dimension has not stopped at personal information. In the face of challenges posed by emerging technologies to traditional rights, the courts have demonstrated their proactivity by extending the scope of protection to the digital persona of individuals. In the '*AI Companion Case*', the court ruled that a natural person's personality rights are not limited to their physical appearance in the real world but also extend to virtual images composed of their real personality elements that can form a stable reference in the public's perception. This provides judicial reference for future regulation of Deepfake and digital avatar technologies and signifies that the protection of personality has

[28] Notes on Law of the People's Republic of China Against Unfair Competition (Revised Draft) (关于<中华人民共和国反不正当竞争法(修订草案)>的说明) (2025) <http://www.npc.gov.cn/npc/c2/c30834/202506/t20250626_446142.html> accessed 28 November 2025.

entered the digital age. In recent years, China has emphasized 'eliminating the digital divide' and 'upholding digital inclusivity' in policy documents such as the Guiding Opinions on Strengthening Digital Government Construction.[29] Digital human rights have become a focal point of official discourse and academic research.[30] In the future, protection of individuals will no longer be confined to personal information but will expand to broader areas ensuring that every individual can participate in the digital society fairly and with dignity, and share in the benefits of digital development.

## 1.6 Conclusion

After more than a decade of institutional development, China has gradually established a sophisticated, multi-tiered data protection legal system with local characteristics. At the theoretical level, this system establishes a national interest protection framework centered on key data through a classification and grading system and the differentiation of rights, and distinguishes between privacy rights and personal information related rights in laws such as the Civil Code and the PIPL. In terms of legal framework, the 'three pillars' of the CSL, the DSL, and the PIPL form the institutional backbone, with administrative regulations, departmental rules, and national standards converting abstract principles into operational compliance obligations. In terms of regulatory structure, China has adopted a multi-stakeholder governance model centered on the CAC, with multi-departmental coordination, industry-specific vertical supervision, and supplementary oversight by social organizations. In judicial practice, landmark cases such as the '*Didi case*', the '*Xiaowangsheng case*', and the '*AI Companion case*' have not only defined the boundaries of national security, commercial data rights, and personality rights protection but also provided judicial guidance for emerging fields.

At the same time, China's digital governance system still faces challenges. On the one hand, the maturity of the system still needs to be improved. While the multi-stakeholder governance framework offers the advantage of broad coverage, it also imposes higher demands on the coordination and consistency of enforcement; the practical standards for certain key concepts, as well as new laws and regulations, still need to be further clarified in the future to enhance the legal certainty of the entire system. On the other hand, China is actively promoting its governance philosophy through initiatives such as the Global Initiative on Data Security, striving to shape a more fair, reasonable, and inclusive global digital governance order.

---

[29] Guiding Opinions on Strengthening Digital Government Construction (国务院关于加强数字政府建设的指导意见) (2022) <https://www.gov.cn/zhengce/content/2022-06/23/content_5697299.htm> accessed 30 November 2025.

[30] Zhang 2022, p. 12.

## References

SHI Jianzhong, 'Deconstruction of Data Concept and Construction of Data Legal System and Discussion on Disciplinary Connotation and System of Data Jurisprudence' (数据概念的解构与数据法律制度的构建兼论数据法学的学科内涵与体系) (2023) 35 *Peking University Law Journal* (中外法学) 23.

XU Chunming Xu and YANG Huanhuan, 'On the Legal Definition of Data' (论数据的法律界定) [2024] *SJTU Law Review* (交大法学) *116*.

WANG Liming, 'On the Legal Protection of the Right to Personal Information: Centered on the Definition of the Right to Personal Information and the Right to Privacy' (论个人信息权的法律保护——以个人信息权与隐私权的界分为中心) (2013) 35 *Modern Law Science* (现代法学) 62

ZHANG Xinbao, 'From Privacy to Personal Information: Theory and Institutional Arrangement of Interest Remeasurement' (从隐私到个人信息:利益再衡量的理论与制度安排) [2015] *China Legal Science* (中国法学) 38

ZHANG Wenxian, 'Theoretical, Institutional and Practical Innovation of Social Governance in China in the New Era' (新时代中国社会治理的理论、制度和实践创新) (2020) 37 *Studies in Law and Business* (法商研究) *3*.

QI Aimin and PAN Jia, 'The Establishment of Data Rights, Data Sovereignty and the Basic Principles of Big Data Protection' (数据权、数据主权的确立与大数据保护的基本原则) (2015) 36 *Journal of Soochow University Philosophy & Social Science Edition* (苏州大学学报(哲学社会科学版)) 64

ZHANG Xinbao and XU Ke, 'The Governance Mode of Cyberspace Sovereignty and Its Institutional Construction' (网络空间主权的治理模式及其制度构建) [2016] *Social Science in China* (中国社会科学) 139

HE Bangwu, 'Cyberspace Governance under the Vision of Digital Jurisprudence' (数字法学视野下的网络空间治理) [2022] *China Legal Science* (中国法学) 74

YE Chuanxing and YAN Wenguang, 'On the Current Situation, Problems and Relief Path of China' s Data Cross-Border Regime' (论中国数据跨境制度的现状、问题与纾困路径) (2024) 37 *Journal of Beijing University of Aeronautics and Astronautics (Social Sciences Edition)* (北京航空航天大学学报(社会科学版)) 57.

ZHANG Wenxian, 'Human Rights Jurisprudence in the New Era' (新时代的人权法理) [2022] Human Rights (人权) 12.

# Chapter 2
# Overview of Data Protection Laws in Japan

**Yuto Noro**

## 2.1 Legal Framework for Data Privacy in Japan

### *2.1.1 APPI*

The central pillar of Japan's data-privacy framework is the Act on the Protection of Personal Information[1] (APPI). It was enacted on 23 May 2003 and promulgated on 30 May 2003. When first enacted, the detailed requirements contained in the APPI applied only to the private sector, and separate statutes set forth the rules for the public sector. The APPI has since incorporated the previous public-sector rules and now sets out concrete requirements for both private and public-sector actors.

The purpose of the APPI is to protect an individual's rights and interests while taking the utility of personal information into account[2] The term 'utility of personal information' encompasses the creation of new industries, the realisation of a dynamic economic society and the enrichment of people's lives.[3] 'Individual rights and interests' refers to all personal and proprietary interests that may be infringed upon by the handling of personal information, and while privacy is a principal example, it is not the only one.[4] Commentators disagree on how these two elements should be balanced: with some arguing that protection of individual rights and

[1] Act on the Protection of Personal Information [個人情報の保護に関する法律].

[2] Art 1 APPI.

[3] Ibid.

[4] Sonobe and Fujiwara 2022, p. 60.

Y. Noro (✉)
TMI Associates, Tokyo, Japan
e-mail: Yuto_Noro@tmi.gr.jp



H. Miyashita et al. (eds.), *The Evolution of Data Protection Laws in China, Japan, and Korea*, https://doi.org/10.1007/978-981-95-8609-7_2

interests is paramount,[5] and others contending that the weight of the two objectives should be assessed on a case by case basis.[6]

Although the protection of privacy is an important element of the APPI's aim to protect individual rights and interests, the statute does not expressly list such protection as an objective. There was a debate during the 2015 revision of the APPI that privacy rights should be explicitly mentioned, but ultimately privacy protection was still not expressly stated as a statutory purpose.[7]

### 2.1.2 *Right to Privacy*

Japan's data-privacy regime also draws upon the right to privacy under the Constitution of Japan (Constitution). The Constitution recognises the right to the pursuit of happiness,[8] and it is generally understood that the right to privacy is one aspect of this right. Constitutional rights operate primarily against public authority, but because courts interpret the Civil Code[9] in light of the Constitution, the right to privacy can also be asserted against private parties. A person whose privacy has been infringed upon may therefore seek damages or an injunction under the Civil Code.

The right to privacy was first recognised in Japan in the 'After the Banquet' case of 1964.[10] The court in such case held that individuals enjoy a 'legal guarantee or right not to have their private life exposed without justification', and that a tort of invasion of privacy occurs if the published content is: (i) private; (ii) secret; and (iii) not already known to the public. Although that judgment was delivered by a district court, the Supreme Court has since referred to the right to privacy or analogous interests in several cases.

The mainstream view is that violations of the APPI and infringements of the right to privacy should be distinguished.[11] Under this separation theory, a violation of privacy rights may be established regardless of whether there is a violation of the APPI.

---

[5] Uga 2021, p. 48.

[6] Okamura 2022, p. 60.

[7] Okamura 2022, pp. 55–56.

[8] Constitution, Art 13.

[9] Civil Code [民法].

[10] Tokyo District Court, 28 September 1964, *Lower Court Civil Cases Reports Compilation* 15(9) 2317.

[11] Kato 2011, pp. 84–85.

## 2.2 Background and Amendments to the APPI

### *2.2.1 Enactment of Local Government Rules (1973-)*

The following section introduces the background to the enactment of the APPI and the history of its revisions.[12] The first legally binding rules on data privacy in Japan were adopted at the municipal level. As local governments began using computers in the 1960s, concerns about their negative impact prompted the introduction of measures to protect personal information. Tokushima City adopted an ordinance on the operation of electronic data-processing systems in June 1973, and Kunitachi City in Tokyo adopted a similar ordinance in March 1975.

### *2.2.2 Personal Information Protection Act for Administrative Computer Systems (1988)*

In the late 1970s and early 1980s, many developed countries enacted data-protection legislation. To harmonise the need to protect privacy with the smooth international flow of personal data, the OECD adopted the Recommendation of the Council concerning Guidelines Governing the Protection of Privacy and Transborder Flows of Personal Data in 1980. As an OECD member, Japan had to revise its domestic law, and after deliberation, the Act on the Protection of Personal Information relating to the Processing by Computer Systems of Administrative Agencies was enacted on 9 December 1988. However, this statute applied only to the electronic processing of personal information by administrative agencies, and until the APPI was enacted in 2003, there was no statutory privacy law applying to the private sector.

### *2.2.3 APPI and Related Statutes (2003)*

Following the OECD's recommendation, momentum for harmonisation increased when the EU Data Protection Directive (DPD)[13] was adopted in 1995. In Japan, several major data-breach incidents underscored the need for legislation. In parallel, the government was preparing the Basic Resident Register Network System (Jūki

[12] For a detailed background and amendment history, see Uga 2021, pp. 1–38 and Okamura 2022, pp. 7–45.

[13] Directive 95/46/EC of the European Parliament and of the Council of 24 October 1995 on the protection of individuals with regard to the processing of personal data and on the free movement of such data.

Net),[14] and therefore decided to legislate on data protection. Five bills were submitted to the Diet and the APPI was enacted on 23 May 2003.

The resulting five statutes were: (i) the APPI; (ii) the Act on the Protection of Personal Information held by Administrative Organs; (iii) the Act on the Protection of Personal Information held by Independent Administrative Institutions, etc. ((ii) and (iii) are collectively referred to as the Public-Sector Personal Information Protection Law.); (iv) the Act on the Establishment of Information Disclosure and Personal Information Protection Review Boards; and (v) the Act on Arrangements for the Enforcement of the Act on the Protection of Personal Information Held by Administrative Organs. The basic provisions of the APPI (Chapters 1–3) applied to both the private and public sectors, but the detailed requirements (Chapters 4–6) applied only to the private sector. The concrete rules for the public sector were contained in the Public-Sector Personal Information Protection Law.

### 2.2.4 2015 Amendment

By 2015, various issues had emerged after more than a decade of experience with the APPI. These included: (i) the proliferation of new types of personal data due to advances in information and communication technology; (ii) the fact that supervision of the private sector by the minister responsible for each business sector made it difficult to address matters cutting across multiple sectors; and (iii) developments overseas where legal regimes were being updated.[15] In response, the 2015 amendment to the APPI was enacted on 28 August 2015, and introduced numerous reforms, including: (1) the establishment of the Personal Information Protection Commission of Japan (PPC); (2) clarification of the definition of personal information; (3) introduction of 'sensitive personal information'; (4) rules for small-scale operators; (5) relaxation of the requirements for changing the purposes of use; (6) introduction of anonymously processed information; (7) stricter opt-out procedures; (8) enhanced traceability; (9) creation of the offence of unlawful provision of personal information databases; (10) consolidation of supervisory powers in the PPC; (11) rules on extraterritorial application and provision of information to foreign enforcement authorities; (12) regulation of overseas transfers to foreign businesses; (13) establishment of a system for accredited personal information protection organisations; and (14) clarification of the position of data-subject rights.[16]

---

[14] Jūki Net [住基ネット] is a nationwide system enabling standardised personal identification by networking the resident-registration records that certify an individual's address. See the Ministry of Internal Affairs and Communications website, "Jūki Net' – what is it?'[「住基ネット」って何?] <https://www.soumu.go.jp/main_sosiki/jichi_gyousei/c-gyousei/daityo/juuki01.html> (Access 30 November 2025).

[15] Uryu 2015, p. 3.

[16] PPC, *Handbook on the Utilisation and Protection of Personal Information* [個人情報の利活用と保護に関するハンドブック] <https://www.ppc.go.jp/files/pdf/personal_280229sympo_pamph.pdf> (Access 30 November 2025).

### 2.2.5 2016 Amendment for the Public Sector

In order to better align the public sector rules with the 2015 amendment, the 2016 amendment of the Public-Sector Personal Information Protection Law was enacted on 20 May 2016. It introduced: (i) the creation of anonymously processed information for the public sector; (ii) consolidation of the supervision of anonymously processed information in the PPC; (iii) clarification of the definition of personal information; and (iv) the establishment of sensitive personal information for the public sector.[17]

### 2.2.6 2020 Amendment

Given the situation where the 2015 amendment required a review every three years, the PPC examined the APPI and identified the following objectives: (i) adopting measures sufficient to protect individuals' rights and interests in light of heightened public awareness of personal information; (ii) ensuring that technological innovation brought benefits in terms of both economic growth and the protection of individuals' rights and interests; (iii) harmonising the regime internationally in view of globally offered services; and (iv) creating an environment in which personal data can be used properly amid increasingly varied forms of data utilisation.[18] On 5 June 2020, the 2020 amendment was enacted, with features including: (1) easing the requirements for requests to stop the use of or erase data; (2) allowing data subjects to choose the means of disclosure; (3) enabling data subjects to request disclosure of records of third-party provision; (4) extending disclosure and other rights to short-term data; (5) narrowing the scope of the opt-out rule; (6) obliging businesses to notify the PPC and the data subject of data breaches; (7) prohibiting improper methods of using personal information; (8) increasing flexibility in the system of accredited personal information protection organisations; (9) creating pseudonymously processed information; (10) introducing restrictions on provision of personally related information to third parties; (11) strengthening penalties for failure to comply with orders or investigations; (12) increasing fines for organisations; (13) enhancing supervision of foreign businesses; and (14) tightening the rules on overseas transfers.[19]

[17] Ministry of Internal Affairs and Communications, 'On the Amendment of the Act on the Protection of Personal Information Held by Administrative Organs, etc.' [行政機関個人情報保護法等改正法について] <https://www.soumu.go.jp/main_content/000440724.pdf> (Access 30 November 2025).

[18] Kiyoshi Sawaki (ed) 2020, p. 1.

[19] PPC, 'Outline of the Act Partially Amending the Act on the Protection of Personal Information and Related Acts' [個人情報の保護に関する法律等の一部を改正する法律(概要)] <https://www.ppc.go.jp/files/pdf/200612_gaiyou.pdf> (Access 30 November 2025).

### 2.2.7 2021 Unification of Public and Private-Sector Systems

The 2021 amendment unified the previously fragmented system so that the PPC would supervise all personal information handling in both the public and private sectors. Its aims were: (i) to increase neutrality and objectivity by having an independent body supervise the public sector; (ii) to align Japan's regime with international trends so as to enhance trust and facilitate cross-border data flows; and (iii) to solve problems caused by compartmentalisation of the regime and thereby promote data utilisation.[20] The amendment law was enacted on 12 May 2021.

The 2021 amendment: (1) merged the APPI with the Public-Sector Personal Information Protection Law and local government personal information legislation into a single statute overseen by the PPC; (2) applied, in principle, the same rules as those in the private sector to public hospitals, universities and other public bodies in the medical and academic fields to unify the regulations in those areas; (3) refined the provisions exempting academic research by making exceptions for each duty rather than providing a blanket exemption; and (4) unified the definition of personal information and clarified the rules for handling anonymously processed information in the public sector.[21]

## 2.3 Overview of the APPI

### 2.3.1 Core Concepts

The APPI defines several core concepts as follows.

(a) **Personal Information**: Information relating to a living individual that is capable of identifying a specific individual by description or otherwise, or that contains a personal identifier[22] is classified as 'personal information.'[23] 'Information relating to an individual' includes not only identifiers but also all facts, judgments and evaluations relating to that person's attributes.[24] 'Capable of identifying a specific individual' means that, based on common social understanding, a person of

---

[20] Tomiyasu and Nakada 2021, p. 1.

[21] PPC, 'Outline of the Act on Developing Related Laws to Form a Digital Society'[デジタル社会の形成を図るための関係法律の整備に関する法律 概要資料] <https://www.ppc.go.jp/files/pdf/seibihou_gaiyou.pdf> (Access 30 November 2025).

[22] 'Personal identifier' is defined in Art 2 para 2 APPI, and includes codes specified by a Cabinet Order of the APPI [個人情報の保護に関する法律施行令] (Cabinet Order), current biometric data (for example, face recognition data) and official numbers (for instance, driver's licence numbers) (Cabinet Order Art 1).

[23] Art 2 para 1 APPI.

[24] PPC, 'Guidelines on the Act on the Protection of Personal Information (General Rules Edition)' [個人情報の保護に関する法律についてのガイドライン(通則編)] (November 2016, updated June 2025) (General Guidelines), 2-1.

ordinary judgment and understanding can recognise the identity between the information and a specific living person.[25] A name by itself is one example of this type of information. Information that can easily be collated with other information to identify an individual also falls within this concept.[26] An online identifier that cannot identify a person by itself may still constitute personal information if it can readily be matched with other information held by the business to identify a person. This concept applies to both the private and public sectors.

(b) **Personal Data**: 'Personal data' means personal information that forms part of a personal information database.[27] A personal information database is a collection of information containing personal information organised so that specific personal information can be searched systematically by computer or organised on paper so that specific personal information can readily be found.[28] For example, an email address book stored in an email program may constitute a personal information database. A paper file of employees indexed in alphabetical order may also be an example. This concept applies only to the private sector.

(c) **Retained Personal Data**: 'Retained personal data' means personal data over which a personal information handling business has the authority to comply with all requests from the data subject (or his or her agent) for disclosure, correction, addition or deletion, suspension of use, erasure and suspension of third-party provision (Disclosure, etc.).[29] This definition ensures that the operator subject to data subject rights must have authority over the data. For example, when personal data processing is outsourced, the data generally remains as retained personal data of the consignor,[30] and the consignee is not bound by the obligations relating to the retained personal data. Nevertheless, data whose existence might harm the public interest if disclosed is excluded from retained personal data.[31] This concept applies only to the private sector.

(d) **Anonymously Processed Information**: 'Anonymously processed information' is information relating to an individual obtained by processing personal information so that a specific individual cannot be identified and the original personal information cannot be restored.[32] Creating anonymously processed information requires appropriate processing measures such as: (i) deleting descriptions that identify specific individuals; (ii) deleting personal identifiers; (iii) deleting codes linking information; (iv) deleting unique descriptions; and (v) other measures

[25] PPC, 'Questions and Answers on the Guidelines on the Act on the Protection of Personal Information' [「個人情報の保護に関する法律についてのガイドライン」に関するQ&A] (November 2017, updated June 2025) (QA) No. 1-1.

[26] Art 2 para 1 APPI.

[27] Art 16 para 3 APPI.

[28] Art 16 para 1 APPI.

[29] Art 16 para 4 APPI.

[30] QA No 1-56.

[31] Art 16 para 4 APPI; Cabinet Order Art 5.

[32] Art 2 para 6 APPI.

appropriate to the nature of the personal-information database.[33] Anonymously processed information does not qualify as personal information, so it may be provided to third parties without the data subject's consent, thereby contributing to the circulation and utilisation of data. [34] This concept applies to both the private and public sectors, although special rules apply to anonymously processed information in the public sector.[35]

(e) **Pseudonymously Processed Information**: 'Pseudonymously processed information' means information relating to an individual obtained by processing personal information so that the individual cannot be identified unless the information is collated with other data.[36] Creating pseudonymously processed information requires measures such as: (i) deleting descriptions that identify specific individuals; (ii) deleting personal identifiers; and (iii) deleting information whose misuse would cause financial harm.[37] Pseudonymously processed information may or may not fall within the definition of personal information. Either way, the restrictions on changing the purposes of use do not apply, allowing for flexible use and facilitating data utilisation.[38] This concept applies to both the private and public sectors, but the public sector is not permitted to create pseudonymously processed information.[39]

(f) **Personally Related Information**: 'Personally related information' means information relating to a living individual that does not fall within personal information, pseudonymously processed information or anonymously processed information.[40] For example, browsing history collected via cookies or similar device identifiers constitutes personally related information.[41] This concept applies only to the private sector.

(g) **Retained Personal Information**: 'Retained personal information' in the public sector means information created or obtained by officials in the course of

---

[33] Art 43 para 1 APPI; Enforcement Regulations of the APPI [個人情報の保護に関する法律施行規則] (Enforcement Regulation) Art 34.

[34] For details, see the PPC, 'Guidelines on the Act on the Protection of Personal Information (Pseudonymised/Anonymised Information Edition)' [個人情報の保護に関する法律についてのガイドライン(仮名加工情報・匿名加工情報編)] (November 2016, updated December 2016) (Pseudonymised/Anonymised Guidelines).

[35] In the public sector, anonymised processed information may be created only if it falls within the special category of administrative-organ anonymised processed information. See 'Questions and Answers on the Act on the Protection of Personal Information (Administrative Organs Edition)' [ 個人情報の保護に関する法律についてのQ&A(行政機関等編)] (Public Sector QA) No. 6-1-1.

[36] Art 2 para 5 APPI.

[37] Art 41 para 1 APPI; Enforcement Regulations Art 31.

[38] See the Pseudonymised/Anonymised Guidelines.

[39] Pseudonymised processed information may not be created in the public sector. See Public Sector QA No. 6-1-1.

[40] Art 2 para 7 APPI.

[41] General Guidelines 2-8.

their duties and recorded in an administrative document that is retained for organisational use.[42] This concept applies only to the public sector.

(h) **Personal Information File**: 'Personal information file' is a collection of retained personal information held for a specific administrative purpose organised either: (i) by computer so that specific retained personal information can be searched (electronic files); or (ii) on paper so that specific retained personal information can readily be searched (manual files).[43] This concept applies only to the public sector.

## *2.3.2 Different Regimes for the Public and Private Sectors*

The APPI distinguishes between the public and private sectors. The public sector comprises public sector organisations;[44] namely: (i) administrative organs; (ii) independent administrative agencies; (iii) local governmental bodies; and (iv) local independent administrative agencies. The private sector comprises personal information handling businesses;[45] namely, entities other than public sector organisations that use a personal information database in the course of business.

Certain public-sector bodies and activities, such as hospitals and universities, are subject to the same rules as the private sector in order to unify the regulation of the medical and academic fields. However, the public-sector rules continue to apply with respect to the requirements of: (1) personal information files; (2) requests for disclosure, etc.; and (3) anonymously processed information.[46]

## *2.3.3 Data Acquisition*

### 2.3.3.1 Rules for the Private Sector

(A) **Specification and Change of Purpose**: Personal information handling businesses must specify the purposes of use of the personal information as much as possible when handling such information.[47] For example, a company may state that it uses personal information 'to ship goods, provide after-sales service and inform customers about new products and services.'[48] When changing the purposes of use, the change must remain within a scope reasonably related to the original purposes,[49]

---

[42] Art 60 para 1 APPI.

[43] Art 60 para 2 APPI; General Guidelines 4-2-4.

[44] Art 2 para 11 APPI.

[45] Art 16 para 2 APPI.

[46] Arts 58 and 125 APPI.

[47] Art 17 para 1 APPI.

[48] General Guidelines 3-1-1.

[49] Art 17 para 2 APPI.

and the business must notify the data subject of, or publicly announce, such new purposes.[50]

(B) **Fair Acquisition**: Personal information handling businesses must not acquire personal information by deception or other wrongful means.[51] For example, it is unlawful to acquire personal information by intentionally providing false information about the identity of the collector or the purposes of use.[52] This rule also covers situations in which a business acquires personal information despite knowing or easily being able to know that a third party is about to violate the restriction on third-party provision.[53]

(C) **Sensitive Personal Information**: As a rule, personal information handling businesses must obtain the data subject's prior consent before acquiring sensitive personal information.[54] Exceptions defined in the APPI apply, such as where acquisition is required by law.[55] Sensitive personal information includes information about race, creed, social status, medical history, criminal history, the fact of having been a victim of crime and other information prescribed by Cabinet Order as requiring special care to prevent unfair discrimination, prejudice or other disadvantage.[56]

### 2.3.3.2 Rules for the Public Sector

(A) **Restriction on Retention**: Heads of public sector organisations may retain personal information only to the extent necessary to perform duties prescribed by law and must specify the purposes of use as much as possible.[57] They must not retain personal information beyond the extent necessary to achieve those purposes,[58] and when changing the purposes, they must remain within a scope reasonably related to the original purposes.[59]

(B) **Fair Acquisition**: The head of a public sector organisation must not acquire personal information by deception or other wrongful means.[60] For example, it would be unlawful to coerce a person to provide personal information that the person is under no obligation to provide as a condition of receiving an administrative service.[61]

---

[50] Art 21 para 3 APPI.

[51] Art 20 para 1 APPI.

[52] General Guidelines 3-3-1 Example 3.

[53] General Guidelines 3-3-1 Example 5.

[54] Art 20 para 2 APPI.

[55] Ibid.

[56] Art 2 para 3 APPI.

[57] Art 61 para 1 APPI.

[58] Art 61 para 2 APPI.

[59] Art 61 para 3 APPI.

[60] Art 64 APPI.

[61] PPC, 'Guidelines on the Act on the Protection of Personal Information (Public Sector Edition)' [個人情報の保護に関する法律についてのガイドライン(行政機関等編)] (January 2022, updated June 2025) (Public Sector Guidelines).

## 2.3.4 *Data Use*

### 2.3.4.1 Rules for the Private Sector

(A) **Limitation by Purpose**: Personal information handling businesses must not handle personal information beyond the scope necessary to achieve the specified purposes of use without the data subject's prior consent,[62] unless one of the exceptions applies.[63]

(B) **Notification or Publication of Purposes**: When personal information is collected, the personal information handling business must, unless the purpose of use has already been publicly announced, promptly notify the data subject of or publish the purposes of use. Businesses often post a privacy policy on their website for this purpose. When personal information is obtained directly from the data subject in writing (including by electronic means), the business must state the purposes of use in advance,[64] such as by providing or sending a contract stating the purposes.[65] There are exceptions, including where the purposes are obvious from the circumstances.[66]

(C) **Prohibition of Improper Use**: Personal information handling businesses must not use personal information in a way that promotes or induces illegal or unjust acts,[67] such as by engaging in unjust discrimination in recruitment based on personal information[68] or providing personal information to a third party where it is foreseeable that the third party will violate the restrictions on third-party provision.[69]

### 2.3.4.2 Rules for the Public Sector

(A) **Restriction on Use**: Heads of public sector organisations may not use retained personal information for any purpose other than the specified purposes of use unless permitted by law.[70] Limited exceptions allow use for other purposes, for example with the data subject's consent or when providing the information to the data subject, or when providing it solely for statistical or academic research.[71] Even where an exception applies, it is unlawful to use retained personal information for another

[62] Art 18 para 1 APPI.

[63] Art 18 para 3 APPI.

[64] Art 21 para 2 APPI

[65] General Guidelines 3-3-4

[66] Art 21 para 4 APPI.

[67] Art 19 APPI.

[68] General Guidelines 3-2 Example 5.

[69] General Guidelines 3-2 Example 4.

[70] Art 69 para 1 APPI.

[71] Art 69 para 2 APPI.

purpose if doing so would unjustly infringe upon the rights or interests of the data subject or a third party.[72]

(B) **Statement of Purpose**: When a public sector organisation obtains personal information directly in writing from the data subject, it must in principle state the purposes of use in advance.[73] Exceptions apply when the purposes are obvious from the circumstances.[74]

(C) **Prohibition of Improper Use**: Heads of public sector organisations must not use personal information in a way that promotes or induces illegal or unjust acts.[75] For example, it would be improper for an administrative body to use personal information to unlawfully discriminate against a person.[76]

## *2.3.5 Data Management*

### 2.3.5.1 Rules for the Private Sector

(A) **Accuracy and Deletion**: Personal information handling businesses must strive to keep personal data accurate and up to date to the extent necessary to achieve the purposes of use.[77] This includes procedures for checking and correcting data when entered into a personal information database, updating records and setting retention periods.[78] Personal information handling businesses must also strive to delete personal data without delay once it is no longer needed,[79] such as when the purposes of use have been achieved or the business in question has ceased.[80]

(B) **Security Measures**: Businesses must take necessary and appropriate measures to prevent leakage, loss or damage of personal data and to otherwise securely manage personal data.[81] The measures must be necessary and appropriate, depending on the scale and nature of the business, the circumstances surrounding the handling of personal data and the nature of the media on which the personal data is recorded, while taking into consideration the extent of the infringement of the rights and interests of the individual in the event of a leakage of personal data.[82] Specific measures are set out in PPC guidelines.[83]

[72] Art 69 para 2 proviso APPI.

[73] Art 62 APPI.

[74] Ibid.

[75] Art 63 APPI.

[76] Public Sector Guidelines 5-2-3.

[77] Art 22 APPI.

[78] General Guidelines 3-4-1.

[79] Art 22 APPI.

[80] General Guidelines 3-4-1.

[81] Art 23 APPI.

[82] General Guidelines 3-4-2.

[83] General Guidelines 10.

(C) **Supervision of Employees**: When employees handle personal data, the business must supervise them as necessary and appropriate in order to ensure the security of the personal data.[84] 'Employees' here includes persons engaged in the business while under the direct or indirect supervision of the business.[85]

(D) **Supervision of Contractors**: When all or part of the handling of personal data is outsourced, the business must supervise the contractor as necessary and appropriate to ensure the security of the personal data. In practice, the business must select an appropriate contractor, conclude a contract requiring the contractor to take equivalent security measures and monitor the contractor's handling of the data.[86]

#### 2.3.5.2 Rules for the Public Sector

(A) **Accuracy**: Heads of public sector organisations must strive, to the extent necessary to achieve the purposes of use, to ensure that retained personal information matches past or present facts.[87] The required period, whether past data, current data or both, varies depending on the purpose and accuracy, and must be ensured accordingly.[88]

(B) **Security Measures**: Heads of public sector organisations must take necessary and appropriate measures to prevent leakage, loss or damage of retained personal information and to otherwise securely manage the same.[89] The measures shall be necessary and appropriate, depending on the scale and nature of the administrative or business operations, the circumstances surrounding the handling of retained personal information, and the nature of the media on which the retained personal information is recorded, while taking into consideration the extent of the infringement of the rights and interests of the individual in the event of a leakage of the retained personal information.[90] Heads of public sector organisations must also supervise contractors. Appropriate measures include: (i) setting criteria for what information and systems contractors may access and for selecting contractors; (ii) including provisions in contracts concerning information management; and (iii) conducting periodic audits.[91]

(C) **Duty of Employees**: Employees of public sector organisations must not, without a justifiable reason, reveal any personal information obtained in the course of their duties to others or use the same for improper purposes.[92] 'Reveal to others'

---

[84] Art 24 APPI.

[85] General Guidelines 3-4-3.

[86] General Guidelines 3-4-4 (1)–(3).

[87] Art 65 APPI.

[88] Public Sector Guidelines 5-2-4.

[89] Art 66 para 1 APPI.

[90] Public Sector Guidelines 5-3-1 (1).

[91] Ibid.

[92] Art 67 APPI.

means disclosing personal information without justification,[93] and 'use for improper purposes' means using personal information for personal or other improper advantage.[94]

## 2.3.6 *Data Provision*

### 2.3.6.1 Rules for the Private Sector

(A) **Provision of Personal Data**: As a rule, a personal information handling business must not provide personal data to a third party without the data subject's prior consent.[95] A 'third party' means anyone other than: (i) the data subject; and (ii) the business providing the data.[96] Provision within the same business (for example, between departments) is not a third-party provision.[97] When obtaining consent, the business must clearly state the information reasonably necessary for the data subject to make a decision.[98] Exceptions defined in the APPI apply, such as where the provision is required by law.[99] When the opt-out procedure is followed and notified to the PPC, personal data may be provided without consent.[100] Provision of personal data through outsourcing, business succession or joint use is not considered third-party provision and is not subject to these restrictions.[101]

(B) **Provision to Foreign Third Parties**: When providing personal data to a foreign third party, the business must do one of the following: (i) obtain the data subject's consent to the international transfer; (ii) transfer the data to a country recognised as having a personal information protection system of a level equivalent to that of Japan; or (iii) satisfy the standard of the safeguard necessary for the third party to continuously take measures equivalent to those required to be taken by personal information handling businesses in Japan.[102] To obtain consent under condition (i), the business must inform the data subject of the name of the foreign country, the foreign data-protection regime and the data-protection measures taken by the recipient.[103] Regarding condition (ii), the countries recognised by the Japanese

---

[93] Public Sector Guidelines 5-3-2.

[94] Ibid.

[95] Art 27 para 1 APPI.

[96] QA 7-1.

[97] General Guidelines 3-6-1.

[98] Ibid.

[99] Art 27 para 1.

[100] Art 27 para 2 APPI.

[101] Art 27 para 5 APPI.

[102] Art 28 APPI.

[103] Art 28 para 2 APPI; Enforcement Regulations Art 17 para 2.

government are currently the EU member states[104] and the United Kingdom.[105] The criteria for condition (iii) are that the implementation of measures is ensured in line with the relevant obligations of the APPI (e.g., concluding data transfer agreements that cover the relevant APPI requirements) or that the recipient is accredited under an international framework (e.g., APEC's CBPR certification).[106] Under condition (iii), the provider must take necessary steps to ensure that the recipient continues to meet the required standards and must inform the data subject of those measures and standards.[107]

(C) **Records of Third-Party Provision**: When personal data is provided to a third party, the business must, in principle, prepare and retain a record of the provision for three years.[108] When personal data is received from a third party, the business must, in principle, confirm and record the circumstances of the provision and retain the record for three years.[109,110]

(D) **Provision of Personally Related Information**: When a business handling personally related information provides such information to a third party in circumstances where the third party is expected to obtain it as personal data, the provider must confirm that the data subject has consented to the provision.[111] Personally related information is generally not subject to the APPI, but the obligation to confirm consent applies where the recipient is expected to combine it with personal data.

---

[104] 'EU member states' here also includes countries that are parties to the EEA Agreement (i.e., Norway, Iceland and Liechtenstein).

[105] Commission Announcement No. 1 of 2019 designates foreign countries with systems for the protection of personal information equivalent to Japan's [個人の権利利益を保護する上で我が国と同等の水準にあると認められる個人情報の保護に関する制度を有している外国等(平成31年個人情報保護委員会告示第1号)].

[106] Art 28 para 1 APPI; Enforcement Regulations Art 16; and PPC, 'Guidelines on the Act on the Protection of Personal Information (Provision to Foreign Third Parties Edition)' [個人情報の保護に関する法律についてのガイドライン(外国にある第三者への提供編)] (November 2016, updated April 2025) 4.

[107] Art 28 para 3 APPI.

[108] Art 29 APPI.

[109] Art 30 APPI.

[110] For details on confirmation and record-keeping, see PPC, 'Guidelines on the Act on the Protection of Personal Information (Confirmation and Record-Keeping upon Third-Party Provision Edition)' [個人情報の保護に関する法律についてのガイドライン(第三者提供時の確認・記録義務編)] (November 2016, updated December 2017).

[111] Art 31 APPI.

#### 2.3.6.2 Rules for the Public Sector

(A) **Restriction on Provision**: Heads of public sector organisations must not provide retained personal information for any purpose other than the specified purposes of use unless permitted by law.[112] This rule parallels the restriction on use described above.

(B) **Provision to Foreign Third Parties for Other Purposes**: When providing retained personal information to a foreign third party for any purpose other than the specified purposes, heads of public sector organisations must obtain the data subject's prior consent.[113] Unlike the private sector, this rule applies only when the provision is carried out outside the original purposes.

### *2.3.7 Response to Data Breaches*

#### 2.3.7.1 Rules for the Private Sector

When a covered data breach occurs, as defined in the Enforcement Regulations of the APPI, the business must report the incident to the PPC and notify the data subject.[114] Covered breaches include leakage, loss or damage of personal data in cases where: (i) sensitive personal information is involved; (ii) personal data with a risk of financial damage through misuse is involved; (iii) the breach has been committed with malicious intent; or (iv) the number of affected persons exceeds 1000.[115] When personal data processing is outsourced, both the consignor and the consignee are responsible for reporting and notification, but the consignee may discharge its duty by notifying the consignor.[116] When it is difficult to notify affected data subjects, substitute measures such as public announcement are required.[117]

#### 2.3.7.2 Rules for the Public Sector

Similar rules apply to the public sector.[118]

---

[112] Art 69 para 1 APPI.

[113] Art 71 APPI.

[114] Art 26 APPI.

[115] Enforcement Regulations Art 7.

[116] Art 26 para 1 proviso; General Guidelines 3-5-3-2.

[117] Art 26 para 2 proviso; General Guidelines 3-5-4-5.

[118] The same rules apply to the public sector, subject to differences reflecting the nature of public bodies. See the Public Sector Guidelines 5-4.

## *2.3.8 Transparency and Response to Data Subject Requests*

### 2.3.8.1 Rules for the Private Sector

(A) **Transparency Regarding Retained Personal Data**: Personal information handling businesses must make certain information regarding retained personal data available to the data subject, including the business's name, address and representative; the purposes of use; the procedures (and fees) for responding to requests from the data subject; the security measures in place; and the contact point for complaints.[119]

(B) **Disclosure, Correction, Suspension of Use and Suspension of Provision to Third Parties**: When the data subject requests notification of the purposes of use, disclosure, correction addition or deletion, suspension of use or erasure, or suspension of provision to third parties of the retained personal data, the business must respond to such requests.[120] If the business refuses, it must strive to explain its reasons for such refusal.[121] The business may stipulate the procedures (including fees[122]) for making requests, and the data subject must follow those procedures.[123] Court proceedings may not commence until two weeks after the business has refused a request.[124]

(C) **Complaints**: Personal information handling businesses must endeavour to deal appropriately and promptly with complaints about the handling of personal information,[125] and must establish internal systems as necessary to achieve that end.[126]

### 2.3.8.2 Rules for the Public Sector

(A) **Prior Notification of Personal Information Files**: When an administrative organ intends to create a personal information file, the head of that organ must notify the PPC in advance of matters such as the name of the file, the name of the organisation and the purposes of use.[127]

(B) **Register of Personal Information Files**: Heads of administrative organs must prepare and publish a register of personal information files held by their

[119] Art 32 para 1 APPI.

[120] Arts 32 para 1, 32 para 2 and 33–35 APPI.

[121] Art 36 APPI.

[122] Art 38 APPI. The data subject may be charged a fee only when requesting notification of the purpose of use or disclosure.

[123] Art 37 para 1 APPI.

[124] Art 39 APPI.

[125] Art 40 para 1 APPI.

[126] Art 40 para 2 APPI.

[127] Art 74 APPI.

organisations, describing matters such as the name of the file, the name of the organisation and the purposes of use.[128]

(C) **Disclosure, Suspension of Use and Suspension of Provision**: When the data subject requests disclosure, correction (including addition or deletion) or suspension of use (including erasure or suspension of provision), the head of the organisation must comply with such request.[129]

### *2.3.9 Enforcement Powers and Penalties*

When the APPI was first enacted, supervision of the private sector was conducted by the ministers responsible for each business sector and supervision of the public sector was conducted by the Ministry of Internal Affairs and Communications. At present, the PPC has unified oversight of both sectors. The PPC may conduct investigations, including requesting reports and conducting on-site inspections.[130] Failure to comply with such investigations may result in fines of up to JPY 500,000.[131] Accordingly, the PPC may provide guidance and advice[132] and issue advisory orders,[133] and failure to comply with such advisory orders may lead to mandatory orders.[134] Violation of a mandatory order is punishable by imprisonment for up to one year or a fine of up to JPY 1 million for individuals,[135] and by a fine of up to JPY 100 million for corporations.[136]

### *2.3.10 Related Regulations and Guidelines*

Regulations and guidelines related to the APPI can be divided into those based on the APPI itself and those based on other laws.

---

[128] Art 75 APPI.

[129] Arts 76-103 APPI.

[130] Arts 146 and 156 APPI.

[131] Arts 182 no 1 and 184 para 1 no 2 APPI (applicable only to the private sector).

[132] Arts 147 and 157 APPI.

[133] Arts 148 para 1 and 158 APPI.

[134] Art 148 para 2 APPI (applicable only to the private sector).

[135] Art 178 APPI (applicable only to the private sector).

[136] Art 184 para 1 no 1 APPI (applicable only to the private sector).

#### 2.3.10.1 Regulations and Guidelines Based on the APPI

For certain sectors the APPI is supplemented by sector-specific guidelines, including:

- **Financial Sector**—Guidelines on personal information protection in the financial sector; practical guidance on security measures; guidelines on credit; guidelines on debt-collection services.
- **Medical Sector**—Guidance on the proper handling of personal information by healthcare and nursing-care providers; guidance for health-insurance societies; guidance for national health-insurance associations; and guidelines on the handling of personal genetic information in the economic and industrial sectors.
- **ICT Sector**—Guidelines on the protection of personal information in the telecommunications industry; guidelines on the protection of personal information of broadcast subscribers; guidelines on the protection of personal information in the postal services sector; guidelines on the protection of personal information in the letter-delivery sector.

#### 2.3.10.2 Regulations Based on Other Laws

Aside from the APPI, other laws regulate the handling of personal information in specific contexts. Among the most important are the rules on direct marketing, cookies and similar technologies, as well as those on recruitment.

(A) **Direct Marketing**: Regulation of data privacy in direct marketing is governed by the Act on Regulation of Transmission of Specified Electronic Mail (ASEM).[137] ASEM defines 'specified electronic mail' as an email sent for the purpose of advertising one's own or another's business.[138] As a general rule, sending such emails requires prior consent.[139]

(B) **Cookies and Similar Technologies**: The Telecommunications Business Act (TBA)[140] contains external transmission rules relating to cookies and similar technologies. When telecommunications providers offer certain services, such as: (i) messaging; (ii) platforms for posting information by unspecified persons (for example, social networks, marketplaces and review sites); (iii) search engines; or (iv) information distribution services, they must notify users or make it easy for users to learn about programs that cause external transmission (for example, web tags or

137 Act on Regulation of Transmission of Specified Electronic Mail [特定電子メールの送信の適正化等に関する法律].

138 Art 2 no 2 ASEM.

139 Art 3 para 1 no 1 ASEM.

140 Telecommunications Business Act [電気通信事業法].

information-collection modules embedded in apps).[141,142] Specifically, they must inform users of the content of the information sent, the name of the entity receiving it and the purposes of use.[143]

(C) **Recruitment**: Data privacy in recruitment is regulated by the Employment Security Act (ESA).[144] The ESA sets out general rules on the handling of personal information of jobseekers.[145] Detailed requirements are provided in the ESA guidelines;[146] which address the collection, storage and use of personal information, management of personal information and compliance with the APPI.[147]

## *2.3.11 Approach in Japan*

### 2.3.11.1 Regulatory Approaches to the Public and Private Sectors

Japan's data privacy framework under the APPI regulates both the public and private sectors. Looking at other Asian data privacy regimes, Korea's Personal Information Protection Act (PIPA)[148] and China's Personal Information Protection Law (PIPL)[149] likewise apply to both sectors. However, whereas the APPI contains two distinct internal structures for the public and private sectors that diverge from the definitional level upwards, the PIPA and PIPL essentially adopt a single framework and merely exempt or supplement certain requirements for the public sector to reflect its particular characteristics.

The coexistence of two regulatory systems for the public and private sectors within the APPI can be explained since Japan's data privacy laws were historically divided into separate statutes for each sector. The persistence of this dual structure, even after the APPI reforms, may also reflect a cultural reluctance to radically overhaul existing legal systems. Turning to European law, the EU General Data

141 Art 27-12 TBA.

142 Art 22-2-27 of the Enforcement Regulations of the TBA [電気通信事業法施行規則] (TBA Enforcement Regulation).

143 Art 22-2-29 of the TBA Enforcement Regulations.

144 Employment Security Act [職業安定法].

145 Art 5-5 para 1 ESA.

146 Ministry of Health, Labour and Welfare, 'Guidelines for Job Placement Businesses, Employers, Recruiters, Recruitment Agents, Providers of Recruitment Information, Labour Supply Businesses and Recipients of Labour Supply, etc., to Properly Address Their Responsibilities and Other Matters' [職業紹介事業者、求人者、労働者の募集を行う者、募集受託者、募集情報等提供事業を行う者、労働者供給事業者、労働者供給を受けようとする者等がその責務等に関して適切に対処するための指針] (ESA Gudelines).

147 ESA Guidelines, Part V (Sections 1–3).

148 Personal Information Protection Act [개인정보 보호법].

149 Personal Information Protection Law of the People's Republic of China [中华人民共和国个人信息保护法].

Protection Regulation (GDPR)[150] likewise covers both public and private sectors, while partially exempting or adding requirements for public-sector processing. In this respect, the GDPR can be viewed as taking a similar direction to the PIPA and PIPL.

Thus, Japan's approach has converged with foreign models in that a single statute now covers both the public and private sectors. At the same time, it remains distinctive in that two different regulatory systems for the public and private sectors still coexist within one and the same law.

#### 2.3.11.2 Regulatory Approaches to Sector-Specific Requirements

Japan's approach to data privacy regulation is to supplement the APPI with sector-specific guidelines and reinforce it with a patchwork of special statutes. Korea's PIPA, China's PIPL and the EU's GDPR likewise introduce additional or complementary rules tailored to particular sectors and can thus be regarded as adopting a broadly similar model. This common approach in data privacy law is rational in that it allows for the general data privacy requirements to be supplemented or tightened in light of the characteristics of each individual sector.

In Japan, an additional consideration is the desire to respect the pre-existing allocation of responsibilities among administrative agencies. The APPI establishes cross-cutting rules, but at the same time adopts an approach that is sensitive to the traditional jurisdiction of each authority. This may again reflect a broader cultural preference in Japan against rapid and radical changes to the structure of legal systems.

## 2.4 Right to Privacy

### *2.4.1 Judicial Development in Japan*

#### 2.4.1.1 Emergence of the Right to Privacy in Japan

The notion of a right to privacy was first advocated in the United States in the late nineteenth century as a 'right to be let alone'.[151] In Japan, the right to privacy became the focus of public debate with the 'After the Banquet' case in 1964,[152] which concerned depictions of a politician's private life in a novel, where the court recognised

[150] Regulation (EU) 2016/679 of the European Parliament and of the Council of 27 April 2016 on the protection of natural persons with regard to the processing of personal data and on the free movement of such data, and repealing Directive 95/46/EC.

[151] Warren and Brandeis 1890, p. 193.

[152] Tokyo District Court, 28 September 1964, *Lower Court Civil Cases Reports Compilation* 15(9) 2317.

a right not to have one's private life disclosed without justification and held the publisher liable for damages. The decision stated that a tort of invasion of privacy is made when the published matter: (i) relates to the person's private life or could reasonably be taken as such (private); (ii) would not be willingly disclosed by the person concerned (secrecy); and (iii) is not yet known to the public (non-publicity).

#### 2.4.1.2 Recognition of the Right to Privacy Through Case Law

Since the 'After the Banquet' judgment, the Supreme Court has recognised, albeit indirectly, rights or interests akin to privacy. In cases involving the state, it has recognised freedoms such as the freedom not to be photographed without justification (Kyoto University Student Federation Case),[153] the freedom not to be compelled to provide fingerprints (Fingerprint Refusal Case)[154] and the freedom not to have one's personal information disclosed to third parties without justification (Jūki Net Case).[155] In cases between private organisations and/or persons, it has recognised interests such as the personality interest in preventing the unjustified revelation of private matters (Non-Fiction 'Reversal' Case)[156] and has stated that 'the personal information … is legally protected as information pertaining to privacy' (Jiang Zemin Lecture Case),[157] 'any individual has a legally protected personality interest against the unjustified photographing of their likeness or appearance' (Wakayama Poisoned Curry Case),[158] and 'the interest in preventing the unjustified disclosure of facts pertaining to one's privacy should be recognised as a legally protected interest' (Google Search Results Deletion Case).[159]

---

[153] Supreme Court Grand Bench, 24 December 1969, *Supreme Court Criminal Cases Reports Compilation* 23(12) 1625).

[154] Supreme Court Third Petty Bench, 5 December 1995, *Supreme Court Criminal Cases Reports Compilation* 49(10) 842.

[155] Supreme Court First Petty Bench, 6 March 2008, *Supreme Court Civil Cases Reports Compilation* 62(3) 665.

[156] Supreme Court Third Petty Bench, 8 February 1994, *Supreme Court Civil Cases Reports Compilation* 48(2) 149.

[157] Supreme Court Second Petty Bench, 12 September 2003, *Supreme Court Civil Cases Reports Compilation* 57(8) 973.

[158] Supreme Court First Petty Bench, 10 November 2005, *Supreme Court Civil Cases Reports Compilation* 59(9) 2428.

[159] Supreme Court Third Petty Bench, 31 January 2017, *Supreme Court Civil Cases Reports Compilation* 71(1) 63.

#### 2.4.1.3 Judicial Differentiation Between APPI Violations and Privacy Torts

Given that the right to privacy in Japan has developed separately from the APPI, the prevailing view is that infringements of the right to privacy and violations of the APPI should be distinguished. According to this separation theory, the APPI is a general statute governing the proper handling of personal information and it was enacted independently of the tortious liability arising from infringements of the right to privacy.[160] As a consequence, a breach of the APPI does not necessarily amount to an infringement of the right to privacy and, conversely, an infringement of the right to privacy may be found even in the absence of a violation of the APPI.

### *2.4.2 Academic Theories in Japan*

#### 2.4.2.1 Legal Basis

Scholars generally locate the right to privacy in Article 13 of the Constitution as part of the right to pursue happiness.[161] Article 13 provides that 'life, freedom and the right to pursue happiness shall, to the extent that it does not conflict with the public welfare, be respected in legislation and other affairs of state', and the right to privacy is understood as one element of that right.

#### 2.4.2.2 Right of Control Over Personal Information

Drawing on American scholarship of the 1960s, Japanese scholars in the 1970s reconceptualised the right to privacy as a right to control one's own information. Under this view, individuals exercise autonomy by deciding how information about themselves is shared. One influential scholar defined the constitutional privacy right as the right of individuals, as morally autonomous beings, to pursue ends which they deem good, to communicate with others, and to decide the extent to which information concerning their existence is disclosed and used.'[162] Under this perspective, only data relevant to individual autonomy were subject to legal protection, while data falling outside that sphere were excluded. However, in view of advances in information technology, critics have observed that information outside the sphere of personal autonomy may also influence how people live socially since it can now be aggregated and rapidly analysed at scale.[163] In response to such critique, a leading recent scholar has reconfigured the right to control one's own information to

[160] Kato (n 11) 84–85.

[161] Shishido 2020, pp. 15–16.

[162] Sato 2020, p. 203.

[163] Sato 2023, pp. 111–112.

include a wide range of information by considering the structure and architecture of information network systems and databases.[164]

#### 2.4.2.3 Right to the Protection of Personal Information / Fair Handling of One's Own Information

In recent years scholars have criticised the self-determination focus of privacy rights. They argue that the right to privacy guaranteed by Article 13 should instead be understood as a right to the protection or fair handling of personal information.[165] A critic has argued that: (i) self-determination or consent plays only a procedural role in the realm of privacy or data protection; (ii) in contemporary information-rich society, the effectiveness of personal data self-determination/consent is increasingly doubtful; and (iii) existing legislation fails to guarantee thorough self-determination, thereby undermining the validity of the informational self-control thesis.[166]

#### 2.4.2.4 Scholarly Differentiation Between the APPI and Privacy Rights

In judicial practice, violations of the APPI are clearly distinguished from infringements of privacy rights. However, within Japanese academia, there is a tendency to essentially equate the theoretical foundation of the APPI with privacy rights. Indeed, the mainstream conception of the right to privacy in Japan discussed thus far (i.e., the right to control one's own information, to the protection of personal information and to fair handling of one's own information) serves to link the APPI with constitutional privacy rights. By contrast, another strand of Japanese commentary differentiates the theoretical bases of the APPI and the right to privacy. Departing from the traditional approach that unified privacy protection and the protection of personal information, this perspective conceptualises the two as coexisting, with neither being integrated into or absorbed by the other.[167] This view is theoretically constructed on the basis of the informational self-determination right (in German: *informationelle Selbstbestimmung*) established by German constitutional case law. Recently, one of the scholars has argued that Japan's personal information protection legislation developed independently from privacy rights, and that traditional theories must be rejected—at least to the extent that they bear no relation to the data protection framework.[168] This scholar further contends that the OECD Guidelines,[169]

---

[164] Yamamoto 2010, pp. 82–85; Yamamoto 2023, pp. 142–152.

[165] Sogabe 2018, pp. 71–78; Otonashi 2021, pp. 193–223.

[166] Sogabe and Yamamoto 2020, pp. 129–130.

[167] Koyama 2012, pp. 120–124.

[168] Takagi 2022, p. 49.

[169] OECD, Recommendation of the Council concerning Guidelines Governing the Protection of Privacy and Transborder Flows of Personal Data.

to which Japanese law aspires, are designed to realise data protection, and that the core of data protection lies in the principle of relevance.

### *2.4.3 Approach in Japan*

In Japan, the concept of the right to privacy has developed in case law, separately from the APPI, within the framework of injunctive relief and damages under the tort provisions of the Civil Code. Although there is theoretical debate as to how the right to privacy should be positioned in the legal system, in judicial practice it is treated as distinct from the APPI and plays an important role within Japan's broader data privacy framework.

Other Asian legal systems also sometimes provide mechanisms for exercising a right to privacy independently of the personal data protection statute. In Korea, if one's private life or portrait rights are violated, damages can be sought under tort law under Article 750 of the Civil Act.[170] Meanwhile, Article 39 of the PIPA works like a special rule for civil damages and provides that a personal information controller is liable for compensation for a PIPA violation unless it proves absence of wrongful intent or negligence. In China, both personal information protection and privacy rights are treated as "personality rights." However, the Civil Code[171] sets out personal information protection and the right to privacy in separate provisions (Articles 1032 and 1034). In addition, the Civil Code introduces preventive regulation for lawful processing of personal data, while the privacy-related provisions are defensive rules aimed at remedying infringements (Articles 1033 and 1035).

In Europe, the EU Charter of Fundamental Rights[172] guarantees the right to privacy in Article 7, which protects respect for private and family life, as well as home and communications, while the right to the protection of personal data is laid down as an autonomous right in Article 8. The GDPR, unlike its predecessor—DPD—does not list the protection of the right to privacy among its objectives (Article 1 of the GDPR). Although there is no settled international consensus on the theoretical status of the right to privacy, at least at the level of institutional design, there is a clear tendency for it to be exercised through mechanisms that are separate from those governing personal data protection.

[170] Civil Act of the Republic of Korea [대한민국 민법].

[171] Civil Code of the People's Republic of China [中华人民共和国民法典].

[172] Charter of Fundamental Rights of the European Union.

## References


Itsuo Sonobe and Shizuo Fujiwara (eds), *Commentary on the APPI* (3rd rev edn, Gyosei 2022) [園部逸夫=藤原静雄編『個人情報保護法の解説(第三次改訂版)』(ぎょうせい、2022年)] 60.

Katsuya Uga, *Article-by-Article Commentary on the New APPI* (Yuhikaku 2021) [宇賀克也『新・個人情報保護法の逐条解説』(2021、有斐閣)] 48.

Hisamichi Okamura, *The APPI* (4th ed, Shojihomu 2022) [岡村久道『個人情報保護法(第4版)』(商事法務、2022)] 60.

Takayuki Kato, 'Observance of Personal Information Protection Rules and Invasion of Privacy Rights: Cases Concerned with Providing Personal Data to a Third Party' (2011) 46(1) ASIA University Law Review [加藤隆之「個人情報保護 制度の遵守とプライヴァシー権侵害」亜細亜法学 46 巻 1 号] 84–85

Kazuhisa Uryu (ed), *Questions and Answers on the 2015 Amendment of the APPI* (Shojihomu 2015) [瓜生和久編『一問一答 平成27年改正個人情報保護法』(商事法務、2015)] 3

Kiyoshi Sawaki (ed), *Questions and Answers on the 2020 Amendment of the APPI* (Shojihomu 2020) [佐脇紀代志編『一問一答 令和2年改正個人情報保護法』(商事法務、2020)] 1.

Taiichirō Tomiyasu and Hibiki Nakada (eds), *Questions and Answers on the 2021 Amendment of the APPI* (Shojihomu 2021) [冨安泰一郎=中田響編『一問一答 令和3年改正個人情報保護法』(商事法務、2021)] 1.

Samuel D. Warren and Louis D. Brandeis, 'The Right to Privacy', *Harvard Law Review* 4(5) (1890) 193.

George Shishido, 'Privacy and Personal Information Protection - Considering Recent Developments in the APPI', in Nishimura & Asahi (eds), *The Complete Guide to the APPI* (Shojihomu 2020) [宍戸常寿「プライバシーと個人情報保護——近時の個人情報保護法制の動向を踏まえつつ」西村あさひ法律事務所編『個人情報保護法制大全』(商事法務、2020)] 15–16

Koji Sato, *Japanese Constitutional Theory*. 2nd ed. (Seibuno, 2020) [佐藤幸治『日本国憲法論(第2版)』(成文堂、2020)] 203.

Koji Sato, *Modern Constitutionalism and the Significance of Human Rights* (Yuhikaku 2023) [佐藤幸治『現代立憲主義と人権の意義』(有斐閣、2023)] 111–112.

Tatsuhiko Yamamoto, 'The Right to Privacy', *Jurist* 1412 (2010) [山本龍彦「プライバシーの権利」ジュリスト1412号(2010年)] 82-85

Tatsuhiko Yamamoto, *(The Counterattack of Hyper Individualism) - A Constitutional Warning to AI Society* (Kobundo 2023) [山本龍彦「プライバシーの権利」ジュリスト1412号(2010年)] 142–152

Masahiro Sogabe, 'Is the Right to Control One's Own Information a Fundamental Right?', *Constitutional Studies* 3 (2018) [曽我部真裕「自己情報コントロールは基本権か?」憲法研究3号(2018)] 71–78

Tomohiro Otonashi, *Reconstructing the Right to Privacy - From the Right to Control One's Own Information to the Right to Fair Handling of One's Own Information* (Yuhikaku 2021) [音無知展『プライバシー権の再構成——自己情報コントロール権から適正な自己情報の取扱いを受ける権利へ——』(有斐閣、2021)] 193–223

Masahiro Sogabe and Tatsuhiko Yamamoto, 'On the Right to Control One's Own Information', *Information Law Review* 7 (2020) [曽我部真裕=山本龍彦「自己情報コントロール権をめぐって」情報法制研究7号(2020年)]129–130

Go Koyama, *Constitutional Protection of Simple Personal Information, Ronkyu Jurist* 1 (2012) [小山剛『単純個人情報の憲法上の保護』論究ジュリスト1号(2012年)] 120–124

Hiromitsu Takagi, 'From Personal Information Protection to Personal Data Protection -Reviewing the Purpose of the System Based on Its Objectives (6)', *Information Law Review* 12 (2022) [高木浩光「個人情報保護から個人データ保護へ-法目的に基づく制度見直しの検討(6)」情報法制研究12号(2022)] 49

# Chapter 3
# The Korean Personal Information Protection Act: An Overview

**Hwan Kyoung Ko, Il Shin Lee, and Ji Hoon Kim**

## 3.1 Basic Regulatory Framework of PIPA

### *3.1.1 Direction of Recent Amendments of PIPA*

Since its enactment in September 2011, Personal Information Protection Act (PIPA) has undergone several amendments to reflect the rapid evolution of the digital environment. Notably, key amendments were made in 2020 and 2023. The 2020 revision integrated into PIPA the provisions on the processing of online personal information that had previously been regulated separately under the Act on Promotion of Information and Communications Network Utilization and Information Protection (Network Act). Influenced by the EU General Data Protection Regulation (GDPR), it also introduced new rules on the additional use and provision of personal information and special provisions on the processing of pseudonymized information for statistical purposes, scientific research, or preservation of public interest records. In 2023, regulations that had been previously separated into online and offline regimes were unified, rules on the cross-border transfer of personal information were refined, and new rights of data subjects, such as the right to request the transfer of personal information, were introduced.

In 2025, Korea experienced a series of unprecedented large scale personal data breaches across sectors closely connected to everyday life, including telecommunications, e-commerce, and financial services. In February 2026, against this backdrop, the National Assembly of Korea passed another amendment package to PIPA. The amendment further strengthens corporate accountability and incident–response obligations. The amendments will enter into force on September 11,

H. K. Ko (✉) · I. S. Lee · J. H. Kim
Lee & Ko, Seoul, Republic of Korea
e-mail: hwankyoung.ko@leeko.com; ilshin.lee@leeko.com; jihoon.kim3@leeko.com



H. Miyashita et al. (eds.), *The Evolution of Data Protection Laws in China, Japan, and Korea*, https://doi.org/10.1007/978-981-95-8609-7_3

2026, except for the data protection certification requirement (effective July 1, 2027).

Separately, in 2021, the European Commission adopted an adequacy decision acknowledging the level of personal information protection in The Republic of Korea (Korea).[1] Under the GDPR, additional mechanisms, such as standard contractual clauses or certification, are generally required for cross-border transfers of personal information. However, with the adequacy decision in place, personal information of EU data subjects can be transferred to Korea without further safeguards being necessary. This development has facilitated the operations of Korean global companies in the EU market and has also enabled smaller Korean enterprises, which previously found compliance with the GDPR's data transfer requirements challenging, to explore business opportunities in the EU. In September 2025, the Korean government recognized the EU's equivalence. As a result, Korea and the EU are now mutually able to conduct cross-border transfers of personal information in either direction without separate consent from data subjects.[2]

### *3.1.2 Relationship with Other Laws*

In certain specific industrial sectors, special laws provide rules on the protection of personal information. In such cases, pursuant to the principle of the 'precedence of special laws,' these sector-specific laws take precedence over PIPA. For example, the Act on the Use and Protection of Credit Information (the Credit Information Act) prevails over PIPA for the processing of personal credit information in the credit and financial sectors; the Act on the Protection and Use of Location Information takes precedence over PIPA with respect to the processing of personal location information; and the Medical Service Act takes priority over PIPA concerning the processing of personal information in the health and medical sectors.

### *3.1.3 Personal Information Protection Commission and Korea Internet & Security Agency*

The Personal Information Protection Commission (the PIPC) is the competent authority responsible for privacy and data protection matters. It oversees compliance with PIPA, conducts investigations, issues decisions, and imposes administrative sanctions such as administrative fines, penalties, and corrective orders, as well

---

[1] Commission, 'Implementing Decision (EU) 2022/254, 17 December 2021, on the adequate protection of personal data by the Republic of Korea' C(2021) 9316, 1.

[2] PIPC, 'Completion of Safe and Free Personal Information Transfer System between Korea and the EU' (Press Release, 17 September 2025).

as formulates policies on personal information protection. The PIPC delegates some of its functions—such as research and studies related to personal information protection, receiving reports on data breaches, and tasks related to the designation of professional personal information management intermediaries—to the Korea Internet & Security Agency (KISA).

## 3.2 Definition and Types of Personal Information

PIPA defines personal information as "information relating to a living individual that identifies or can identify a particular individual." More specifically, it includes:

- information that identifies a particular individual by his or her full name, Resident Registration Number, etc.;
- information which, even if it does not by itself identify a particular individual, may be easily combined with other information to identify a particular individual. In such cases, whether the information can be easily must be determined by reasonably considering the time, cost, technology, and other factors required to identify the individual; and
- **pseudonymized information: information that has been processed in such a way that a particular individual cannot be identified without the use or combination of additional information required for restoration to its original state. Pseudonymized information is considered personal information but is subject to special provisions (as set out in Sect.** 3.4).

By contrast, information that can no longer be used to identify an individual even when combined with other information and taking into account reasonable factors such as time, cost, and technology, is not subject to PIPA, as it is excluded from the definition of personal information.

## 3.3 General Obligations for Data Handlers

A 'data handler' refers to a person that, directly, or through a third party, handles personal information in order to use or carry out any operation of personal information files in the course of its work or in relation to its business. A data handler may be a public agency, a corporation, an organization, or an individual. In this regard, the concept of a data handler is similar to that of a 'controller' under the GDPR. However, compared with the GDPR's controller, PIPA's data handler characterized by its express reference to the "operation of personal information files" and PIPA does not recognize a concept equivalent to the GDPR's 'joint controller.'

Many provisions of PIPA designate data handlers as obligated parties and impose various obligations on them. The main obligations of data handlers under PIPA are as follows:

### *3.3.1 Collection and Use of Personal Information, and Its Provision to Third Parties*

PIPA prescribes duties that data handlers must observe throughout the processing of personal information.

When the data handler intends to **collect and use** personal information, any of the following legal bases must be met:

(1) Where the data handler notifies a data subject of matters prescribed by PIPA (e.g., the items listed below), and consent is obtained from the data subject;

- Purpose of collection and use of personal information
- Items of personal information to be collected
- Retention and use period of personal information
- The fact that the data subject has the right to refuse consent and the disadvantages, if any, resulting from the refusal of consent

(2) Where special provisions exist in other statutes or it is inevitable to comply with statutory obligations;
(3) Where it is unavoidable for a public institution to perform its duties prescribed by laws and regulations;
(4) Where it is necessary to take measures at the request of a data subject in the course of performing a contract concluded with the data subject or concluding a contract (amended in 2023 from "Where it is inevitably necessary for the conclusion and performance of a contract with the data subject");
(5) Where it is deemed clearly necessary for the protection, from imminent danger, of life, bodily and property interests of a data subject or a third party;
(6) Where it is necessary to attain the legitimate interests of the data handler, provided such interests clearly outweigh the rights of the data subject. (In such cases, processing shall be allowed only to the extent the processing is substantially related to the legitimate interests of the data handler and does not go beyond a reasonable scope); or
(7) Where it is urgently necessary for public safety and security, public health, etc. (newly added in the 2023 amendment in light of the need to process personal information for public health purposes during the spread of COVID-19).

When a data handler intends to **provide** a data subject's personal information **to a third party**, one of the following legal bases must be satisfied:

(1) Where the data handler notifies a data subject of matters prescribed by PIPA (e.g., the items listed below), and consent is obtained from the data subject;

- Recipient (third party) of personal information
- Purpose of use of personal information by the recipient
- Items of personal information to be provided
- Retention and use period of personal information by the recipient

- The fact that the data subject has the right to refuse consent and the disadvantages, if any, resulting from the refusal of consent

(2) Where the provision of information falls within the scope of the purposes for which it was initially collected under the legal bases for collection and use as defined in items (2), (3), (5), (6), and (7) above.

The PIPC had previously taken a restrictive approach to recognizing legal bases other than the data subject's consent for the collection and use of personal information and for its provision to third parties. It is now moving toward a broader and more flexible recognition and application of alternative legal bases. In particular, prior to the 2023 PIPA amendment, the collection and use of personal information without the data subject's consent was possible 'where it was strictly necessary' for the conclusion and performance of a contract with the data subject, which significantly limited the application of that legal basis. However, with the removal of the term 'inevitably' in the 2023 PIPA amendment, the PIPC now interprets that personal information can be collected and used without separate consent based on mutual trust, within a reasonable scope that the data handler and the data subject can mutually expect in relation to the contract.[3] Furthermore, while the PIPC previously took a strict position when applying the legal basis in subparagraph (6), it has recently been gradually expanding its scope of application, for example, by providing guidance that legitimate interests can constitute a substantive legal basis for collecting and using publicly disclosed personal information for AI training and services.[4]

When seeking **consent** from a data subject, a data handler must obtain each item of consent separately and clearly. For instance, if personal information is processed for marketing or promotional purposes, separate opt-in consent must be obtained, and refusal of such optional consent must not result in denial of service. Further, as a follow-up to the 2023 amendments to PIPA, the Enforcement Decree effective from September 15, 2024, explicitly provides that valid consent must be given freely and voluntarily by the data subject, "allowing them to make an uninfluenced choice as to whether to consent." While it had been common practice in Korea for data handlers to request consent from data subjects in a mandatory manner during the collection of personal information, following the amendment of the Enforcement Decree, efforts are being made to reorganize consent procedures so that the data subject's free will is better reflected.

Data handlers must use or provide personal information only **within the scope of the purposes for which it was initially collected**, unless exceptions are prescribed by law. Violations are subject to criminal and administrative penalties, and thus, the PIPC and the courts have tended to interpret "the scope of the initially collected purpose" strictly.

---

[3] PIPC, 'Comprehensive Guide to Personal Information Processing' (Guideline, 2025) 41.

[4] PIPC, 'Guidelines on Processing Publicly Disclosed Personal Information for AI Development and Services' (Guideline, 2024) 6.

Influenced by the GDPR, the 2023 amendment to PIPA permits the limited additional use or provision of personal information without consent, if such use or provision is reasonably related to the original purpose of collection, taking into account whether the data subject may be adversely affected and whether appropriate safeguards, such as encryption, have been implemented. The PIPC recently published a guideline providing concrete examples of when personal information can be additionally used or provided without the data subject's consent under the amended law, related interpretations are accumulating. A typical example is where a data handler utilizes a user's personal information for AI training and development in a manner that is reasonably related to the purpose for which it was originally collected.[5]

### 3.3.2 *Outsourced Processing of Personal Information*

The provision of personal information to a third party and the outsourced processing of personal information both involve the transfer of personal information from a data handler to a third party; however, there are important differences. Third-party provision involves a case where the recipient (third party) has its own independent purpose for processing information, whereas outsourced processing refers to a case where a data handler entrusts a data processor with handling personal information solely to achieve the data handler's own business purposes.[6]

In the case of third-party provision, the right to control and manage personal information is transferred to the recipient, and the provider is generally not legally responsible for the recipient's processing of personal information. On the other hand, in the case of outsourced processing of personal information, the data handler still retains the right to control and manage personal information even after it has been transferred; therefore, should the data processor violate PIPA and cause damage to data subjects, the data handler may be held liable for compensation.

As such, distinguishing the legal nature of personal information transfer as either third-party provision or outsourced processing is practically very important in terms of legal liability. There are numerous significant cases where the distinction between third-party provision and outsourced processing has been a key issue, such as the case of Homeplus, a major Korean hypermarket chain, selling personal information to insurance companies, and the case of Kakao Pay, a major Korean FinTech company, transferring personal information to Alipay.

Unlike third-party provision, the outsourced processing of personal information does not require separate consent from a data subject. Instead, the data handler must enter into a written contract with the data processor specifying details of the entrusted tasks and the identity of the data processor, both of which must be

[5] PIPC, 'Comprehensive Guide to Personal Information Processing' 76–80; PIPC, 'Guideline on Personal Information Processing for Generative AI Development and Utilization' (Guideline, 2025) 12–13.

[6] Supreme Court of Korea, 7 April 2017, 2016Do13263, Judgement.

disclosed in the data handler's privacy policy. In addition, the data handler is also required to manage and supervise the data processor to ensure compliance with PIPA.

### *3.3.3 Special Categories of Personal Information (Personal Information of Children, Sensitive Information, Unique Identification Information)*

PIPA imposes more stringent obligations for particular categories of information that require special protection.

(1) **Personal Information of Children:** When a data handler is required under PIPA to obtain consent under PIPA to process personal information of children under the age of 14, the data handler must obtain consent from the child's legal representative (e.g., parent) and verify such consent. In 2021, an incident occurred where a company developing an AI chatbot was sanctioned by the PIPC for collecting personal information of children without the consent of their legal representative.[7]

(2) **Sensitive Information:** This includes data that pose a significant risk to the privacy of data subjects, such as ideology or beliefs, political views, health or sexual information, genetic data, criminal records, and biometric data. Processing sensitive information requires separate consent in addition to general consent for personal information processing, or a specific legal basis under applicable laws. In 2024, the Worldcoin Foundation was sanctioned by the PIPC for collecting sensitive information, such as iris data of Korean data subjects, without a legitimate legal basis for processing.[8]

(3) **Unique Identification Information:** This refers to identification information assigned to individuals in Korea for the purpose of uniquely distinguishing them, such as Resident Registration Numbers, passport numbers, driver's license numbers, and Aline Registration Numbers. Processing unique identification information also requires separate consent in addition to general consent or a statutory basis. However, the processing of the **Resident Registration Numbers** is prohibited unless there is a specific legal basis, even if consent is obtained from the data subject.

[7] PIPC, 28 April 2021, 2021-007-072, Decision.

[8] PIPC, 25 September 2024, 2024-016-234, Decision.

### 3.3.4 *Obligation to Destroy Personal Information*

When the retention or use period of personal information notified to the data subject expires, or when the purpose of processing personal information has been achieved, the data handler must destroy such personal information without delay son that it cannot be recovered or reused. If other laws require continued retention of personal information, the data handler must store and manage such information separately from other personal information.

### 3.3.5 *Measures to Ensure Security of Personal Information*

Data handlers must implement measures to prevent the loss, theft, leakage, forgery, alteration, or damage of personal information. These security measures include technical, managerial, and physical safeguards, such as establishing and implementing internal management plans, controlling and restricting access to personal information processing systems, and securing storage facilities using locking devices or other physical protections. The minimum specific requirements for these security measures are detailed in the Standards for Ensuring the Safety of Personal Information (PIPC Notification). The major articles are specified below:

- Establishment, Implementation, and Review of Internal Management Plans
- Management of Access Authority
- Access Control
- Encryption of Personal Information
- Retention and Review of Access Records
- Prevention of Malicious Programs, etc.
- Physical Security Measures
- Destruction of Personal Information

A violation of the duty to implement security measures is itself subject to administrative fines (up to KRW 30 million, approximately USD 20,000). If a data breach occurs and the duty to implement security measures has not been fulfilled, administrative penalties may also be imposed, as detailed in Sect. 3.3.6 below. Accordingly, the fulfillment of security obligations is an important factor in determining whether to impose administrative penalties and, if so, at what level in the event of a data breach.

The 2026 amendment of PIPA introduces mandatory ISMS-P (Personal Information & Information Security Management System) certification requirements for certain large-scale data handlers. Under the previous regime, obtaining ISMS-P certification was generally voluntary for most data handlers and was often pursued to enhance external credibility regarding the robustness of their data protection practices. The PIPC has also indicated that it may actively consider revocation of ISMS-P certification in cases involving serious violations relating to personal data protection.

### 3.3.6 Obligation to Take Action in the Event of Data Breach

In the event of a data breach, the data handler must notify the affected data subject of the breach within 72 hours of becoming aware of the breach. Under the 2026 amendment of PIPA, even prior to confirmation of a data breach, where a data handler becomes aware of the possibility of a data breach, the duty to notify data subjects may arise. The data handler must also report to the PIPC or the KISA within 72 hours if: (i) personal information of 1000 or more data subjects has been leaked; (ii) sensitive information or unique identification information has been leaked; or (iii) personal information has been leaked due to hacking or other unauthorized access from the outside.

Investigation and administrative disposition for data breach incidents are among the primary responsibilities of the PIPC. If any deficiencies in security measures are found as a result of investigations, administrative penalties may be imposed. Under PIPA, a data handler may be subject to an administrative penalty of up to 3% of the data handler's total annual revenue (calculated as the average over the preceding three (3) years and excluding any income unrelated to the violation). In addition, under the 2026 amendment of PIPA, the cap on administrative penalties may now be imposed at up to 10% of total annual revenue (on the same basis as above) in the following circumstances: (i) if a violation constituting grounds for an administrative penalty is committed within three (3) years from the date of receiving a previous administrative penalty, with intent or gross negligence; (ii) if a violation constituting grounds for an administrative penalty is committed with intent or gross negligence, and the number of affected data subjects is 10 million or more; or (iii) where a data breach occurs as a result of failure to comply with a corrective order.

In recent years, Korea has experienced multiple major data breaches involving large companies. Notably, in 2025, several significant hacking incidents resulted in large-scale leaks of personal information affecting telecommunication providers, credit card companies, and other entities handling substantial volumes of personal information. In response to heightened awareness of data breaches, regulatory oversight by the PIPC has become more stringent, resulting in increased administrative penalties. Against this backdrop, there has also been a corresponding rise in disputes and complaints from data subjects, highlighting the growing public demand for stronger data protection and security measures. Notably, in August 2025, the PIPC imposed its largest-ever administrative penalty of KRW 134.8 billion (approximately USD 92 million) on SK Telecom, South Korea's largest mobile carrier, following a personal information leakage incident.[9]

[9] PIPC, 27 August 2025, 2025-018-243, Decision.

### 3.3.7 *Designation of Chief Privacy Officer*

The Chief Privacy Officer (CPO) must be appointed directly by the business owner or representative, or designated at the executive level. If there is no executive level officer, the head of the department responsible for personal information processing may be appointed. Particularly for large organizations, it is required to designate a professional with experience in data privacy as the CPO. The data handler must ensure the CPO's independence. The major tasks of the CPO are specified below:

- Establishment and implementation of personal information protection plans
- Managing qualified personnel and securing the budget necessary for the protection of personal information (under the 2026 amendment)
- Reporting to the representative and the board of directors on the status of personal information protection and other related matters of importance (under the 2026 amendment)
- Periodic investigation and improvement of personal information processing status and practices
- Handling of complaints and redress of damage related to personal information processing
- Establishment of an internal control system for preventing leakage, misuse, and abuse of personal information
- Establishment and execution of personal information protection training plans
- Protection, management, and supervision of personal information files
- Establishment, modification, and enforcement of privacy policy
- Management of human and material resources and data related to personal information processing
- Destruction of personal information when processing purpose is achieved or retention period expires

Recently, discussions have been underway to further strengthen the authority and status of the CPO. In the recent SK Telecom personal information leakage incident, the PIPC ordered SK Telecom to clearly establish the responsibilities and roles of the CPO.[10]

Under the 2026 amendment of PIPA, the representative (e.g., CEO) or business owner bears ultimate responsibility for the secure processing of personal information and the protection of data subjects' rights, and must effectively implement comprehensive management measures, including the allocation of qualified personnel and sufficient budgetary support. Furthermore, certain large-scale data handlers are now subject to obligations to (i) obtain board approval when appointing, changing, or dismissing the CPO; and (ii) report matters concerning the appointment, change, or dismissal of the CPO to the PIPC.

[10] Ibid.

- **Comparison with Chief Information Security Officer** (CISO): Under the Network Act, online business operators are required to designate a CISO, and those above a certain scale business must report their designated CISO to the Ministry of Science and ICT. The roles of the CISO and the CPO can be held concurrently.

### *3.3.8 Establishment and Public Disclosure of Privacy Policy*

The data handler must establish a privacy policy and publicly disclose such policy on its website or other channels. The privacy policy must include the following items:

- Categories of personal information processed
- Purpose of processing personal information
- Retention and use period of personal information
- Details concerning the provision of personal information to a third party and outsourced processing
- Procedures and methods for the destruction of personal information
- Possibility of disclosure of sensitive information and methods for opting out such disclosure
- Matters concerning the processing of pseudonymized information
- Measures taken to ensure the security of personal information
- Methods and procedures for the data subject's exercise of rights
- Name and contact information of the CPO or the department in charge of personal information protection
- Matters concerning the use of cookies
- Details concerning the cross-border transfer of personal information
- Name of countries from which personal information is directly collected

Data handlers are not required to obtain consent from data subjects regarding the privacy policy itself. Instead, the privacy policy must include various details in addition to the matters that must be notified to data subjects when obtaining consent for the collection, use, or third-party provision of personal information, such as details concerning outsourced processing, procedures and methods for the destruction of personal information, and the possibility of disclosure of sensitive information and methods for opting out of such disclosure. With the 2023 amendment to PIPA, a privacy policy assessment system was newly introduced, allowing the PIPC to select and assess large-scale data handlers and recommend improvements.

## 3.4 Processing of Pseudonymized Information

The 2020 amendment introduced special provisions for the processing of pseudonymized information. This was adopted by referring to the regulations concerning pseudonymization under the GDPR, and this regulatory framework aims to minimize privacy risks to data subjects while facilitating the active use of data to promote new industry development, such as utilizing data for AI training. PIPA also includes regulations regarding the combination of pseudonymized information between different data handlers.

Pseudonymized information falls within the scope of personal information, but it significantly differs from general personal information in that it may be processed without obtaining consent from data subjects when used for statistical purposes, scientific research, or preservation of public interest records. 'Statistical purposes' include commercial statistics, such as market research, and 'scientific research' covers basic and applied research as well as industrial research for the development and demonstration or validation of new technologies, products, or services.[11]

Data handlers must not process pseudonymized information for the purpose of identifying a specific individual. They are required to implement protective measures, such as separately storing additional information necessary for re-identification, to prevent restoration to the original state.

## 3.5 Cross-Border Transfer of Personal Information

Cross-border transfer of personal information encompasses the provision and outsourcing of personal information to third parties outside the territory of Korea, as well as accessing or storing personal information abroad. In addition to complying with the legal bases necessary for third-party provision or outsourcing of personal information, additional legal criteria apply to cross-border transfers. These include notifying data subjects of the cross-border transfer, obtaining separate consent, or disclosing relevant information regarding overseas transfers in the privacy policy (which shall be limited to cases of outsourced processing or storage of personal information).

Furthermore, to align with international standards and facilitate global data exchange and cooperation, the 2023 amendment to PIPA expanded the legal bases for cross-border transfers, including:

- **Where legal provisions, treaties to which Korea is a party, or other international agreements provide specific rules on cross-border transfers**: however, to date, no such laws or treaties involving Korea exist regarding cross-border transfer.

[11] PIPC, 'Guidelines on Processing of Pseudonymized Information' (Guideline, 2024) 11–12.

- **Cross-border Transfer Certification**: where the overseas recipient of personal information obtains certification from the PIPC and takes necessary security measures; however, no cases certified by the PIPC to date.
- **Recognition of Equivalence by the PIPC**: where the PIPC recognizes the data protection level of a specific country or international organization as equivalent to the level under PIPA. This system is similar to the GDPR's adequacy decision. As noted above, in September 2025, the PIPC recognized the EU's equivalency, establishing mutual recognition of adequacy and equivalence of data protection between Korean and the EU. While no other equivalence determinations have been made other than the EU, the PIPC intends to expand the list over time.

Meanwhile, the amended PIPA also grants the PIPC the authority to order the suspension of cross-border transfers. Specifically, where cross-border transfers of personal information are ongoing or further transfers are anticipated, the PIPC may order the data handler requiring the data handler to suspend such transfers if: (i) the transfer violates PIPA provisions cross-border transfers; or (ii) the recipient of personal information, or the country or international organization; to which such personal information is transferred, fails to ensure a level of protection equivalent to that under PIPA, thereby causing, or posing a substantial risk of causing, harm to the data subjects. Recently, the PIPC has been actively imposing sanctions relating to cross-border transfers of personal information, such as the case in which Kakao Pay a major Korean Fintech Company, was subject to an administrative penalty for the problematic transfer of user personal information to Alipay.[12]

## 3.6 Rights of Data Subjects

PIPA also stipulates the rights that data subjects hold against the data handler. The key rights are outlined as follows:

- **Right to Request Access:** A data subject has the right to request access to his or her personal information. The data handler must allow access within ten (10) days upon receipt of such request, unless there are exceptional circumstances, such as where access is prohibited or restricted by law.
- **Right to Request Rectification and Deletion:** Upon accessing his or her personal information, a data subject may request the rectification or deletion of such personal information. However, deletion may be restricted where other laws require that such personal information be retained for a prescribed period.
- **Right to Request Suspension of Processing:** A data subject may request a temporary suspension of the processing of his or her personal information. The data handler cannot refuse such a request unless it falls under the exceptions prescribed by law and must notify the data subject of the reasons for any refusal.

[12] PIPC, 22 January 2025, 2025-001-002, Decision.

Recently, telecommunications users filed a lawsuit against the carriers, citing this right, to request the suspension of pseudonymization of their personal information. However, in July 2025, the Supreme Court of Korea rejected the claim, ruling that the pseudonymization of personal information is not subject to the exercise of the right to request suspension of personal information processing.[13]

- **Right to Data Portability:** This is the right for data subjects to request the transfer of their personal information from a data handler to another entity, forming the legal basis for the so-called 'MyData' in Korea. Initially introduced in the financial sector with the 2020 Credit Information Act regarding personal credit information, the right to data portability was subsequently incorporated into PIPA through the 2023 amendment and took effect in March 2025. The concept is largely divided into two forms, with the right to request transmission to oneself and the right to request transmission to a third party.

  The request for transmission to a third party is further divided into those sent to general recipients and those processed through specialized personal information management intermediaries. Transfers to general recipients are limited to cases where the transfer is necessary for verifying the authenticity of information collected in the course of the recipient's own business activities. Even so, general recipients must implement appropriate security measures and maintain certain facilities and technical capabilities. Professional personal information management intermediaries are entities that either (i) act as intermediaries facilitating the transmission of personal information from the data handler to other institutions or companies (specialized intermediary institutions), or (ii) perform management and analytical services for information received from data handlers (general and specialized institutions). The request for transmission to a third party is conducted through standardized API-based systems via intermediary institutions to ensure security and reliability.
- **Right to Automated Decision-Making:** Where decisions with significant effects on a data subject's rights or obligations are made solely by automated means (including AI-based systems), data subjects have the right to object to those decisions or request relevant explanations from the data handler. Unless there is a legitimate reason, the data handler must not apply such automated decisions and must provide explanations and necessary measures such as re-processing through human intervention to fulfill the data subject's request. This right was introduced through the 2023 PIPA amendment to serve as a social safeguard amid the increasing adoption of AI-based services, ensuring data subjects can safely use such technologies.

[13] Supreme Court of Korea, 18 July 2025, 2024 Da210554, Judgement.

## 3.7 Extraterritorial Application

While PIPA does not specifically limit the scope of its application, it fundamentally governs personal information processing in Korea. However, the PIPC explains that PIPA may apply to an overseas data handler (i) when the handler provides goods or services targeting Korean data subjects, (ii) when the handler's processing of personal information affects Korean data subjects, or (iii) when the handler has a place of business within the territory of Korea.[14]

However, the determination of PIPA's applicability to overseas data handlers may vary depending on the specific facts of the case.

## 3.8 Designation of Domestic Agents

A 'domestic agent' is an individual or entity that acts on behalf of an overseas data handler regarding (i) handling complaints and providing remedies for damages related to personal information processing (CPO's task), (ii) notifying and reporting data breach, and/or (iii) submitting materials for PIPA investigations. If the domestic agent violates PIPA concerning the duties mentioned above, the data handler shall be deemed to have committed such act.

The obligation to designate a domestic agent applies to an overseas data handler if any of following apply:

- The total (global) sales revenue (for the immediately preceding business year) is KRW one (1) trillion or more (considering the average exchange rate of the preceding year)
- The daily average number of Korean data subjects whose personal information is stored and managed for the three (3) months immediately preceding the end of the previous year is one (1) million or more
- The PIPC determines that the designation is necessary

If an overseas data handler has a Korean corporation (i) which is established by the data handler, or (ii) over which the data handler exercises control, the data handler must designate that corporation as a domestic agent. When designating a domestic agent, the data handler must disclose the domestic agent in the privacy policy.

[14] PIPC, 'Guidelines on Applying the Personal Information Protection Act to Foreign business operators' (Guideline, 2024) 9–16.

## 3.9 Outlook

Since its enactment in 2011, PIPA has evolved to pursue two seemingly competing goals—safeguarding individual privacy and enabling flexible data processing to promote the development of the data industry. As the age of AI fully unfolds, discussions concerning regarding the need to reconsider the concept of personal information and the legal bases for processing, as the current PIPA framework faces challenges in adequately regulating personal information processing related to AI. In line with global trends, the acquisition and use of data to advance the AI industry has emerged as a significant issue in Korea. The PIPC has also announced plans for legislative reform plans aimed at facilitating the use of original data for AI, broadening the legal bases for personal information processing, and enhancing related regulatory frameworks. Continued attention should therefore be paid to the evolution of PIPA in response to advancements in AI technology.

# Part II
# Biometric Data Protection Law

# Chapter 4
# The Evolution and Mechanism of China Personal Biometric Data Legal Protection System

**Haotian Ma**

## 4.1 Introduction

In the era of digital transformation, biometric technology has become deeply embedded in the fabric of societal operations, revolutionizing identity authentication and enabling a myriad of commercial applications. However, The rapid proliferation and utilization of personal biometric data have concurrently given rise to profound challenges, including widespread over-collection, unauthorized use, and commercial exploitation of such sensitive information, highlighting an urgent need for robust legal safeguards.

China's journey in constructing a legal protection system for personal biometric data reflects its distinct developmental trajectory and jurisprudential logic, evolving from fragmented regulations across various legal domains towards a more integrated and hierarchical framework. This article seeks to systematically examine the evolution, institutional design, and operational mechanisms of China's legal protection system for personal biometric data. It will trace the historical development from early criminal provisions and civil law incorporations to the landmark enactment of the Personal Information Protection Law (PIPL) in 2021, analyze the specific rights and obligations established for data subjects and processors, explore the enforcement dynamics involving judicial and administrative bodies, and situate China's approach within comparative international models. By doing so, this article aims to provide a comprehensive understanding of the characteristics, achievements, and ongoing challenges within China's legal framework for safeguarding personal biometric data.

H. Ma (✉)
Renmin University of China, Beijing, China





H. Miyashita et al. (eds.), *The Evolution of Data Protection Laws in China, Japan, and Korea*, https://doi.org/10.1007/978-981-95-8609-7_4

## 4.2 Defining Personal Biometric Data Under China Law

With the development of biological science, the technology for collecting and identifying biological information has gradually matured. Biological information has been linked to citizens' personal identities, gradually revealing its commercial value. The compound annual growth rate of China's biometric recognition market was 50% from 2002 to 2015.[1] By 2025, the scale of China's biometric recognition market is expected to reach approximately 45 billion yuan, and it is projected to grow to over 80 billion yuan by 2030.[2] Against this backdrop, the legal protection of biometric data has become an urgent issue to be addressed, and the abuse of biometric data by related industries cannot be ignored. According to a 2018 report by the Consumers' Association, as many as 91 apps were found to be over-collecting personal biometric data.[3] These applications often collect personal biometric data without permission.[4] Some industries even openly sold personal biometric data.[5] There is a serious mismatch between the market for personal biometric data and the supporting legal system, and it is necessary to identify, define, and protect it legally.

Under China's legal system, personal biometric data is classified as a type of personal information as stipulated in the Civil Code of the People's Republic of China. According to Article 1034, Paragraph 2 of the Civil Code, personal information refers to various types of information recorded in electronic or other forms that can identify a specific natural person either alone or in combination with other information. As for personal biometric data, there is no legal definition. In academic and practical field, it refers to personal biometric feature information obtained through biometric recognition technology, which can identify the identity of a natural person either alone or in combination with other information, including but not limited to fingerprint, facial, iris, palmprint, vein, voiceprint, eyeprint, gait, handwriting, and other biometric sample data and templates.[6] Personal biometric data, due to its nature of being able to indicate the specific identity of a natural person, is

---

[1] Caixia 2018, p. 62.

[2] 'China Biometric System Industry Market Development Trends and Outlook Strategic Analysis Research Report 2025–2030'(Docin.com, 2019) <https://www.docin.com/p-4874356258.html> accessed 1 August 2025.

[3] China Consumers Association, *Personal Information Collection and Privacy Policy Evaluation Report for 100 Apps (100款App个人信息收集与隐私政策测评报告)* (2018) <http://www.cca.org.cn/jmxf/detail/28310.html> accessed 1 August 2025.

[4] Li 2019, p. 20.

[5] '170,000 "facial recognition information" Items Publicly Sold, Covering Over 2,000 People!'*(17万条"人脸数据"遭公开售卖，覆盖超2000人!)* (Sohu.com, 2 September 2019) <http://www.sohu.com/a/343495053_100017041> accessed 1 August 2025.

[6] Sun Ge and Zhang Rongzhao, 'Investigation of Overseas Personal Biometric Data Protection Models'*(域外个人生物识别信息保护模式考察)* , *People's Court Daily(人民法院报)*, (24 January 2025), sec 1 <https://www.chinacourt.cn/article/detail/2025/01/id/8685349.shtml> accessed 1 August 2025.

classified under the legal concept of 'personal information' and has been protected under the same standards as other personal information for a period of time.

However, personal biometric data, due to its nature, requires more comprehensive protection measures than other personal information. Compared with other personal information, personal biometric data has the following unique characteristics: First, the definition and collection of biometric data need to rely on certain technical means. Secondly, biometric data is derived from inherent physiological and behavioral characteristics of the human body, featuring exclusivity, uniqueness, high sensitivity and immutability. Exclusivity and uniqueness mean that biometric data obtained through biometric technology can be directly linked to a specific natural person, and the biometric data collected from a specific individual can identify the corresponding natural person without the need to combine it with any other information. High sensitivity refers to the fact that personal biometric data has bears personal rights and interests and is closely related to other important information.[7] Immutability means that the connection and correspondence between a specific individual and specific biometric data cannot be erased or changed, and once collected, such data remains valid for life. This nature is particularly evident in biometric data based on physiological features such as fingerprints, palm prints, voice prints, and facial images.[8] Due to these properties, biometric data has higher accuracy and reliability in the identification of natural persons' identities than general personal information, and is also more closely related to personal privacy.

## 4.3 Historical Development of Legal System about Personal Biometric Data Protection in China

Around 2020, many scholars in China had already fully recognized the significance of personal biometric data in their research,[9] and the government had also issued some administrative regulations and industry standards. However, before the promulgation of the Personal Information Protection Law (PIPL) in 2021, China's laws still lacked a comprehensive and integrated regulatory system regarding personal biometric data. The enactment of the PIPL marks the improvement of relevant laws in China. The following text will systematically review the development process of China's personal biometric data protection legal system.

[7] Chuyao 2025, pp. 67–68.

[8] Li 2019, p. 19.

[9] In the legal research database CNKI (China's version of Google Scholar), legal papers related to personal biometric data began appeared around 2019. After 2020, the number of such papers increased significantly.

### 4.3.1 Pre-PIPL Legal Phase: General and Additional Regulations

The Chinese legal system has undergone a long process of development regarding the regulations concerning personal information, including personal biometric data. The protection of personal information first emerged in the criminal domain.[10] The Amendment VII to the Criminal Law of the People's Republic of China of 2009 first explicitly stipulated the crime of infringing upon citizens' personal information, which states:

> Any staff member of a State organ, or an institution of finance, telecommunication, transportation, education, or health care, etc., who in violation of State regulations, sells or illegally provides citizens' personal information obtained by the aforesaid entity during the course of performing duties or providing services shall, if the circumstances are serious, be sentenced to a fixed term of imprisonment of not more than three years or criminal detention and be concurrently imposed with a fine, or shall be imposed with a fine alone. Any person who illegally obtains the aforementioned information by theft or other means shall, if the circumstances are serious, be punished in accordance with the provisions of the preceding paragraph.

However, the main participants this time were limited to the staff members form state organ and members from financial and telecommunications units and there is no specific definition of personal biometric data.

The earliest specific regulation on personal biometric data was Cybersecurity Law implemented in 2017. Article 44 of Cybersecurity Law first stipulates: '*no individual or organization shall steal or illegally obtain citizens'personal information, nor shall they illegally sell or provide citizens'personal information to others*'. Article 76, Paragraph (5), in terms of definition, clearly states that personal information includes personal biometric data. In general civil legal field, by the revision of the Civil Code in 2020, Article 1034 of the Civil Code stipulates that personal biometric data belongs to one type of personal information, completing the supplementation of regulations on personal biometric data in the civil legal field.

From 2009 to 2020, China gradually built a relatively complete legal system for the regulation of personal information and deepened the understanding of this sensitive area. However, in the issue of personal biometric data, China lacks targeted standards at the legal level. During the period when relevant laws were lacking, it was the administrative regulations, judicial interpretations and other less powerful laws that played the main role. These legal documents have a lower legal force than laws, but before the specialized laws for the protection of personal biometric data are enacted, they have played an important guiding role in the relevant fields.

The most valued and experienced area of personal biometric data in China is facial recognition. In the civil field, there are several judicial interpretations related to facial recognition like the Provisions of the Supreme People's Court on the Application of Law in Civil Cases Related to the Use of Facial recognition

[10] Juan and Dengfeng 2022, p. 145.

Technology Processing Personal Information in 2021. This judicial interpretation focuses on the relevant issues of facial recognition, treating facial recognition information as a sub-item of personal biometric data, and providing detailed regulations in accordance with the Civil Code. In the criminal field, there is the Interpretation on the Application of Law in Criminal Cases Involving the Illegally Trading of Personal Information. This interpretation classifies personal information into sensitive information, important information, and general information, but does not clearly specify which type of information biometric data belongs to.

In terms of more sensitive personal biometric data, there are also specialized administrative regulations, which stipulate more stringent protection measures and specific regulatory authorities, demonstrating more public domain control rather than coordination under private law. The representative example is genetic information, also known as human genetic resources. In 2019, the State Council issued the Regulation on the Management of Human Genetic Resources of the People's Republic of China, which is aiming to effectively protect and utilize human genetic resources while maintaining public health, national security, and social public interests. The regulation confirms that the National Health Commission is the main responsible and supervisory department, and specifically stipulates the requirements and obligations of genetic data processors.

According to the Regulation, the collection and preservation of human genetic resources must meet the following conditions: (1) possess legal person status; (2) the purpose of preservation is clear and legal; (3) the preservation plan is reasonable; (4) the source of the human genetic resources to be preserved is legal; (5) undergo ethical review; (6) have the department responsible for human genetic resources management and preservation management systems; (7) have places, facilities, equipment, and personnel that comply with national human genetic resources preservation technical norms and requirements. In addition, it must be approved by the National Health Commission. Foreign organizations, individuals, and their established or controlled institutions are not allowed to collect, preserve, or provide Chinese human genetic resources within China, nor are they allowed to provide such resources to foreign countries.[11]

In terms of obligations, genetic data processors must not harm the health of the Chinese public, national security, and social public interests, and must protect the privacy rights of the providers, abide by technical norms. They are not allowed to trade human genetic resources, and can only pay or receive reasonable costs.[12] According to the provisions of the Regulation on Human Genetic Resources Management, the collection, preservation, and circulation of genetic information related to human genetic resources are not general market behaviors but scientific research behaviors subject to national regulation. Its management scope is relatively

[11] Regulation of the People's Republic of China on the Management of Human Genetic Resources (Promulgated by the State Council, 10 May 2019, effective 1 July 2019), art 7.

[12] Ibid arts 8–10.

closed, and the significance of market regulation for other personal biometric data-related markets is relatively small.

The trend of uniformly defining and protecting personal biometric data is mainly reflected in relevant administrative laws, judicial interpretations, and departmental regulations such as the Regulation on Exit and Entry Administration of the People's Republic of China, Information Security Technology—Personal Information Security Specification, Personal Financial Information Protection Technical Specification, Provisions of the People's Procuratorate on Handling Network Crimes, and Guidelines for Internet Personal Information Security Protection. These rules all have special definitions and classifications for personal biometric data, and some provisions and standards even stipulate more stringent protection measures. For instance, the industry standard Information Security Technology—Personal Information Security Specification formulated by the National Information Security Standardization Technical Committee in 2020, Article 3.2, lists personal biometric data under 'Personal Sensitive Information', and clearly states in 8.4(f) that personal identification information shall not be publicly disclosed. Moreover, it adds several new requirements, including before collecting personal biometric data, the information processor should separately inform the personal subject of the purposes, methods, scope, storage time and other rules for collecting and using personal biometric data. The information processor should obtain the express consent of the personal subject, and personal biometric data should be stored separately from personal identity information; in principle, the information processor should not store the original personal biometric data. After using facial recognition features, fingerprints, palm prints, iris scans, etc. to achieve identity recognition and authentication functions, the original images that can extract personal biometric data should be deleted. The 'Personal Financial Information Protection Technical Specification' formulated by the National Financial Standardization Technical Committee in 2020 clearly states that personal biometric data belongs to the highest level of user identification information, emphasizing the huge harm of personal biometric data leakage, and explains the corresponding security technologies and management measures throughout the information processing cycle.

These regulations and standards have provided valuable experience, a large amount of clear standards and legislative experience has been accumulated in specific fields such as facial recognition information. However, due to their weak enforcement, the protective effect they can achieve is limited. The lack of legislation has left individuals in a disadvantaged position when facing enterprises that collect biometric data.[13] On the other hand, the dispersion of relevant regulations leads to insufficient supply of the system. From the perspective of reducing the cost of legal regulation,[14] and in order to establish a comprehensive and targeted regulatory system in a short period of time,[15] China needs a specialized legislation.

[13] Haina and Geng 2021, p. 87.

[14] Mingjun 2021, p. 95.

[15] Xiaoshuai 2021, p. 157.

### 4.3.2 PIPL Features: Classification and Integration

The PIPL was officially implemented in November 2021 and is one of the departmental laws of the country. This law is the fundamental law of China in the field of personal information protection and holds a core position in this field, as well as having the functions of leading, guiding and coordinating the system.[16] In terms of the nature of the law, the PIPL is both a hybrid law combining public law and private law, and also integrates the scattered provisions from other departmental laws to form a comprehensive law for protecting personal information. The PIPL not only regulates the relationships between equal civil entities, but also regulates the relationship between the state authorities as the personal information processors and the personal information subjects.[17] It includes both rights content norms and procedural norms such as rights relief and public interest litigation.

The PIPL has taken a further step in the classification and protection of personal information compared to civil code, absorbing beneficial experiences from general laws and industry standards, and making a more detailed definition and hierarchical management of personal information. Article 28 of the PIPL uniformly defines biometric data, specific identities, medical health and other information as 'sensitive personal information', and stipulates that the processing of sensitive personal information must be carried out under specific purposes and sufficient necessity, and with more strict protection measures than usual personal information. Based on the provisions of the PIPL, China has established a binary protection system for sensitive and non-sensitive information. To some extent, this is also an absorption of the achievements of previous industry standards.

In addition, the PIPL for the first time stipulates which departments is responsible for personal information protection. Article 60 of the PIPL stipulates that the Cyberspace Administration of China is the department responsible for coordinating the work of personal information protection and related supervision and management. The relevant departments of the State Council and the relevant departments of county-level and above local governments are responsible for personal information protection and supervision and management within their respective duties, and together with the cyberspace administration department, they are collectively referred to as the departments fulfilling the duties of personal information protection. Article 62, Paragraph (2) stipulates that the cyberspace administration department has the right to formulate specific personal information protection rules and standards for small-scale personal information processors, processing sensitive personal information, and new technologies and applications such as facial recognition and artificial intelligence based on the PIPL. The departments fulfilling the duties of personal information protection have the power to question and investigate the parties conducting personal information processing activities and require the personal information processors to conduct compliance audits. The departments fulfilling the

[16] Yong 2022, p. 68.

[17] Peizhi 2024, p. 137.

duties of personal information protection have the obligation to handle complaints and reports from any individual or organization.[18]

In terms of penalty measures, the PIPL can conduct administrative penalties based on its own provisions and clearly stipulates the connection with the criminal law. Article 66 stipulates that the departments fulfilling the duties of personal information protection will first give a warning, order correction, and confiscate the illegal gains. Serious cases shall be ordered to rectify by the departments responsible for protecting personal information at the provincial level or above, and the illegal gains shall be confiscated. A fine of no more than 50 million yuan or 5% of the previous year's business turnover shall be imposed. The business may be ordered to suspend operations or undergo a period of suspension and rectification, or be notified to the relevant competent authorities to revoke the relevant business license or be ordered to close down. The directly responsible supervisors and other directly responsible personnel shall be fined between 100,000 yuan and 1 million yuan, and may be prohibited from serving as directors, supervisors, senior managers, or information protection officers of relevant enterprises for a certain period. If a crime is constituted, it shall be dealt with in accordance with the provisions of the Criminal Law.

Overall, the introduction of the PIPL has, on a macro level, improved China's legal system related to personal information protection, filling the gap in the original standards for personal biometric data. PIPL has become the main legal source for protecting biometric data and coordinated different legal and administrative regulations. The mechanism integrating civil, administrative and criminal measures is established on the basis of PIPL. However, this model of the PIPL also means that China did not choose to adopt independent legislation on the issue of personal biometric data, but instead protected it as a subcategory of sensitive personal information. At the same time, the PIPL does not define personal biometric data separately. China's modern legal system defines 'sensitive personal information' through a general definition combined with specific enumeration, and various effective laws and regulations have mentioned it. The definition is not very clear in terms of definition, and it may be given different meanings in different scenarios.[19] This also brings certain ambiguity to the protection of sensitive personal information including personal biometric data. In actual infringement cases, how to deal with this kind of ambiguity becomes the task of judicial institutions such as courts and procuratorates.

### *4.3.3 Law in action: Consistency and Protection*

Chinese legal practice focus on maintaining the consistency of definitions in multiple related laws, emphasizing the possible damage to individuals caused by the abuse of personal biometric data or the social harm to the unspecified public, in order to

[18] Personal Information Protection Law of the People's Republic of China, arts 63–65.

[19] Xiaodong 2025, p. 171.

protect the personal information rights of individuals and enhance the attention obligation and responsibility of information processors. Courts attached great importance to the impact of the abuse of personal biometric data on the rights of individuals during the judicial process. In 2020, the first case of facial recognition in China, the court ruled that the defendant's collection of the plaintiff 's biometric data was invalid and ordered the defendant to delete the plaintiff's facial and fingerprint information. At that time, the legal regulation of personal biometric data was not very complete. The court, from the perspective of protecting the interests of the parties involved, made a decision in favor of the plaintiff's claim. After the introduction of the PIPL, cases related to personal biometric data will be defined by listing personal biometric data and treating it the same as the legally defined sensitive personal information. In the case of the People's Procuratorate of Xiaoshan District, Hangzhou City, Zhejiang Province v. Yu Shenglong for a civil public interest lawsuit on personal information protection, the court determined that the defendant, knowing that the software and tutorials for AI face swapping might be used for illegal purposes, still provided them, '*clearly violating the basic security obligations for the processing of sensitive personal information or biometric data, significantly increasing the risk of the sensitive personal information of the users' faces being infringed upon by the unspecified public entities in society.*'[20] Therefore, the court ruled that the initiation of public interest litigation should be supported and the defendant should bear the liability for compensation.

In the criminal aspect, although the judicial interpretation did not clearly define which type of personal information personal biometric data belongs to, in Guiding Case No. 192, the court referred to the provisions of the PIPL and recognized personal biometric data as sensitive personal information, and based on this, judged the defendant's act of stealing 'facial information' by using the 'appearance level detection' software involved in the case had clear social harmfulness, as having committed the crime of infringing upon personal information.[21]

In these cases, the consideration of damage to the interests of subjects played a significant role in driving the outcome. During this process, the previously disparate laws demonstrated consistency through interpretation, and specialized laws such as the PIPL were also implemented in courts.

Administrative cases usually are not prosecuted to courts but handled by the procuratorate and public security department, which urges relevant departments to establish and improve protection systems. The administrative supervision of the procuratorate is usually accomplished through suggestions. These suggestions do not have legal coercive force, but if the administrative agency does not cooperate, the procuratorate has the right to file an administrative lawsuit.[22] In 2022, the People's Procuratorate of Wangcheng District, Changsha City, Hunan Province

[20] *Zhejiang Province Hangzhou City Xiaoshan District People's Procuratorate v Yu Shenglong*, (Hangzhou Internet Court, 4 August 2023, Case No. (2023) Zhe 0192 Min Chu 4563).

[21] *Guiding Case No 192 of the Supreme People's Court* (Shanghai Fengxian District People's Court, 23 August 2021, Case No (2021) Hu 0120 Xing Chu No 828).

[22] Administrative Litigation Law of the People's Republic of China, art 25.

received a report from the public, claiming that the District Health Bureau was collecting excessive personal biometric data. The procuratorate suggested that the District Health Bureau improve the way of seeking informed consent and avoid excessive collection of fingerprint or facial recognition personal biometric data; improve technical and management measures to prevent unauthorized access and the leakage, alteration, or loss of personal information. The procuratorate also suggested that the District Public Security Bureau handle the illegal acts of 17 medical and health institutions that failed to fulfill the responsibility of cybersecurity level protection in accordance with the law. At the same time, the above procuratorial suggestions were copied to the Wangcheng District Cyberspace Administration Department to urge the Health Bureau and the Public Security Bureau to urge the administrative agency to take the 'backup sealing + local complete deletion + expiration complete deletion' approach to deal with the excessive collected personal biometric data data, eliminate security risks, and further carry out technical rectification.[23] On the other hand, the public security departments are responsible for conducting reviews and imposing penalties on information processors based on the evaluations provided by specialized institutions such as the Network and Information Security Notification Center, which may affiliated with the national cyberspace administration department or public security department. These evaluations mainly assess whether information processors have fulfilled their relevant obligations.

Due to insufficient legal definition for biometric data in China, court's approach is of great significance in cases. On the other hand, the procuratorate plays a supervisory role, urging the public sector that collect personal information to improve relevant systems. Public security departments are responsible for the specific inspections and enforcement, ensuring that market entities fulfill their obligations of protection and assessment. The legal provisions and guiding cases jointly constitute the system for identifying and regulating infringement of personal biological data in China. When it comes to how to properly utilize biological data and promote orderly participation from all parties, China has also provided a relatively detailed system of rights and obligations based on previous relevant rules.

## 4.4 The Specific Mechanism of China Personal Biometric Data Legal Protection

The promulgation of the PIPL marks the entry of China's personal information protection into a new era, establishing a hierarchical protection model centered on 'sensitive personal information'. Moreover, the greatest contribution of the PIPL lies in clarifying the rights and obligations in the information processing process,

[23] Supreme People's Procuratorate, 'Good News | Changsha Selected as One Case! Supreme People's Procuratorate Releases Typical Cases of Public Prosecution for Protecting Personal Information' (3 April 2023) <http://www.changsha.jcy.gov.cn/jcyw21/gyss/202304/t20230403_4075927.shtml> accessed 1 August 2025.

and thereby constructing a detailed regulatory system. During the process of biological data processing, different rights and obligations have been stipulated for each party, enabling the protection and utilization of biological data to be carried out in an orderly manner.

### *4.4.1 Rights in the Processing of Personal Biometric Data*

The right holder of personal biometric data is the individual, that is, the natural person who has their personal information collected and used by the information processor. Under the category of civil ownership rights, Chinese scholars believe that legal persons cannot yet constitute subjects.[24] In civil prospective, the individual enjoys the right related to personal information, which is a mixed right, including but not limited to the right of reputation, portrait right, privacy right, and the right not to be discriminated against.[25] The personal information right has the characteristics of cross-law departments, diversity, and integration of public and private aspects.[26] These characteristics are caused by the fact that the rights of personal information are covered by various different laws.

Article 1034(2) of the Civil Code stipulates that private information in personal information shall be governed by the relevant provisions on privacy rights; if there are no such provisions, the relevant provisions on personal information protection shall apply. Thus, in China, the protection of personal information and the protection of privacy rights do not entirely fall under the same category. The protection scope of personal information includes privacy rights and is broader than the category of privacy rights, requiring special legal protection. Professor Wang Liming believes that '*in general, the concept of personal information far exceeds the scope of privacy rights.*'[27] In the Civil Code and other related laws, the interests related to personal information are not called rights but called interests. They contain the meaning of benefits that are not explicitly stipulated by law but are widely recognized by society.[28] Chinese scholars believe that the attached interests to personal information are a non-specific personality right, and the specific content of the rights is determined by the content and protection model.[29] In practical application, personal information rights include but are not limited to privacy rights, equality rights, and property rights. Basic rights demonstrate a composite feature of personality and property by the provisions in laws such as the Civil Code and the PIPL.[30]

---

[24] Peizhi 2024, p. 156.

[25] Heqing 2022, pp. 112–113.

[26] Hanhua 2020.

[27] Liming 2013, p. 62.

[28] Hualv.com, 'Legal Consultation Platform'(2025) <https://www.66law.cn/question/49210859.aspx> accessed 1 August 2025.

[29] Jing and Zhuonan 2021, p. 4.

[30] Xiaoshuai 2021, pp. 153–154.

In PIPL fields, the rights of individuals including know and decide, access and copy, rectification and supplementation, deletion, request for explanation right. There are also rights for deceased people's information. In the fields of biometric data, the right of know and decide is the most important right, which means that the individual can make an effective consent only after fully understanding the processing mode of the processor. In the field of personal biometric data, the individual has the right to separately consent to the authorization of personal biometric data under full knowledge, and in certain circumstances, written consent is required.[31] Other rights allow individuals to access and inspect the personal biometric data collected and used by an information processor, to request access to and copying of their personal information, to request the transfer of personal information to a designated personal information processor, and to request the information processor to correct, supplement inaccurate or incomplete personal information, withdraw their authorization to the information processor and request the information processor to delete personal information related to themselves, to request the personal information processor to explain the rules governing the processing of their personal information.

When these rights requests are rejected, the individual has the right to file a lawsuit to a court or seeking relief from regulatory authorities. Additionally, the national cyberspace administration can determine specific organizations to file a public interest lawsuit regarding cases that infringe upon the rights of numerous individuals, along with consumer associations and the people's procuratorate, both of which are eligible parties for public interest lawsuits as determined by law.[32]

In China's legal system, the rights about biological data have different legal sources. The provisions of the Civil Code and PIPL are different, and there are also disputes regarding their relationship in the academic community. However, in actual civil disputes, each provisions can be invoked. At the administrative level, individual have the right to file complaints and reports with relevant departments to exercise the right of supervision.[33]

### *4.4.2 Obligations in the Processing of Personal Biometric Data*

The entities that carry out a series of actions such as collection, processing, analysis, and use of personal biometric data are collectively referred to as personal information processors, which are the entities that have relevant obligations for the protection of personal biometric data. Given the classification as sensitive personal

[31] Personal Information Protection Law of the People's Republic of China, (n 18) arts 28–29; Facial recognition Technology Application Security Management Measures (issued by the Cyberspace Administration of China and other departments, 16 July 2021), arts 5–6.

[32] Personal Information Protection Law of the People's Republic of China, (n18). art 70.

[33] The PIPL, and laws such as the Regulation on Human Genetic Resources Management all stipulate that the competent authorities have the duty to accept relevant complaints and reports from the public. See Article 61(2) of the PIPL, and Article 35 of the Regulation on Human Genetic Resources Management (promulgated by the State Council, 10 May 2019, effective 1 July 2019).

information, the processing of personal biometric data is subject to all general principles and, crucially, to a set of stricter, additional obligations designed to address its unique risks. According to PIPL, the processing of personal biometric data must follow the principles of legality, necessity, propriety, and security, and ensure the truthfulness, accuracy, and completeness of personal information in order to avoid adverse impacts on the individuals. A lawful basis under Article 13 is mandatory. Critically, for sensitive information like biometric data, PIPL imposes a heightened consent standard. According to Article 29, processing such data requires obtaining the separate consent of the individual, meaning consent must be given voluntarily, explicitly, and for a specific processing activity. Public sector do not need to obtain consent authorization from individual to process personal information, but still need to follow the principles mentioned above. Especially Article 8 for accuracy and updated in a timely manner. In special scenarios such as epidemic prevention and control, or the capture of criminals, individuals should not abuse rights such as the right to deletion at will and have the obligation to cooperate with the information processor.[34]

Articles 51 to 59 of PIPL stipulate the obligations of personal information processors. Apart from the obligations necessary for realizing the rights of the individuals, personal information processors also have other obligations.

The first is the obligation to carefully store, and Article 51 of PIPL stipulates that personal information processors must adopt measures such as systems, classification, and technology to ensure that personal information processing activities comply with the provisions of laws and administrative regulations and prevent unauthorized access as well as the leakage, alteration, or loss of personal information. In the case of sensitive personal information such as personal biometric data, personal information processors also have additional obligations of impact assessment and record-keeping.

The second is the supervision obligation, and personal information processors that process personal information reaching the specified quantity by the national cyberspace administration department shall appoint a personal information protection officer to be responsible for supervising the personal information processing activities and the measures taken for protection. Personal information processors shall conduct regular compliance audits of their processing of personal information in accordance with the law and administrative regulations.

The third is the obligation to report regularly. Article 58 of the PIPL stipulates that personal information processors providing important internet platform services, with a large number of users, and complex business types shall establish corresponding system frameworks, regularly issue reports, and accept external members and public supervision. The Facial Recognition Technology Application Security Management Measures stipulates that personal information processors shall, starting from the date when the storage quantity of facial information processed by the application reaches 100,000 people, complete the filing procedures with the relevant

---

[34]Yongqi 2024, p. 134.

cyberspace administration department at the provincial level or above and accept the supervision of the local cyberspace administration department in 30 days.

The fourth is to establish an impact assessment mechanism and the obligation to notify the subject and relevant departments in case of information leakage. Article 55(1) of PIPL stipulates that when handling sensitive personal information including personal biometric data, a protection impact assessment should be conducted in advance and the handling situation should be recorded. The impact assessment should include the purpose of the processing, the legality, legitimacy, necessity of the processing method, the impact on personal rights and interests, and the security risks, the legality, effectiveness, and adaptability of the protection measures to the risk level, and should be retained for at least three years.[35]

Article 57 stipulates that if there is or may be a leakage, alteration, or loss of personal information, the personal information processor shall immediately take remedial measures and notify the department and individual responsible for personal information protection. If the personal information processor can effectively avoid the harm caused by information leakage, alteration, or loss by taking measures, the personal information processor may not notify the individual; if the department responsible for personal information protection believes that it may cause harm, it has the right to require the personal information processor to notify the individual. The notification should include: (1) the types of information, the cause, and the possible harm of the information leakage, alteration, or loss; (2) the remedial measures taken by the personal information processor and the measures that the individual can take to mitigate the harm; (3) the contact information of the personal information processor.

In terms of legal liability, except the administrative, criminal liability mentioned before, there are other provisions for information processors. According to Article 69 of the PIPL, the liability of personal information processors adopts the principle of fault presumption. If personal information processors cannot prove that they have no fault, they shall bear the liability for compensation. Apart from the penalty measures stipulated in Article 66, Article 67 also stipulates the legal liability of being recorded in the credit file and public announcement, further strengthening the penalty for violations.[36] For the public sector, Article 68 stipulates that if state organs fail to fulfill the personal information protection obligations stipulated in this law, their superior organs or the departments responsible for personal information protection shall order corrections; the directly responsible principal officers and other directly responsible personnel shall be legally punished; If the staff members of the

[35] Personal Information Protection Law of the People's Republic of China, (n18) art 56.

[36] The credit record is a report issued by an independent third party (credit reporting agency) in accordance with international standards, which has been approved by the national administrative authority. It can help customers assess and control credit risks, and has an impact on the reputation and operation of the business operators. For details, please refer to the Regulation on the Credit Industry, Opinions of the General Office of the Central Committee of the Communist Party of China and the General Office of the State Council on Establishing a Social Credit System and other documents.

department responsible for safeguarding personal information fail to perform their duties properly, abuse their power, or engage in malpractice for personal gain, and such actions do not constitute a crime, they shall be subject to disciplinary action in accordance with the law.

The rights and obligations set forth in Chinese law aim to protect the personal rights of individuals to the greatest extent while actively requiring organizations with public responsibilities to participate and safeguard the public interests that may be involved in the processing of personal biometric data, and ensuring that the actions of information processors are subject to strict supervision. Meanwhile, it also require the accuracy from individuals, in order to ensure the public interest. From the perspective of legal provisions, information processors not only need to be responsible to individuals, but also to the competent authorities. The processing scenarios of personal information involve the three parties of the processors, individuals, and the competent authority, and all three parties can participate in and influence the processing process. Information processors not only need to fulfill the duty of due care during information collection, but also have the obligation to take positive measures such as establishing protection systems. This is closely related to the complexity of personal information, which has both private and public interests. In the case of personal biometric data, additional obligations have been added, such as conducting impact assessments and promptly notifying relevant departments and individuals, in order to minimize the damage caused by information leakage.

## 4.5 Comparison and Summary of China Biometric Data Legal Protection

Through the roles and responsibilities of individuals, processors, and judicial institutions in the protection of personal biometric data, a protective model with clear rights and responsibilities which involving multiple parties can be seen. This mechanism is based on general personal information protection. In the field of biometric information data, it particularly emphasizes the roles of information processors and official departments. From a comparative law and systematic perspective, the Chinese model has its unique institutional characteristics, which is profoundly influences its future development direction.

In the international context, the protection of personal biometric data mainly falls into three models: specialized legislation protection, comprehensive legislation protection, and industry standard protection.[37] Examples of specialized legislation protection include the biometric data Privacy Act in Illinois, USA, and the Biometric Privacy Act in Washington State. These models are characterized by clear definitions, with the informed consent principle as the core, strict protection, and comprehensive coverage of the information processing cycle, with emphasis on civil

[37] Ge and Rongzhao (n 6).

litigation remedies in case of infringement. Examples of comprehensive legislation protection include the General Data Protection Regulation in the European Union, which features the proposal of several protective principles, unified protection of personal biometric data along with other personal information, and higher protection standards for personal biometric data based on its sensitivity and personal relevance. Compared to the specialized legislation protection model, the comprehensive legislation protection model offers more diverse remedies for personal biometric data, typically enabling the establishment of a complete 'civil - criminal - administrative' remedy mechanism. The industry standard model is a set of behavioral guidelines formulated and implemented by industry associations, organizations, or enterprises themselves, featuring flexibility and forward-looking nature, and capable of promptly responding to the needs of technology, market, and consumers regarding the protection of personal biometric data, better addressing the technical risks and legal challenges brought by new technologies. However, it lacks a mandatory accountability mechanism.

China's protection model is more similar to the comprehensive legislation protection model, which is determined by China's legislative situation and diversified demands. As in the category of comprehensive legislation, China, Japan and South Korea share similarities in their legal protection of biometric data. All three countries have specific legislation related to personal information, and emphasize it by categorizing it as sensitive personal information, etc. The use of information is subject to the individual's consent. However, China has a diverse legal sources and departments for governing biometric data, unlike Japan and South Korea which rely on a unified personal information protection committee for supervision and guidance.[38]

Before the PIPL, China realized that the related rights of personal information could not be fully covered by the privacy rights stipulated in civil law, thus it was necessary to introduce the right of personal information rights and provide specialized legislative protection. At the same time, adopting this protection model is conducive to leveraging the existing achievements of administrative regulations, industry standards, and other relevant rules, and enabling relevant departments to intervene promptly to provide remedies for personal information. In addition, it also allow recognized public organizations to offer professional advice to make up for the deficiencies in governance. During the development process, China has taken criminal amendments and judicial interpretations as the lead, and gradually established legal provisions in the civil and administrative fields, and further unified and specialized the relevant provisions in the PIPL. After the introduction of the PIPL, China's protection model still emphasizes the role of industry management and self-governance. The law requires information processors to formulate compliance systems and platform rules, and the state departments have the responsibility to formulate industry standards and provide guiding opinions. On this premise, there are much of legislative and judicial practice in facial recognition area, which

[38] *Overview of Foreign Facial Recognition Legal Systems*, The People's Junior Court (Shuozhou Intermediate People's Court, 15 July 2025) <https://sxszzy.shanxify.gov.cn/article/detail/2025/07/id/8902847.shtml> accessed 1 August 2025; Zhixuan et al. 2025, p. 65.

accumulated much protective experience. Overall, China's protection approach is based on comprehensive protection, while exploring specific scenarios of personal biometric data protection through industry standards, judicial interpretations, and guiding cases, achieving a diverse and self-consistent legal protection mechanism.

The main problems faced by China's protection of personal biometric data still lie in the fact that relevant norms are scattered across various laws and administrative regulations, with an insufficiently specific rule system, resulting in insufficient institutional supply.[39] In the digital age, individuals have weak control over their own information, and the information processing process is complex. Information processors are reluctant or unable to clearly inform individuals of the processing methods, leading to the virtualization of the right to informed consent.[40] In response to this, Chinese scholars believe that the fragmentation of legislation is a norm, and it does not necessarily undermine the overallity and applicability of the legal system. Since a single civil law, administrative law, or criminal law cannot achieve the realization of diversified value goals, multiple legislation is necessary.[41] The key lies in how to improve the connection between legal norms and achieve a positive interaction between laws. Regarding the issue of the dilution of the right to informed consent, Chinese scholars believe that the obligations of information processors should be made more specific, diversified, and hierarchical, with clear and diverse notification methods, in order to ensure that the right to informed consent of individuals is effectively implemented. Additionally, throughout the entire process of information processing, the participation level of individuals should be continuously enhanced to ensure that they can smoothly exercise the right to withdraw based on the circumstances.[42] For the protection of personal biometric data in China in the future, it is necessary to clearly define the definition and importance of personal biometric data in legislation, shift to a multi-party collaborative governance system, enhance the enthusiasm of all parties to participate in governance, refine relevant certification, review, and assessment standards, and improve legal-level remedies and regulations to ensure that personal biometric data can be quickly identified, protected, and remedied. This will be a further goal.

## References

Wu Caixia, 'Exploration of Biometric Technology Applications in the Financial Field'*(金融领域生物识别技术应用探析)*, (2018)12, Financial Theory & Practice*(金融理论与实践)*, 62.

Wang Li, 'Abuse of biometric data Gives Rise to a Gray Industry'*(生物识别信息滥用催生灰色产业)* (2019) 24 Fangyuan*(方圆)* 20.

Song Chuyao, 'Conceptual Definition of Personal biometric data'*(个人生物识别信息的概念界定)* (2025) 4 China Terminology*(中国科技术语)* 67–68

---

[39] Yuangao 2025, p. 154.

[40] Peizhi 2024, p. 156.

[41] Yongqi 2024, p. 195–196.

[42] Yuangao 2025, p. 167.

Xu Juan and Qin Dengfeng, 'Construction of Personal Information Protection Models'*(个人信息保护模式的建构)*, 2022/2 (2022), Qinghai Social Sciences*(青海社会科学)*, 145.

Lu Haina and Zhao Geng, 'Legal Regulation of Commercial Use of Personal biometric data: Comparison and Reflection on US State Legislative Experience' *(个人生物识别信息商业利用的法律规制:美国州立法经验的比较与反思)* (2021) 2 Human Rights Studies*(人权研究)* 87

Liu Mingjun, 'Legal Regulation of Facial recognition Technology Applications from the Perspective of Law and Economics'*(法经济学视域下人脸识别技术应用的法律规制)* (2021) 33(4) Journal of Sichuan Police College*(四川警察学院学报)* 95

Wu Xiaoshuai, 'Legal Regulation of Personal biometric data Security in the Big Data Context'*(大数据背景下个人生物信息识别安全的法律规制)* (2021) 2 Legal Forum*(法学论坛)* 157

Zhang Yong, *Research on Personal Information Protection from the Perspective of Criminal-Civil Integration* (Commercial Press 2022) 68.

Zhu Peizhi, *Research on Legal Protection of Personal biometric data* (China Procuratorate Press 2024) 137.

Ding Xiaodong, 'Interpretive Reconstruction of the Sensitive Personal Information Protection System'*(敏感个人信息保护制度的解释性重构)* (2025) 2 China Legal Science*(中国法学)* 171.

Yang Heqing, *Interpretation of the Personal Information Protection Law of the* People's Republic of China (Law Press China 2022) 112–113

Zhou Hanhua, 'Legal Positioning of Personal Information Protection'*(个人信息保护的法律定位)* (2020) 3 Studies in Law and Business*(法商研究)*.

Wang Liming, 'On the Legal Protection of the Right to Personal Information: Centered on the Distinction Between Personal Privacy and Information Rights' *(论个人信息权的法律保护——以个人隐私权和信息权的界分为中心)* (2013) 4 Modern Law Science*(现代法学)* 62

Wu Jing and Shang Zhuonan, 'Research on Legal Regulation of Personal biometric data'*(个人生物信息的法律规制研究)* (2021) 7 Legal System and Society*(法制与社会)* 4.

Wang Yongqi, *Research on Legal Systems for Personal Information Processing in the Digital Age* (Chinese People's Public Security University Press 2024) 134

Wu Zhixuan, Nora Santalu, and Liang Shirong, 'Biometric Recognition: the Legal Comparation between Europe and Asia-Pacific Region'*(生物识别:欧洲与亚太地区的法律比较)* , March 2025, Hong Kong Lawyer*(香港律师)*, 65.

Liang Yuangao, 'Systematic Approach to biometric data Protection in Multiple Application Scenarios'*(多重应用场景下生物识别信息保护的体系化进路)* (2025) 4 Law Science Magazine*(法学杂志)* 154.

# Chapter 5
# Neuroprivacy: Mind, Body, and Integrity

**Hiroshi Miyashita**

## 5.1 Brain as a New Domain of Privacy

### *5.1.1 Decoding Brain*

According to Japanese medical researchers Yu Takagi and Shinji Nishimoto, a non-invasive neural decoding method has enabled the reconstruction of visual images perceived by individuals, based on brain activity measured through functional Magnetic Resonance Imaging(fMRI).[1] Using high-resolution image reconstruction techniques with latent diffusion models, their research demonstrated the ability to generate visual images that closely resemble what a person has seen, based solely on fMRI scans of brain function. Their study underscores the growing capacity of neurotechnology, which can be defined as devices and procedures used to access, monitor, investigate, assess, manipulate, and/or emulate the structure and function of the neural systems of natural persons,[2] to translate inner mental states into observable data, challenging traditional boundaries of privacy.

This chapter was supported by the Toyota Foundation under Grant of Co-Creating New Society with Advanced Technologies, 'Brain Liberty: Neuroprivacy' (D23-ST-0006). The author gratefully acknowledges the Foundation's generous support, which made this research possible. The author declares that there are no conflicts of interest relevant to this study.

[1] Takagi and Nishimoto 2023.

[2] OECD, 'Recommendation of the Council on Responsible Innovation in Neurotechnology' (2019).

H. Miyashita (✉)
Chuo University, Tokyo, Japan
e-mail: hmiya.64r@g.chuo-u.ac.jp



H. Miyashita et al. (eds.), *The Evolution of Data Protection Laws in China, Japan, and Korea*, https://doi.org/10.1007/978-981-95-8609-7_5

The regulation of neurotechnology can be divided into medical and non-medical applications. For medical use in Japan, the Pharmaceuticals and Medical Devices Act as a medical product safety regulation requires that devices obtain marketing approval from the Minister of Health, Labour and Welfare prior to being placed on the market (Article 23-2(1)).[3] The first neurotechnology device for medical use, specifically in neurosurgery, was approved in December 2016, when Israel-based INSIGHTEC Ltd. introduced the Exablate Neuro (ExAblate 4000) to the Japanese medical market. This device enables treatment of essential tremor and Parkinson's disease by using focused ultrasound (FUS) to non-invasively ablate targeted brain tissue without opening the skull. Subsequent approvals include Century Medical's BrainsWay TMS system for the treatment of depression in 2019, Daiichi Sankyo's DELYTACT as a gene therapy for malignant glioma in 2021, and MIREVO, a software-based neuropsychological testing programme for dementia screening via eye-tracking technology, approved in 2023. The Ministry also published a list of pharmaceuticals prohibited from personal importation for the purpose of enhancing brain function.[4] In South Korea, the Ministry of Food and Drug Safety issued in December 2015 approval guidelines specifically for electrical brain-stimulation devices used in psychotherapy, indicating that, at that time, the regulatory focus for such devices was on therapeutic applications.[5] Neurotechnology has facilitated the advancement of medical interventions such as cochlear implants, which restore sensory functions like hearing, and deep brain stimulation (DBS), employed in the treatment of tremors. Additional neuro devices continue to emerge under this medical regulation.

### *5.1.2 Expansion of Neurotechnology: From Sleeping Track to Reading the Room*

Since the 1970s, researchers have seeking 'neurometrics'[6] to provide quantitative information about brain activity. This early effort to capture and analyze the brain's electrical signals laid important groundwork for what later came to be defined as the brain–computer interface (BCI). BCI can be defined as 'a system that measures

[3] The EU General Product Safety Regulation (Regulation 2023/988) may cover the consumer BCI products. See Elisabeth Steindl 2024, p. 105945.

[4] Ministry of Health, Labour and Welfare, 'Notice: On the Handling of Personal Importation of Pharmaceuticals and Similar Products Claiming to Enhance Brain Function' [厚生労働省「脳機能の向上等を標ぼうする医薬品等を個人輸入する場合の取扱いについて」] 26 November 2018.

[5] Choi 2025, p. 104951.

[6] Roy John et al. 1977, p. 1393 (stating that '[t]he goals of neurometrics are to gather accurate data sensitive to this variety of brain functions, to extract and quantify critical features of these data, and to classify the resulting profiles into clusters sharing common features of brain function by using statistical analysis and numerical taxon').

CNS [central nervous system] activity and converts it into artificial output that replaces, restores, enhances, supplements, or improves natural CNS output and thereby changes the ongoing interactions between the CNS and its external or internal environment'.[7] BCI has two different functions, which can be integrated in a hybrid mode: namely, the goal selection in BCI instructs the application 'what to do' (for instance, in application to the movement of a motorised wheelchair, moving the wheelchair to a specific location), whereas process control instructs it 'how to do' it (for instance, controlling the wheelchair's direction, speed, and braking).[8] Recent developments in neurotechnology have enabled non-invasive BCIs to be integrated into compact wearable devices, including earplug-like EEG systems.[9] BCIs can be extensively used for therapeutic applications such as rehabilitation, assessment of consciousness, and communications to affective state detection, and human enhancement or augmentation.[10] They are increasingly deployed not only to enhance physical or cognitive capability, but also to monitor, infer, or analyse an individual's mental states, thereby raising significant concerns regarding mental or physical integrity within the framework of human rights law.[11]

In Japan, non-medical applications of neurotechnology for interacting and even rewriting brain activities by stimulation have expanded without requiring scientific approval from the Ministry. For example, NeuroSpace's sleep monitoring device has been used in major companies such as Yoshinoya, the beef bowl restaurant chain, and other companies as part of an employee sleep improvement programme.[12] It has also been implemented by the Toyoko Inn hotel chain, in collaboration with KDDI, to monitor guests' sleep patterns through sensors embedded in the mattress.[13] Despite not being directly classified as a neurotechnology, the robot 'OriHime-D' responds to the eye movements of patients with amyotrophic lateral sclerosis (ALS) to support daily living, which may be potentially applied to neuro-related field in the future.[14] There are more examples on deploying neural devices in business such as tourism to measure the satisfaction through the headphone style neural devices,[15] automobile companies to develop sounds that are easier for pedes-

[7] Wolpaw and Wolpaw 2012, p. 1. BMI (brain-machine interface) 'does not reflect the reality that a computer and the brain are partners in the interactive adaptive control needed for effective BCI (or BMI) operation'. Ibid 5.

[8] Ibid 9–10.

[9] Takashi Nakamura, et al., 'Automatic Sleep Monitoring Using Ear-EEG' (proposing the design and validation of a novel wearable in-ear EEG sensor for sleep monitoring).

[10] Nam et al. 2018.

[11] *See* Ienca and Andorno 2017, p. 5.

[12] CFIEC, 'Case Studies on Japan-Israel SMEs Collaboration' 17 November 2020. <https://www.cfiec.jp/activities/toho-tec_en/> (access 1 June 2025).

[13] Toyoko Inn, 'Sleep PJ' <https://www.toyoko-inn.com/feature/sleep_pj>.

[14] Barbareschi et al. 2022, p. 36.

[15] World's First: Brainwave-Based Tourism Navigation System "NEURONAVI" [世界初、脳波を活用した観光ナビゲーションシステム「NEURONAVI」] 28 June 2017 <https://prtimes.jp/main/html/rd/p/000000001.000026766.html>.

trians to hear when electric vehicles approach by measuring the brain waves,[16] and mental treatment for traumatic stimuli provoking brain reactions after the earthquake in Japan.[17]

In Japanese culture, the practice of 'reading the room' is a deeply embedded social norm. In an effort to render this tacit interpersonal awareness more visible, brain activity analytics have been introduced in both corporate and educational settings. In 2019, Tokyu Land Corporation, a real estate company, implemented a BCI to assess employees' states across five dimensions: stress, concentration, interest, comfort, and excitement, with the aim of fostering a more motivated and productive work environment, which was enhanced by the presence of green trees within the office space.[18] In education, giga school project aims to target the individual student data. An experiment by using fNIRS was conducted to measure the real-time concentration of each student throughout brain activity at high school.[19]

In the global market of neurotechnology, its market expands from $1.74 billion in 2022 to $6.2 billion by 2030, with the Asia-Pacific region expected to experience the highest growth during this period.[20] Several national brain research strategies have been launched in response to this rapid development, including the U.S. BRAIN Initiative (2013), the EU Human Brain Project (from 2013), China's Brain Project (2016),[21] and Korea Brain Initiative (2017).[22] The neural data also is shared to the third parties in the name of consent click or publishing a privacy policy. According to Neurorights Foundation report, among the major neurotechnology companies, '29 of the 30 companies (96.67%) can and may transfer data to third parties'.[23]

In the wake of BCI, the modern right to privacy is increasingly intertwined with the concept of cognitive liberty and the inner living space of human being, which

---

[16] Macnica Holdings Inc., 'Sound development for mobility using brainwave analysis[脳波"分析を活用した、モビリティの音開発]' (20 June 2023) <https://www.macnica.co.jp/business/ai/manufacturers/innereye/143752/>.

[17] Okamoto et al. 2011, p. 13.

[18] Tokyu Land Corp. 'Press Release: Visualisation of the "Work Reform" as the Chosen Office' [「働き方改革」の見える化を実現し、選ばれるオフィスへ], 30 September 2019. (in Japanese) https://www.tokyu-land.co.jp/news_data/d44eb0b5f4f6f5adbeba0eaad72d8e2e.pdf>.

[19] Mainichi Newspaper, 'Effectiveness of ICT Classes Probed by 'Red Brain Activity Display' by the University of Tokyo Team' [「赤い脳活動表示」で探る ICT授業の効果 東大チーム], 27 May 2019. (in Japanese) <https://mainichi.jp/articles/20190527/k00/00m/040/190000c>.

[20] Grand View Research, 'Brain Computer Interface Market Size, Industry Report, 2030'. <https://www.grandviewresearch.com/industry-analysis/brain-computer-interfaces-market#>.

[21] It is reported that, as a government sponsored project, Chinese employees working in factories, in the military, and on trains are being given hats and helmets equipped to monitor their brain waves for sudden changes in their emotional state. Erin Winick, 'With Brain-scanning Hats, China Signals it Has no Interest in Workers' Privacy' *MIT Technology Review* 30 April 2018. <https://www.technologyreview.com/2018/04/30/143155/with-brain-scanning-hats-china-signals-it-has-no-interest-in-workers-privacy/>

[22] Researchers at KAIST developed a novel online BCI system using speech imagery and ear-EEG, enabling users to control home appliances through imagined speech commands. Kaongoen et al. 2022, p. 107022.

[23] Genser et al. 2024, pp. 52–54.

may be called as 'the right to control one's inner cognition'.[24] Considering the fact that BCI is already used in the rehabilitation, the puzzling question is the baseline of using BCIs. Should BCIs be limited to restoring lost functions, or can they be employed to enhance human capabilities beyond their natural limits? This question lies at the heart of 'transhumanism', an idea aimed at overcoming the inherent limitations of the human condition, including ageing, physical and psychological constraints, and suffering.[25] It is beyond the scope of this chapter, yet it is obvious that the mental and physical privacy in the context of BCI now becomes a reality.

## 5.2 Neurorights Within the International Frameworks

### *5.2.1 Toward a Legal Framework for Neurorights*

The potential threat of neurotechnology to human being does not stop privacy and data protection. The US Supreme Court noted that '[o]ur whole constitutional heritage rebels at the thought of giving government the power to control men's minds'.[26] This constitutional heritage of resistance to undue influence or manipulation is grounded in a constellation of fundamental rights designed to safeguard personal integrity, individual autonomy, and human dignity. These intertwined of rights, particularly in the context of neurotechnology, serve to safeguard individuals from undue influence or manipulation of human behaviour via brain activity. The bundle of these rights can be named as 'neurorights'. As defined by Marcello Ienca, neurorights represent the 'freedom or entitlement relating to a person's cerebral and mental domain',[27] consisting of the freedom of thought and conscience, the right to privacy, and the right to mental integrity.

Whether we call these bundle rights 'neurorights' or not,[28] what matters is not its name, but its substance to protect human brain from arbitrary powers. The fundamental issue lying in privacy in relation to neuro devices is where to draw the line between forms of permissible persuasion and unacceptable manipulation.[29] Unlike the traditional right to privacy as being left alone, the emerging concept of 'mental

[24] Richard Glen Boire 'On Cognitive Liberty Part III', 2 The Journal of Cognitive Liberties.

[25] Farahany 2023, p. 191.

[26] *Stanley v. Georgia*, 394 U.S. 557, 565 (1969).

[27] Ienca 2021, p. 701258. See also Marcello Ienca & Roberto Andorno, 'A New Category of Human Rights: Neurorights' 26 Apr 2017 <https://blogs.biomedcentral.com/bmcblog/2017/04/26/new-category-human-rights-neurorights/> (access 1 June 2025).

[28] For a critical observation, see Borbón and Borbón 2021, p. 703121 (noting that free will on human rights seems deeply complicated in conceptual terms).

[29] Council of Europe, 'Declaration by the Committee of Ministers on the manipulative capabilities of algorithmic processes, 1337th meeting of the Ministers' Deputies', Decl(13/02/2019)1 (February 2019).

privacy'[30] concerns the (in)direct access to an individual's mind or brain through certain characteristic elements such as thoughts, judgments, desires, and intentions.[31] The question here is not its name, but the catalog of rights which the neurotechnology imposed.

The most progressive developments in neurorights were seen in Chile. Chile's 2021 constitutional amendment marked a historic milestone, establishing legal recognition for neurorights by mandating special protection for brain-related data. Article 19(1) provides that '*Scientific and technological development shall be at the service of people and shall be carried out with respect for life and physical and psychological integrity. The law shall regulate the requirements, conditions and restrictions for its use on people, and shall especially protect brain activity, as well as the information coming from it*'.[32] It clarified to protect 'brain activity, as well as the information coming from it' in terms of 'respect for life and physical and psychological integrity'. Chile's strong commitment to human rights from a historical tragedy of coup and the legislative initiatives stemming from science and medicine motivated the Constitutional amendment.[33] In its landmark decision in *Girardi v. Emotiv* on August 9, 2023, the Chilean Supreme Court affirmed the constitutional protection of neurorights. The Court held that the processing of neural data requires the explicit and informed consent of the data subject, which cannot be used for different purposes without knowledge and approval of the data subject.[34] The Chilean constitutional reform is of considerable interest. However, further scrutiny is required to examine whether it is consistent with existing international disability and human rights norms.[35]

The emergence of so-called 'neurorights' whether or not designated by that term brings a profound evolution in the landscape of human rights law. The human brain, which was considered as the final frontier of privacy, autonomy, and dignity, must not remain legally exposed to unregulated technological incursion. The law must

[30] The concept of 'mental privacy' appears to presuppose a mind–body distinction as mental/physical privacy, and insofar as this is the case, it confronts the problems inherent in mind–body dualism, as well as the practical implications for the right to respect for physical and mental integrity (EU Charter of Fundamental Rights Art3(1)). Thus, this article titled 'neuroprivacy', as the concept of privacy to protect neurodata, instead of the narrower scope of 'mental privacy'. Brain privacy consists of 'perceptions, memories, and thoughts, or privacy of health information pertaining to the status of the brain'. Fischbach and Mindes 2011, p. 365.

[31] Lavazza and Giorgi 2023, p. 11 (noting that mental privacy is different from the general privacy by kind, content, and rank).

[32] Isabel Cornejo-Plaza and Saracini 2023, p. 1177720.

[33] Einhorn and Yuste 2022, p. 29.

[34] Isabel Cornejo-Plaza et al. 2024, p. 1330439; Cornejo-Plaza and Cippitani 2025, p. 210; Micaela Mantegna, Neural Data on Trial: Chile's Supreme Court addresses the First Global Neurorights Case, Medium, 17 August 2023. <https://abogamer.medium.com/neural-data-on-trial-chiles-supreme-court-addresses-the-first-global-neurorights-case-2ddad0e2b06b>. The original judgement is GIRARDI/EMOTIV INC. Rol 105065-2023, Corte Suprema (in Spanish).

[35] Fins 2022, p. 26 (noting the possible risks of disaggregation by a technical intervention may violate the UN Convention on the Rights of Persons with Disabilities).

confront the normative and doctrinal challenges posed by direct or indirect access to mental or emotional states through brain activity.

### 5.2.2 International Frameworks on NeuroData

Several international frameworks have been developed for the risk of neural data processing and responsible innovation for neurotechnology. The 2019 OECD Recommendation on Responsible Innovation in Neurotechnology encourages the beneficial use of neurotechnologies for health and well-being, while emphasising the need to safeguard human rights, especially privacy, cognitive liberty, and autonomy of individuals.[36] The Council of Europe' Committee on Bioethics under the Oviedo Convention (Convention on Human Rights and Biomedicine (ETS No 164)) published the Strategic Action Plan on Human Rights and Technologies in Biomedicine in 2020–2025 recognises the 'issues of privacy, personhood, and discrimination'.[37] The Strategic Action Plan raises a question 'whether … issues can be sufficiently addressed by the existing human rights framework or whether new human rights pertaining to cognitive liberty, mental privacy, and mental integrity and psychological continuity, need to be entertained in order to govern neurotechnologies'. In October 2023, the EU Telecommunications and Digital Ministers adopted the León Declaration on European Neurotechnology, calling for a human-centric and rights-based approach to innovation. The declaration emphasised that '[m]anipulating, collecting, retaining, processing, and storing brain data is of utmost sensitivity', underscoring the urgent need for ethical and legal safeguards to protect fundamental rights. The UNESCO's published ethical reports, aiming at a global governance framework on neurotechnology.[38] In 2024, the Global Privacy Assembly adopted a resolution outlining principles for the processing of personal information in the context of neuroscience and neurotechnology.[39] The resolution elaborates on how existing data protection and privacy principles, such as lawful basis and consent, purpose specification, data minimisation, accuracy, transparency, and security, should be interpreted and applied to neurotechnologies and neuroscience.

Several national data protection or human rights commissions published reports complementing international instruments in the area of neurotechnology. For instance, the Spanish Data Protection Authority (AEPD) highlighted the sensitivity of brain data, which 'can be used for predictive purposes and opens new

[36] OECD, note (2).

[37] Council of Europe, 'Strategic Action Plan on Human Rights and Technologies in Biomedicine (2020-2025)' Adopted on 19–21 November 2019, 9.

[38] UNESCO, International Bioethics Committee, 'Ethical issues of Neurotechnology' (2021); 'Unveiling the Neurotechnology Landscape: Scientific Advancements Innovations and Major Trends' (2023).

[39] 46th Closed Session of the Global Privacy Assembly, 'Resolution on Principles regarding the Processing of Personal Information in Neuroscience and Neurotechnology' (2024).

possibilities in representations of the individual through data'.[40] The subsequent AEPD–EDPS 'TechDispatch on Neurodata' report further cautions that 'certain uses of neurodata pose unacceptable risks to fundamental rights and are likely unlawful under EU law',[41] referring to the prohibited AI practices under the EU AI act.[42] The UK Information Commissioner's Office mapped the sector-specific applications of neurotechnology such as healthcare, well-being, sports, workplace, consumers, and education in different scenarios, recognising the potential 'to not only observe and collect neurodata, but modulate neuropatterns and alter behaviour'.[43] Similarly, the Australian Human Rights Commission recognised human rights risks in that '[n]eural data is more sensitive and valuable than all other categories of personal data'.[44] It discussed right to privacy, freedom of thought, conscience and religion of brief, and right to equality and non-discrimination. In the United States, the Senators have introduced the Mind Bill, directing that the Federal Trade Commission to undertake a study on the governance of neural data.[45] In Asia, the 2024 Chinese 'Guidelines for Research Ethics in Brain-Computer Interface', issued by the Ministry of Science and Technology, draw attention by outlining six ethical criteria for BCI research and therapeutic applications: scientific soundness, beneficence, autonomy, minimum harm, privacy, and fairness and justice.[46]

The common ground among these international or domestic instruments does not advocate the immediate establishment of a new legislative framework. Rather, they reaffirm the applicability of existing human rights norms to the governance of neurotechnology. At the same time, the Council of Europe has undertaken a series of expert studies and reports to assess the ethical and legal implications of neurotechnologies, with a particular focus on identifying potential regulatory gaps and evaluating whether the emergence of cognitive and neural interface technologies necessitates normative development beyond the current legal architecture.[47]

---

[40] AEPD (Agencia Española de Protección de Datos), Neurodata: Privacy and Protection of Personal Data (II), 18 January 2023 <https://www.aepd.es/en/prensa-y-comunicacion/blog/neurodata-privacy-and-protection-of-personal-data-II>.

[41] EDPS and AEPD, 'Neurodata' EDPS TechDispatch 2024-1, (2024).

[42] Aimen 2025, p. 1 (clarifying the notion of manipulative AI to better safeguard cognitive autonomy); Daniel Susser et al., 'Technology, Autonomy, and Manipulation' (2019) 8(2) *Internet Policy Review* 1 (exploring the autonomy harm that results from exploiting their decision-making vulnerabilities); Neuwirth 2022, p. 901 (proposing the concept of legal synaesthesia).

[43] UK Information Commissioner's Office 2023, p. 6.

[44] Australian Human Rights Commission, 'Protecting Cognition: Background Paper on Human Rights and Neurotechnology' (2024) 14.

[45] S. 2925, MIND (Management of Individuals' Neural Data) Act of 2025, 119th Congress (introduced 29 September 2025). See Luguri and Strahilevitz 2021, p. 43 (providing the empirical evidence of dark patterns that user interfaces designed to manipulate decisions by exploiting cognitive biases).

[46] Poo 2024, p. nwae154; Wang 2024, p. 131. The original Guidelines are available at <https://www.most.gov.cn/kjbgz/202402/t20240202_189582.html>.

[47] See Marcello Ienca, 'Common Human Rights Challenges Raised by Different Applications of Neurotechologies in the Biomedical Field' (2021) Report Commissioned by the Committee on Bioethics(DH-BIO) of the Council of Europe; Bertoni and Ienca 2024.

## 5.3 Reconsidering Data Protection Frameworks

This sub-section critically analyzes the risks to privacy and data protection posed by emerging neurotechnology from a legal perspective, while recognising that these concerns have also been the subject of inquiry in diverse disciplines, including neuroscience, neuroengineering, behavioral science, and psychology. How could the existing data privacy laws address this challenge?

### *5.3.1 Denial of Mind-Body Dualism: Brain as Death Controversy in Japan*

AI brings a question of relationship between body and intelligence: whether intelligence emerges through the embodied experiences of the human body. Put another way, is intelligence merely a process confined within the brain, or is it cultivated through interaction by the body? Mind reading has increasingly taken the form of brain reading, as advances in neuroscience and machine learning now enable researchers to infer certain mental states from patterns of neural activity.[48] These developments rely on computational algorithms that decode brain signals into interpretable representations. As a result, traditional philosophical questions about the mind–body relationship are now being recast in terms of the brain–body relationship. Although this complex issue exceeds the scope of this legal book, it has been the subject of extensive debate in philosophy, cognitive science, and social theory. These interdisciplinary discussions highlight the significance of 'embodiment'[49] as foundational to understanding human intelligence.

Descartes noted in '*Discourse on Method*' that 'So that this Me, to wit, my Soul, by which I am what I am, is wholly distinct from the Body'.[50] This reflects the foundation of Cartesian mind–body dualism. It is a hallmark of certain strands of Western philosophical thought, though not universally accepted, that conceptualises the mind as separate from the physical body, often elevating the brain as the central organ to be protected.[51]

In contrast, mind–body dualism is not native to Japan or many other Asian cultures, where more integrated views of the self, such as the holistic unity of mind and

---

[48] Blitz 2018, p. 18.

[49] Kuniyoshi et al. 2004, p. 203 (stating that some global information structure will emerge from the natural dynamics of the body-environment system); Clark 2008, p. 219 (stating that human mind emerges at the productive interface of brain, body, and social and material world).

[50] Descartes 1649, p. 52.

[51] It is needless to say that not all the Western discourses support mind-body dualism. See Merleau-Ponty 1983, p. 210 (considering the mind as structural integration since 'duality is not a simple fact'). Michel Foucault's concept of discipline may also offer a critical lens on disembodiment in AI, insofar as '[a] body is docile that may be subjected, used, transformed, and improved'. Foucault 1977, p. 136.

body, are traditionally embraced. Typically, the Buddhist concept of 'mind and body as one' clearly rejects the mind-body dualism, as the Indian Supreme Court held that '[t]he body and the mind are inseparable elements of the human personality'.[52] The Chinese holistic views make virtually no distinction between body and mind and spirit, all of which are identified as '*qi*'.[53] Brain research in Korea has progressed relatively slowly, partly due to the legacy of Confucian cultural values, which emphasise the preservation of bodily integrity after death and thus discourage practices such as autopsy.[54] Japanese Shinto holds that the soul resides within the human body, embodying a fundamental unity of mind and body rather than a dualistic separation. In Shinto belief, defilement as *kegare* refers to death and blood, and it is also associated with the departure of spiritual energy from the body.[55] In the cultural context, the leading Japanese ethicist Tetsuro Watsuji observed that 'carnal interconnection is always found wherever there is betweenness' (*aidagara*, 間柄)[56] as a person being in the network of intersubjective places.[57] It suggested that the fundamental mode of being human must be understood as the unity of mind and body, or the 'oneness of body and mind' (*shinjin ichinyo*, 心身一如).[58] The conventional Japanese intellectuals presupposed that 'there is no distinction between the mind and the flesh'.[59] Traditional Japanese cultural values help explain the sense of resistance toward BCI rehabilitation, especially concerning the treatment of individuals as body of mere physical objects.[60] While recent scholarship has challenged the extent to which East Asian thought can be characterised as purely holistic, it remains impossible to discuss mind–body dualism in Asia without acknowledging the enduring influence of its own traditions and religions such as Confucianism.[61] In sum, mind-body dualism reflects 'a long-standing divergence between the intellectual histories of East and West',[62] suggesting that the conceptual framing and analytical treatment of the brain may likewise differ across cultures.

While most Japanese people do not adhere to formal religious beliefs, the Japanese cultural understanding of death significantly influenced the national debate over brain death, particularly during the introduction of the Organ Transplantation

---

[52] Judgment of the Supreme Court of India, *Justice K.S.Puttaswamy(Retd) And Anr. vs Union of India And Ors.*, 24 August, 2017 para169 (English translation available at <https://indiankanoon.org/doc/91938676/?utm>.

[53] Raphals 2023, p. 2.

[54] Jeong et al. 2019, p. 390; Yoo et al. 2023, p. e193.

[55] Tomoko 2020, p. 103.

[56] Hanakawa et al. 2003, pp. 301.

[57] Research indicates that in BCI-related research, ingroup and loyalty emerge as a distinctive moral foundation among Japanese speakers. Iijima et al. 2025, p. 40.

[58] Yuasa et al. 1987, p. 49.

[59] Ibid 25. For Japanese thought, a person is not so much a consciousness through time but a conscious body in space. Fukushi et al. 2017, p. 445.

[60] Orito et al. 2025, p. 397.

[61] Slingerland 2019.

[62] Ibid 46.

Bill, which was later enacted into law in 1997. During the preparatory phase, a governmental advisory panel reporting to the Prime Minister issued a report in 1992 stating that 'it seems reasonable to consider brain death as human death in both social and legal contexts'.[63] However, minority opinions within the report, criticising Cartesian mind–body dualism, highlighted that traditional Japanese conceptions of death include the belief and funerary ritual (*mogari*, 殯) of the deceased's body being temporarily kept in a special place before burial, allowing time for the soul to part and for the death to be confirmed. Thus, the minority opinion opposed brain death because it would undermine the unity of soul and body of the person based on the traditional Japanese perspective on life and death since ancient times.

Apart from life and death, brain may adapt the cultural environment through biological adaptation. In Japan and other East Asian countries, traditional abacus training remains part of elementary education. Researchers found that expert users develop a 'mental abacus,' allowing them to perform complex calculations by visualising bead positions through visuospatial/visuomotor information.[64] The fMRI studies have shown that expert abacus users engage parietal brain regions associated with spatial processing, illustrating a culturally shaped cognitive strategy for arithmetic processing that differs from the common linguistic processing.[65]

In sum, neuroprivacy requires 'a culture-specific context',[66] affirming the universal fundamental rights such as right to private life and personal data protection. Although cultural reductionism must be treated with caution, especially given that responses differ across technologies,[67] Japanese discourse on brain privacy is frequently contextualised, as emphasised by the Japanese neuroethical scholars,[68] through classical literature and a cultural tradition that resists Cartesian mind–body dualism. Moreover, cultural factors play an important role in shaping both positive and negative attitudes toward the harvesting of non-conscious data,[69] influencing how the concept of privacy is understood within different cultural contexts.

---

[63] Provisional Committee for Brain Death and Organ Transplantation, 'Report on the Significant Issues relating to Brain Death and Organ Transplantation' [脳死及び臓器移植に関する重要事項について(答申)](in Japanese)(January 1992). Available the report at (1992) 1001 *Jurist* 34, 44.

[64] Kitayama and Park 2010, p. 113.

[65] Hanakawa et al. note (56) 301.

[66] Yuste et al. 2017, p. 162.

[67] Research on cyborg acceptance indicates that 'perceived risk does not significantly influence the intention to use insideables, in either Japan or Spain'. Murata et al. 2019, pp. 129, 135.

[68] Fukushi et al. 2017, p. 442.

[69] Mantello et al. 2023, p. 430.

### 5.3.2 Sensitivity of Neurodata

Neurodata, corresponding to 'personal brain data' in the OECD recommendation, is defined as 'data relating to the functioning or structure of the human brain of an identified or identifiable individual that includes unique information about their physiology, health, or mental states'.[70] Neurodata have the potential to reveal information that may not be known or even consciously accessible to the individual themselves. The processing of neurodata may thus occur in ways that are beyond the individual's awareness or control.[71] It can also serve as 'representations of the individual'[72] by capturing and predicting the most intimate aspects of cognition and emotion in a way that goes beyond conventional forms of personal data. If 'neuro-exceptionalism'[73] is to be acknowledged, it may rest on the premise that neurodata exhibit exceptional qualities that may not be adequately addressed by the existing assumptions underpinning data protection law.

From a data protection law perspective, first, neural data is personal data as long as it is identified or identifiable of an individual. As brain is data repository of humans, the mere monitoring brain activity for a wellness, safety, and productivity application, may be seen as personal data.[74] Secondly, more controversially, neurodata can be situationally categorised as the special categories of personal data as well as a part of biometric data, to infer possible criminals by 'neuroprediction'.[75] However, objections may arise against categorising all neural data as special categories of personal data under data protection law. This is partly because certain neural data may simply reflect ordinary physical movements, such as walking or shaking hands, which are not inherently sensitive or subject to special regulation. Such an expansive interpretation of sensitive data risks triggering 'an inflation effect',[76] potentially encouraging data controllers to circumvent the stricter requirements imposed on the processing of sensitive data.

Yet, neural data, even when derived from seemingly mundane activities may reveal or infer the feeling, emotion, or mood on the inner parts during walking or shaking hands. Moreover, the secondary use or the combination of neural data with other datasets, can significantly increase the sensitivity of the originally collected information beyond its initial context or purpose. The EDPS-AEPD report acknowledges that neurodata 'often'[77] but not always qualify as special categories of personal data under Article 9 of the GDPR. Therefore, the report wrote the types of data processed into three categories, namely, data regarding the structure of the

[70] OECD, note (2).

[71] Hallinan et al. 2014, p. 65.

[72] Ibid.

[73] Hallinan et al. 2023, p. 21.

[74] Rainey et al. 2020, p. 9.

[75] Tortora et al. 2020, p. 220.

[76] Quinn and Malgieri 2022, p. 1584.

[77] EDPS-AEPD, note (41) 15.

brain, data regarding the function and activity of the brain, and data related to the peripheral system. In practice, the high potential for share or misuse, such as the sale of biometric data or re-identification through data aggregation, creates substantial privacy risks.[78] This has prompted some jurisdictions to proactively regulate neural data. Indeed, some US state privacy laws provide neural data.[79] Most notably, the Colorado Privacy Act[80] and the California Consumer Privacy Act[81] by amending their Acts include 'neural data' under their definitions of sensitive data, requiring controllers to obtain consumer consent before processing such information or to limit its use. Thus, unless neural data is strictly separated from other possible sensitive data, in light of privacy by design, it should be afforded the same level of protection as special categories of personal data such as genetic or health data.[82]

### 5.3.3 *Privacy and Personal Data Protection*

The foundation of unlawful manipulation has traditionally been understood as the invasion of privacy of minds.[83] Now the EU AI act explicitly prohibit the AI practices of deploying manipulative or deceptive techniques (Art.5(1)(a)), with Recital 29 citing 'machine-brain interfaces' as a concrete example (recital 29). Similarly, the US state privacy laws of regulating neural data can also be interpreted as targeting so-called 'dark pattern', defined as user interface designs or manipulations that substantially impair a consumer's autonomy, decision-making, or choice.[84] Accordingly, it can be said that the root of regulating manipulative techniques and dark patterns lies in the unjust or exploitative stimulation of the brain and neural process.

Privacy and data protection laws share a common regulatory spirit against undue interference with neural data. The core data privacy principles are designed to address such interference, which results in manipulative or deceptive practices including dark patterns. In addition to the special categories of personal data, which

---

[78] Magee et al. 2024, p. 3019.

[79] At the federal level, a bill on 'Management of Individuals' Neural Data Act of 2025' was submitted to the Senate in September 2025. <https://www.commerce.senate.gov/services/files/A175D9D8-6CF8-4733-B2F6-43C19FE4CB74f>.

[80] 'Data concerning the activity of the human brain and wider nervous systems, or "neural data", is extremely sensitive and can reveal intimate information about individuals, including information about health, mental states, emotions, and cognitive functioning'. 222 Consumer and Commercial Transactions Ch.68, Section 1(1)(d).

[81] 'Neural data' means information that is generated by measuring the activity of a consumer's central or peripheral nervous system, and that is not inferred from nonneural information'. 1798.140. (ae)(1)(G)(ii).

[82] Ienca et al. 2022, p. 24.

[83] Packard 1957, p. 266.

[84] California Consumer Privacy Act, 1798.140 (l).

were discussed above, the following principles, among others, should be particularly considered.

First, much of the neural data collected is often unnecessary for the immediate purpose, thereby conflicting with the data minimisation principle. The continuous and large-scale collection of such data, often beyond the user's awareness or control, risks violating the minimisation requirement of data protection law. The controllers must be aware of potential periodical deletion of neural data which can be automatically acquired beyond the necessary purposes. At the same time, in light of the principle of data protection by design and by default, data controllers must also be mindful of the need for periodic deletion of neural data that may be automatically processed beyond what is necessary for the specified purposes in the neurotechnology domain. The famous judicial warning notes that '[t]he mere storing of data relating to the private life of an individual amounts to an interference'[85] to the private life.

Secondly, under the accuracy principle, given the dynamic and constantly changing nature of neural data, data controllers must ensure the reliability of predictions or inferences derived from such data via BCIs. Scientific studies in 2020 indicate that emotional AI systems achieve unstable accuracy,[86] and similar doubts are likely to arise regarding the accuracy of brainwave-based measurements.[87] Inaccuracies in these inferences may lead to significant disadvantages for data subjects, such as false positives in lie detection scenarios.

Thirdly, in terms of purpose limitation, the multiple processing of the same general brain recordings may lead to the use of neural data for purposes that extend far beyond the original, specified intent.[88] Such secondary or repurposed uses risk violating the purpose limitation principle, which requires that personal data be collected for specified, explicit and legitimate purposes and not further processing in a manner 'incompatible'[89] with those purposes. This is particularly concerning in the context of BCIs, where the same neural inputs can yield various inferences. Thus, the open-ended utility or recording of brain data necessitates strict safeguards to prevent re-identification, tracking, the use as unique identifiers for data linkage, as well as profiling, singling out, and the risk of 'functional creep'.[90]

Fourthly, transparency and fairness will come into play. These principles require that data subjects be clearly informed about how their neural data is processed for what purposes. In the context of neurotechnology, however, the complexity of BCIs

---

[85] ECtHR, *S and Marper v United Kingdom* (2008) Applications nos. 30562/04 and 30566/04 para 67.

[86] See Dupré et al. 2020, p. e0231968.

[87] The study on reliability of consumer EEG-based drowsiness detection system remains questionable in practical and occupational settings. See LaRocco et al. 2020, p. 553352.

[88] Rainey et al. note (74) 3.

[89] Article 29 Data Protection Working Party, 'Opinion 03/2013 on Purpose Limitation' WP203, 21. (noting that the 'compatibility test could be formal or substantive').

[90] Kindt 2022, p. 380 (noting these risks in the Eurodac system and the Indian biometric database of Aadhaar).

and affective computing systems can make it difficult for users to fully understand the nature and consequences of data processing. This information asymmetry poses a serious challenge to meaningful consent and undermines the data subject's autonomy. Moreover, fairness requires that data processing should not lead to unexpected consequences, such as discrimination ('neurodiscrimination'[91]), manipulation, or exploitation. This is particularly true when neural data is used to infer sensitive traits such as mental status or cognitive capacity. Ensuring that individuals are not subjected to unexpected, opaque, biased, or misleading forms of neural data processing is thus central to protecting fundamental rights.

Precedents on facial recognition technologies may similarly apply to the regulation of neurodata. In China, the Supreme People's Court has issued two landmark judgments on facial recognition and facial swapping technologies (See Chap. 4), and in Korea, comparable cases involving facial recognition have resulted in monetary sanctions imposed by the Personal Information Protection Commission. In contrast, in Japan, the Act on the Protection of Personal Information (APPI) provides no direct regulation of neurotechnology, and the absence of a legal framework for biometric data, such as facial recognition, remains a notable regulatory gap. In Japan, the regulatory vacuum has led to confusion. For instance, regarding the installation of facial identification cameras to detect ex-convicts or suspicious individuals in JR East railway stations, the Personal Information Protection Commission initially acknowledged the necessity of such surveillance, however, following public criticism, JR East was ultimately compelled to modify their operation.[92] The APPI together with other guidelines encourage meaningful consent for processing neurodata. However, it is questionable that unlikely to resolve the complex challenges posed by biometric technologies, including those involving neurodata. First, significant information asymmetries between data subjects and controllers may lead to unforeseen consequences, such as discriminatory outcomes based on neural inferences. Second, many data controllers share or repurpose neurodata in ways that exceed users' expectations, undermining the very premise of informed consent (see Chap. 6). And third, due to its sensitivity, once neurodata is processed and analysed, it may generate non-revocable profiles of individuals' inner states, traits, or vulnerabilities, making it difficult for individuals to reclaim control or mitigate future harms.

The question arises whether data protection laws apply when non-manipulative neurotechnology is deployed in the case of emotional AI systems that do not involve individual identification.[93] If identifiability is the threshold for the application of

[91] UK ICO, note (43) 3.

[92] Takashi Ogawa and Yasukazu Akada, 'Plan to Use Facial Recognition at JR East Stations to Spot Ex-cons Iced', Asahi Newspaper, 22 September 2021. <https://www.asahi.com/ajw/articles/14445523>.

[93] Leijten and Lodder 2025, p. 110 (noting that 'the EU regulatory framework is insufficiently equipped to protect the fundamental rights that may be compromised by the deployment of non-identifying emotional AI'); Peggy, Clifford and Dessers 2021, p.76 (noting that scholars question whether the ECHR's existing protections are adequate to counter the manipulative capabilities of emotional AI).

data privacy law, this raises broader concerns related to human dignity and respect to individuals. Neural data protection relates to several fundamental rights provisions such as integrity of person, freedom of thought, freedom of expression, due process, and privilege against self-incrimination. The following sections consider each legal topic.

### 5.3.4 *Neurorights Beyond Traditional Privacy: Integrity of Person*

First, neural data relates to integrity of person. The EU Charter of Fundamental Rights explicitly protects 'the right to respect for his or her physical and mental integrity' (Art.3(1)). The CJEU interpreted that the right to human integrity 'encompasses, in the context of medicine and biology, the free and informed consent of the donor and recipient'.[94] The CJEU also affirmed 'the right of transgender people to personal development and physical and moral integrity'[95] under Art. 3 as well as Art. 7 of protection of private life. Mental integrity may also be interpreted as involving 'the individual's mastery of their mental states and brain data so that, without their consent, no one can read, spread or alter such states and data in order to condition the individual in any way'.[96] A recent study on mental self-determination also underscores the importance of transcending the traditional mind–brain dualism, arguing that 'all mental phenomena supervene on (or at least correlate with) neuronal processes'.[97]

While Japanese law does not explicitly recognise the concept of personal integrity as an independent legal right, concerns relating to the manipulation or intrusion upon an individual's mental autonomy have surfaced in various legal contexts. One illustrative example is the regulation of religious donation practices. The 2022 Act on Preventing Unjust Solicitation of Donations by a Corporation prohibits solicitation that causes confusion or impairs a person's capacity for rational judgment. Japanese courts have addressed such conduct under Article 90 of the Civil Code, which nullifies legal acts that violate public order, particularly when a person's will is undermined by psychological pressure or undue influence.[98] This reflects a legal sensitivity to the exploitation of cognitive or mental vulnerability, even if not explic-

---

[94] C-377/98, *Netherlands v Parliament and Council*, ECLI:EU:C:2001:523 para78.

[95] C-247/23, *VP v Országos Idegenrendészeti Főigazgatóság*, ECLI:EU:C:2025:172 para 47.

[96] Andrea Lavazza, 'Technology Against Technology: A Case for Embedding Limits in Neurodevices to Protect Our Freedom of Thought', in Marc Jonathan Blitz and Jan Christoph Bublitz (eds), *The Law and Ethics of Freedom of Thoughts, Volume 1* (Palgrave Macmillan 2021) 259, 275.

[97] Bublitz and Merkel 2014, p. 56. See also Schleim 2025, p. 19.

[98] Judgement of the Supreme Court on 11 July 2024, 78(3) *Minshu* 921 <https://www.courts.go.jp/app/files/hanrei_jp/196/093196_hanrei.pdf> (in Japanese). Article 90 of the Civil Code provides that '[a] juridical act that is against public policy is void'.

itly framed as a violation of personal integrity. As brain-monitoring technologies become more sophisticated, capable of recording, interpreting, or even influencing neural activity, questions arise as to whether existing Japanese civil and consumer protection laws are sufficient to safeguard the core aspects of personal integrity.

Beyond the concept of personal integrity, similar legal discourse in Japan has centered on the principles of bodily autonomy and the right to self-determination, particularly in matters involving life and death.[99] In a landmark case concerning a Jehovah's Witness who refused a blood transfusion on religious grounds, the Supreme Court found that medical practitioners had infringed the patient's right to decision-making rights by failing to provide adequate information in light of her clearly stated refusal.[100] The Tokyo High Court further affirmed the importance of right to self-determination, writing that '[r]ecognising that individuals may hold values they are willing to risk their lives for based on their beliefs and act in accordance with those beliefs should not be deemed unlawful so long as these actions do not infringe upon the rights of others or violate the public interest or order'.[101] Although the courts grounded their reasoning primarily in the right to self-determination, this right may be understood as constituting a core element of what is conceived as personal integrity, at least in the Japanese context. That is, the capacity to live in accordance with one's beliefs, especially when those beliefs inform deeply personal, bodily, or existential decisions, reflects the underlying normative commitment of personal integrity to the protection of an individual's coherent and autonomous sense of self.

In other words, the concept of personal integrity is still unmatured, insufficient, or varied to address the entire risks of neurotechnology. Other fundamental rights, in particular, the right to self-determination can reinforce the core value of personal integrity.

### 5.3.5 Freedom of Thought and Conscience

Second, the scope of 'thought' is not clear enough whether to cover such as 'mood', 'emotion', 'feeling', 'memory', or 'dream'. Mood-based music recommender earplugs, for example, are capable of detecting and responding to users' emotional states.[102] Similarly, researchers at Kyoto University have demonstrated the ability to decode dream content by fMRI with approximately 60–70% accuracy by analysing

---

[99] The European context of personal integrity covers the issues relating to medical treatment and death. See Marshall 2009, p. 165. In the United States, a considerable jurisprudential and scholarly corpus has developed on bodily privacy, encompassing privacy protections in the context of abortion. See Henkin 1974, p. 1410.

[100] Judgement of the Supreme Court, 29 February 2000, 54(2) *Minshu* 582 <https://www.courts.go.jp/app/hanrei_en/detail?id=478> (in Japanese).

[101] Judgement of the Tokyo High Court, 9 February 1998, 51(1) *Kosai Minji Hanreishu* 1.

[102] *See* Daly 2023, p. 624.

brain activity during the sleep-onset period.[103] Andrew McStay has explored the concept of 'leaky emotions', which means emotional states involuntarily revealed through EEG and other physiological sensing devices, and raises concerns about 'emotional sincerity' in legal contexts such as depositions.[104] These technological developments pose a constitutional question on freedom of thought.

The Universal Declaration of Human Rights recognises the right to freedom of thought, conscience and religion (Art.18). It established as a cornerstone of being human protected under international law. The classic caselaw on freedom of thought means that, for instance, the US Supreme Court held '[f]reedom of thought, which includes freedom of religious belief, is basic in a society of free men. ... Heresy trials are foreign to our Constitution'.[105] Similarly, the European Court of Human Rights affirmed that '[f]reedom of thought, conscience and religion is one of the foundations of a 'democratic society' within the meaning of the Convention. It is, in its religious dimension, one of the most vital elements that go to make up the identity of believers and their conception of life'.[106]

While freedom of thought has been traditionally understood as enjoying absolute protection so long as thoughts remain within the mind, it may require reconsideration in the face of neurotechnology. Jan Christoph Bublitz noted that '[t]houghts are understood broadly including mental states such as fantasies, opinions, desires, inner images and perhaps even dreams and emotions'.[107] Nita Farahany similarly advocates 'the right not to reveal one's thought'[108] against thought surveillance or thought crime. At the same time, Farahany cautions that if we 'define freedom of thought as the prohibition of every attempt to read each other's minds, we risk criminalizing human understanding'.[109] These attempts for broad understanding may represent the need to reconsider the legal scope of 'thought' as traditionally protected. Continuous monitoring or manipulating of brain activity without consent may infringe upon the mental processes that constitute thought itself, not merely its external expression. If current legal frameworks protect only the outward articulation of thought, they may fail to address the more intimate and complex inner cognitive and emotional processes now accessible through neurotechnology.

In Japan, the historical roots of freedom of thought and conscience can be traced back to Edo era of Persecution of Christians known as 'Fumie': refusal to step on the image of Jesus Christ was interpreted as proof of Christian belief, which could lead to imprisonment. In light of this breach of inner freedom, the Constitution of Japan explicitly protects freedom of thought and conscience.[110] The broader inter-

---

[103] Horikawa et al. 2013, p. 640.

[104] McStay 2018, p. 72.

[105] *United States v. Ballard*, 322 U.S. 78 (1944).

[106] ECtHR, *Kokkinakis v. Greece*, App. No. 14307/88, ECHR (1993).

[107] Bublitz 2014, p. 24.

[108] Farahany 2023, p. 84.

[109] Ibid 71.

[110] 'Freedom of thought and conscience shall not be violated'. (Art. 19).

pretation of thought defines 'inner mental functions related to the formation of personality, such as worldview, philosophy of life, personal beliefs, and convictions'.[111] The court, in a case involving a court-ordered newspaper apology following defamation, considered whether it could compel a public apology that effectively forces an inner thought into the public domain.[112] While the majority upheld the order, the dissenting opinion objected on the grounds of the 'freedom to remain silent' as a component of the freedom of thought.[113] Extending this trajectory into the technological context, Masatoshi Kokubo introduced the possibility of a constitutional interpretation to include mental or cognitive processes as a part of 'thought' in the wake of neurotechnology.[114] While freedom of thought and conscience has long been regarded as a foundational right, its application in the context of neurotechnology remains largely unexplored. At the same time, there remains an unresolved tension as to whether issues raised by neurotechnology should be treated solely as matters of freedom of thought. Framing them too narrowly in that context risks overregulating natural and intuitive forms of interpersonal understanding and relations.

### 5.3.6 *Freedom of Expression*

Third, neural data can be understood as a source of self-expression. As thoughts, emotions, and intentions shape the basis of communications and opinions, the neural signals that infer these mental or emotional states represent the raw material of expressive conduct. Continuous monitoring of neural activity without consent may produce a chilling effect,[115] discouraging individuals from thinking and speaking freely due to the fear of surveillance. Moreover, attempts to manipulate or unduly influence neural activity raise serious concerns, as they may amount to a new technological form of 'censorship'[116] or have 'the potential to subvert free will'.[117] In this sense, the protection of neuro data should be recognised not only as a matter of privacy or data protection, but as an essential dimension of freedom of expression and speech.

---

[111] Ashibe 2000, p. 104.

[112] Judgement of the Supreme Court, 4 July 1956, 10(7) *Minshu* 785. The Civil Code provides that '[t]he court may order a person that has defamed another person to take appropriate measures to restore the reputation of the victim in lieu of or in addition to compensation for loss or damage, at the request of the victim' (Art. 723).

[113] Ibid (dissenting opinion by Justice Katsumi Tarumi).

[114] Kokubo 2020, p. 392. See also Komamura 2025.

[115] Unger 2023a, p. 1484.

[116] Farahany 2023, p. 76.

[117] European Parliament, Resolution (2344) on the Brain-Computer Interface: New Rights or New Threats to Fundamental Freedoms? (2020).

The strong tradition of the U.S. free speech doctrine illustrates that prevalent neurotechnology may violate the First Amendment prohibition against compelled speech unless it meets the strict scrutiny.[118] In *West Virginia State Board of Education v. Barnette*, the Supreme Court held that the government cannot force individuals to express beliefs they do not hold, famously stating that 'no official, high or petty, can prescribe what shall be orthodox in politics, nationalism, religion, or other matters of opinion'.[119] This principle was reaffirmed in *Wooley v. Maynard*, where the Court emphasised that, '[t]he right to speak and the right to refrain from speaking are complementary components of the broader concept of "individual freedom of mind"'.[120] These well-established free speech principles on prohibition of compelled speech raise serious concerns if brain-computer interfaces or other neurotechnologies are used to extract, manipulate, or disclose thoughts against a person's will, potentially amounting to a modern form of compelled expression.

Interestingly, the compelled speech doctrine is closely tied to the concept of personal integrity or 'speaker's autonomy interest'[121] in that it protects individuals from being forced to affirm beliefs they do not hold. As Larry Alexander noted, '[h]e is not in his mind "affirming" what he does not believe'.[122] In this sense, compelled speech and personal integrity can be seen as deeply intertwined, both serving as constitutional safeguards against intrusions that threaten the integrity and autonomy of the individual.

### 5.3.7 Due Process and Privilege Against Self-Incrimination

Fourth, acquiring and sharing neural data, even called as 'brain fingerprinting',[123] must meet due process of law and privilege against self-incrimination. Though not directly related to neural data, the US Supreme Court in *Rochin v. California* formulated 'shocks the conscience',[124] holding the illegal breaking into the privacy of an induvidual by forcing to open one's mouth and remove what was there. Justice

---

[118] Unger 2023a, p. 1454. See also Marks 2023, p. 469 (proposing cognitive content moderation toward the information-based theory of the First Amendment).

[119] *West Virginia State Board of Education v. Barnette*, 319 U.S. 624, 642 (1943).

[120] *Wooley v. Maynard*, 430 U.S. 705, 714 (1977). *See also* Agency *for International Development v. Alliance for Open Society International, Inc.*, 570 U.S. 205 (2013), noting that 'freedom of speech prohibits the government from telling people what they must say'.

[121] Volokh 2018, p. 368.

[122] Alexander 2006, p. 159.

[123] *Harrington v. State*, 659 N.W.2d 509, 516 n6 (Iowa 2003) (a post-conviction case where the defendant introduced computer-based 'brain fingerprinting' as newly discovered evidence; the court cited expert testimony asserting that the suspect's brain did not contain information about the murder, but did not examine the scientific validity or admissibility of this evidence). Regarding the types of neuroimaging technologies for criminal investigation, see Jonathan Blitz 2018, p. 60.

[124] *Rochin v. California*, 342 U.S. 165 (1952).

Frankfurter opinioned by referring to the California Supreme Court '[h]ad the evidence forced from the defendant's lips consisted of an oral confession that he illegally possessed a drug... he would have the protection of the rule of law which excludes coerced confessions from evidence...[We] find no valid ground of distinction between a verbal confession extracted by physical abuse and a confession wrested from defendant's body by physical abuse[125]'. By analogy, the compelled extraction of neural data, particularly through coercive or deceptive means, may similarly constitute a violation of due process.[126] The brain holds even more of 'the privacies of life'[127] than a modern cell phone that is subject to constitutional scrutiny. Despite ongoing disputes over the scientific reliability of neural truth-finding, the brain must nevertheless be treated 'as an inviolable frontier'[128] that cannot be used as 'undue "functionalization" of persons'.[129] Therefore, any neural evidence obtained without free and informed consent should be excluded from admissibility.

Certain strands of case law may also offer insights relevant to the future regulation of neurotechnology. In Japan, polygraph examinations administered by police are admissible as evidence with the consent of the suspect since coercive brain-reading may be constitutionally prohibited confession and self-incrimination,[130] even 'freedom to be silence' as a part of freedom of thought and conscience.[131] The Japanese polygraph system measures physiological responses within the cardiovascular system, including blood pressure, skin blood flow, and normalized pulse wave amplitude. The Supreme Court has upheld lower court decisions admitting polygraph evidence, emphasising that such evidence was reliably produced through accurate scientific documentation of each examination's process and results, and that the examiner possessed the requisite technical expertise and experience.[132]

[125] *Ibid* 167.

[126] *See Kyllo v. United States*, 533 U.S. 27, 34 (2001) (noting that 'obtaining by sense enhancing technology any information regarding the interior of the home that could not otherwise have been obtained without physical "intrusion into a constitutionally protected area," constitutes a search at least where (as here) the technology in question is not in general public use'); *Carpenter v. United States*, 585 U.S.296 (2018) (noting that 'individuals have a reasonable expectation of privacy in the whole of their physical movements'). *See also* Unger 2023b, p. 321.

[127] *Riley v. California*, 573 U.S. 373, 403 (2014).

[128] Monti 2025, p. 43.

[129] Merkel 2015, p. 1355.

[130] Constitution Art.38 provides that '[n]o person shall be compelled to testify against himself. 2. Confession made under compulsion, torture or threat, or after prolonged arrest or detention shall not be admitted in evidence. 3.No person shall be convicted or punished in cases where the only proof against him is his own confession'. Traditionally, the Japanese Supreme Court narrowly interpreted the scope of this privilege, holding that the so-called right to remain silent guarantees that no person shall be compelled to testify against themselves on matters that may expose them to criminal liability (Judgement of the Supreme Court, 2 May 1962, 16(5) *Keishu* 495).

[131] Judgement of the Supreme Court, 4 July 1956, 10(7) *Minshu* 785(dissenting opinion by Justice Katsumi Tarumi).

[132] Decision of the Supreme Court on 8 February 1968, 22(2) *Keishu* 55.

A theoretical framework in *Saunders v. United Kingdom* of distinguishing between testimonial evidence and physical evidence[133] may provide a clue for brain reading technologies in criminal procedures and fair trial. Yet, the absence of a universally accepted concept of 'testimony' under different criminal systems and practices has led to diverging opinions on whether brain-reading technologies should be classified as producing testimonial evidence.[134] In practice, the applicability of the privilege depends on the nature and intensity of the pressure exerted, the presence of procedural safeguards, and the intended use of the obtained information.[135]

In sum, though this chapter does not delve deeply into criminal procedures,[136] it is fair to state that precedents like *Rochin* and *Saunders* underscore the importance of protecting individuals from compelled disclosures of their inner mental life and ensuring a fair trial. Without a clear legislation, the use of brain-derived data risks undermining fundamental right to the privilege against self-incrimination, which is ultimately derived from human dignity and the rule of law.

## 5.4 Beyond Privacy: Cognitive Liberty

### *5.4.1 The Roots of Cognitive Liberty*

By its nature, the law must take human cognition seriously, as legal processes, including the evaluation of evidence and witness testimony, fundamentally rely on memory, perception, and emotion.[137] Neurotechnology raises fundamental questions for contemporary legal theory concerning the nature of human cognition and personality, extending far beyond traditional concerns of privacy and data protection. It engages core rights such as personal integrity, freedom of thought and conscience, freedom of expression, due process, and the privilege against self-incrimination. However, existing legal concepts and frameworks were not designed to situate human cognition within the legal order nor to address the unprecedented forms of intrusion and control enabled by neurotechnology. As a result, these traditional understandings of freedom and rights may prove insufficient to fully confront the legal and ethical issues emerging in the neurotechnological era. By enabling the enhancement or augmentation of cognitive and affective functions, it risks altering personal identity and undermining the conditions of 'authenticity'[138] that undergird personhood of an individual. The fundamental question is how the law can evaluate personhood itself through its generative capacity, mental state, or

[133] ECtHR, *Saunders v. United Kingdom*, Application no. 19187/91, 17 December 1996.
[134] Escobar Veas 2025, p. 1.
[135] Ligthart 2022, p. 197.
[136] See Billing 2016.
[137] *See* Nadel and Sinnott-Armstrong 2013.
[138] Errigo 2020, p. 205.

physical performance, when these human attributes are reshaped through technological intervention into cognitive sovereignty.

The concept of cognitive liberty may be classically rooted in Mill's 'the inward domain of consciousness',[139] Descartes's 'cogito',[140] or Berlin's 'the inner citadel'.[141] In the legal discourse such a concept emerged in Richard Glen Boire's article on 'cognitive liberty' in 2000, claiming the 'right to control one's own consciousness' as 'the quintessence of freedom'.[142] Jan-Christoph Bublitz explained cognitive liberty as 'a right to mental self-determination' guaranteeing 'individuals sovereignty over their minds'.[143] Nita Farahany developed cognitive liberty, which includes 'the right to informational self-determination to access information about ourselves, the right to choose how we will change our own brains and mental experiences, and the right to our capacity to choose by making it unlawful to disable or control a person's mind'.[144] In a similar vein, but more closely aligned with privacy discourses, Neil Richards conceptualised 'intellectual privacy' as comprising three elements: freedom of thought and belief, the right to read and engage in intellectual exploration, and the confidentiality of communications.[145] There is no single concept of cognitive liberty, yet, it does have some components including privacy.

### *5.4.2 Cognitive Liberty as 'Penumbras'*

Traditional fundamental rights may still have force, yet, what was once termed as 'penumbras'[146] of these rights would shape and clarify the legal right of cognitive liberty. The right to cognitive liberty, if it exists, is not an independent right, rather a bundle of the constitutional rights of personal integrity, freedom of thought and conscience, freedom of expression, due process, and the privilege against self-incrimination. Most of the Constitutions do not explicitly protect cognitive liberty, mind control or manipulation constitutes a violation of fundamental constitutional principles, including right to privacy and self-determination, the freedom of thought and conscience, and, often, the right to equal protection and privilege against self-incrimination. In practice, courts and data protection authorities may assess the applicability of each constitutional or legal provision on a case-by-case basis. However, conceptualising cognitive liberty as a bundle of fundamental rights serves to clarify and reinforce the underlying normative values that define and protect

---

139 Mill et al. 2015, p. 15.

140 Descartes 2015, p. 29.

141 Isaiah Berlin and Henry Hardy 2002, p. 181.

142 Glen Boire 2000, p. 7.

143 Bublitz 2013, p. 241. See also Bublitz 2015, p. 1309.

144 Farahany 2023, p. 214.

145 Richards 2015, p. 108.

146 *Griswold v. Connecticut*, 381 U.S. 479, 484 (1965).

being human and personhood. This holistic approach provides a coherent framework for addressing the complex legal and ethical challenges posed by emerging neurotechnology. Framing cognitive liberty as a legal interest not only enriches the substantive meaning of mental privacy but also illuminates its integral relationship with the broader architecture of fundamental rights and constitutional values.

Cognitive liberty may be conceptualised as a foundational stratum of fundamental rights or the condition of being human, which may be shaped by cultural adaptations of mind–body dualism. It may have both positive and negative dimensions. In a negative aspect, cognitive liberty includes the right to silence such as the freedom not to speak, not to disclose, and not to be subject to mental intrusion. The freedom of thought and conscience under the Constitution of Japan is understood as guaranteeing 'the freedom to remain silent for those who wish to do so'.[147] Silence is not merely the absence of words. Silence gives meaning as a space between words, allowing inner thoughts the necessary pause to take form before being expressed outwardly.[148] Silence is a part of one's moral integrity and autonomy.[149] On the other hand, in a positive aspect, cognitive liberty shapes one's thoughts, beliiefs, and identity in order to reinforce autonomy toward self-determination. Joseph Raz praised autonomy in the legal order, noting that '[a]ll three conditions, mental abilities, adequacy of options, and independence admit of degree'.[150] Mere non-interference by the state is insufficient; rather, genuine autonomy requires not only freedom from coercion but also the presence of adequate and worthwhile options, sufficient mental capacities, and an environment that fosters meaningful reflection and choice. In this sense, the right to cognitive liberty emerges as a foundational interest that sustains the preconditions for autonomy itself.

In sum, cognitive liberty embraces, what Louis Brandeis termed as 'man's spiritual nature, of his feelings and of his intellect',[151] which was indeed the source to connect the right to privacy and the freedom of speech, 'freedom to think as you will and to speak as you think'.[152] In other words, the century-long discourse on privacy may be seen as a particular manifestation of the fundamental principle of cognitive liberty.

---

[147] Judgement of the Supreme Court, 4 July 1956, 10(7) *Minshu* 785 (dissenting opinion by Justice Katsumi Tarumi). Freedom of thought extends to 'the right to not remember and even to forget' as memory is the interplay between recall and forgetting. Forgetting is 'by and large, not under our conscious control'. Bublitz and Dresler 2015, pp. 1294–1295.

[148] Michael Seidman 2007 p.2.

[149] Green 1999, p. 661; Kent Greenawalt 1992, p. 193.

[150] Raz 1988, p. 373.

[151] *Olmstead v. United States*, 277 U.S. 438, 478 (1928) (Brandeis, J., dissenting).

[152] *Whitney v. California*, 274 U.S. 357, 375 (1927) (Brandeis, J., concurring).

## References

Elisabeth Steindl, 'Consumer Neuro Devices within EU Product Safety Law: Are We Prepared for Big Tch Ante Portas?' (2024) 52 *Computer Law & Security Review* 105945.

Sinu Choi, et al., 'Ethical, Legal, Social, and Cultural Implications of the Non-clinical Use of Transcranial Direct Current Stimulation (tDCS) in Korea and Japan' (2025) 219 *Neuroscience Research* 104951.

E. Roy John et al., 'Neurometrics' (1977) 196(4297) *Science* 1393.

Jonathan R. Wolpaw, Elizabeth Winter Wolpaw, 'Brain–Computer Interfaces: Something New under the Sun', in Jonathan Wolpaw and Elizabeth Winter Wolpaw (eds), *Brain–Computer Interfaces: Principles and Practice* (OUP 2012) 1.

Chang S. Nam, Anton Nijholt, and Fabien Lotte (eds), *Brain–Computer Interfaces Handbook* (CRC Press 2018).

Marcello Ienca and Roberto Andorno, 'Towards New Human Rights in the Age of Neuroscience and Neurotechnology' (2017) 13 *Life Sciences, Society and Policy* 5.

Giulia Barbareschi, et al., 'Accessible Parallel Embodiment of Multiple Robotic Avatars in a Cafe'(2022) 29(2)*XRDS* 36.

Eika Okamoto, et al., 'EEG Activities Evoked by Trauma Stimuli Related to Earthquakes and Personality Features Associated with Trauma,' 4(1) *International Journal of Intelligent Computing in Medical Sciences & Image Processing* 13.

Netiwit Kaongoen, Jaehoon Choi, and Sungho Jo, 'A Novel Online BCI System Using Speech Imagery and Ear-EEG for Home Appliances Control' (2022) 224 *Computer Methods and Programs in Biomedicine* 107022.

Jared Genser, Stephen Damianos, and Rafael Yuste, 'Safeguarding Brain Data: Assessing the Privacy Practices of Consumer Neurotechnology Companies' Neurorights Foundation Report (2024).

Nita A. Farahany, *The Battle for Your Brain: Defending the Right to Think Freely in the Age of Neurotechnology* (St. Martin's Press 2023).

Marcello Ienca, 'On Neurorights' (2021) 15 *Front Hum Neurosci* 701258.

Diego Borbón and Luisa Borbón, 'A Critical Perspective on NeuroRights: Comments Regarding Ethics and Law' (2021) 15 *Front Hum Neurosci* 703121.

Ruth Fischbach and Janet Mindes, 'Why Neuroethicists are Needed', in Judy Illes and Barbara J. Sahakian (eds), *Oxford Handbook of Neuroethics* (OUP 2011) 343.

Andrea Lavazza and Rodolfo Giorgi, 'Philosophical Foundation of the Right to Mental Integrity in the Age of Neurotechnologies' (2023) 16 *Neuroethics* 10.

María Isabel Cornejo-Plaza and Chiara Saracini, 'On Pharmacological Neuroenhancement as Part of the New Neurorights' Pioneering Legislation in Chile: a Perspective' (2023) 14 *Front Psychol* 1177720.

Emily Einhorn and Rafael Yuste, 'Neurorights and the Chilean Initiative', in Marello Ienca et al. (eds) *The Cambridge Handbook of Information Technology, Life Sciences and Human Rights* (CUP 2022) 26.

María Isabel Cornejo-Plaza, et al., 'Chilean Supreme Court Ruling on the Protection of Brain Activity: Neurorights, Personal Data Protection, and Neurodata' (2024) 15 *Front Psychol* 1330439.

Isabel Cornejo-Plaza & Roberto Cippitani, 'Principles of Research with Neurotechnologies and Artificial Intelligence: A Comparative Analysis of Latin American and European Laws, in Pablo López-Silva (ed) *Contextualizing Neuroprotection: Latin American Perspectives on the Impact of Neurotechnological Development in Life and Society* (Springer 2025) 205.

Joseph J. Fins, 'The Unintended Consequences of Chile's Neurorights Constitutional Reform: Moving beyond Negative Rights to Capabilities' (2022) 15 *Neuroethics* 26.

Taimur Aimen, 'Cognitive Freedom and Legal Accountability: Rethinking the EU AI act's Theoretical Approach to Manipulative AI as Unacceptable Risk' (2025) 1(e20) *Cambridge Forum on AI: Law and Governance* 1.

Rostam J. Neuwirth, 'Law, Artificial Intelligence, and Synaesthesia' (2022) 39 *AI & Society* 901.
Jamie Luguri & Lior Jacob Strahilevitz, 'Shining a Light on Dark Patterns' (2021) 13 *J Legal Analysis* 43.
Mu-ming Poo, 'China's New Ethical Guidelines for the Use of Brain–computer Interfaces' (2024) 11(4) *National Science Review* nwae154.
Xue-Qin Wang, et al. 'Challenges and Suggestions of Ethical Review on Clinical Research Involving Brain-Computer Interfaces' (2024) 39(2) *Chinese Medical Sciences Journal* 131.
Marc Jonathan Blitz, *Searching Minds by Scanning Brains: Neuroscience Technology and Constitutional Privacy Protection* (Palgrave Macmillan 2018).
Yasuo Kuniyoshi, et al., 'From Humanoid Embodiment to Theory of Mind', in Fumiya Iida et al. (eds), *Embodied Artificial Intelligence* (Springer 2004) 202.
Andy Clark, *Supersizing the Mind: Embodiment, Action, and Cognitive Extension* (OUP 2008).
Maurice Merleau-Ponty, Alden Fisher (trans.), *The Structure of Behavior* (Duquesne University Press 1983).
Michel Foucault, *Discipline and Punish: The Birth of the Prison* (Vintage Books 1977).
Lisa Raphals, *A Tripartite Self: Mind, Body, and Spirit in Early China* (OUP 2023).
Sung-Jin Jeong, et al., 'Korea Brain Initiative: Emerging Issues and Institutionalization of Neuroethics' (2019) 101(3) *Neuron* 390.
Sang-Ho Yoo, et al., 'Development of Korea Neuroethics Guidelines' (2023) 38(25) *J Korean Med Sci* e193.
Iwasawa Tomoko, 'Philosophical Implications of Shinto', in Bret W. Davis (ed) *The Oxford Handbook of Japanese Philosophy* (OUP 2020) 97.
Takashi Hanakawa et al., 'Neural Correlates underlying Mental Calculation in Abacus Experts: Functional Magnetic Resonance Imaging Study' (2003) 19 *Neuroimage* 296.
Kazuki Iijima et al., 'Moral Characteristics Underpinning Concerns for Brain-Computer Interfaces: A Cross-Cultural Study' (2025) 18 *Neuroethics* 40.
Yasuo Yuasa, Nagatomo Shigenori and Thomas P. Kasulis trans., *The Body: Toward an Eastern Mind-Body Theory* (State Univ of New York Pr 1987).
Tamami Fukushi, et al., 'Neuroethics in Japan', in L. Syd M Johnson and Kare S, Rommelfanger (eds) *The Routledge Handbook of Neuroethics* (Routledge 2017) 442.
Yohko Orito et al., 'Social Risks of Brain-Machine Interface Usage: Questionnaire Survey of People with and without Disabilities' (2025) *Ethical and Social Impacts of Information and Communication Technology* 397.
Edward Slingerland, *Mind and Body in Early China: Beyond Orientalism and the Myth of Holism* (OUP 2019).
Shinobu Kitayama & Jiyoung Park, 'Cultural Neuroscience of the Self: Understanding the Social Grounding of the Brain' (2010) 5 *SCAN* 111.
Rafael Yuste, et al., 'Four Ethical Priorities for Neurotechnologies and AI' (2017) 551 *Nature* 159.
Kiyoshi Murata, Mario Arias-Oliva, and Jorge Pelegrín-Borondo, 'Cross-cultural study about cyborg market acceptance: Japan versus Spain' (2019) 25(3) *European Research on Management and Business Economics* 129.
Peter Mantello, et al., 'Machines that Feel: Behavioral Determinants of Attitude towards Affect Recognition Technology- Upgrading Technology Acceptance Theory with the Mindsponge Model '(2023) 10 *Humanities and Social Sciences Communications* 430.
Dara Hallinan, et al., 'Neurodata and Neuroprivacy: Data Protection Outdated?', (2014) 12(1) *Surveillance & Society* 55.
Dara Hallinan, et al., 'Legal Neuroexceptionalism: Framing a Concept' (2023) 14(2) *European Journal of Law and Technology* 21.
Leda Tortora, et al., 'Neuroprediction and A.I. in Forensic Psychiatry and Criminal Justice: A Neurolaw Perspective' (2020) 11 *Front. Psychol* 220.
Stephen Rainey et al., 'Is the European Data Protection Regulation Sufficient to Deal with Emerging Data Concerns Relating to Neurotechnology?' (2020) 7(1) *Journal of Law and the Biosciences* 1.

Paul Quinn and Gianclaudio Malgieri, 'The Difficulty of Defining Sensitive Data: The Concept of Sensitive Data in the EU Data Protection Framework' (2022) 22(8) *German Law Journal* 1583.

Patrick Magee, Marcello Ienca, and Nita Farahany, 'Beyond Neural Data: Cognitive Biometrics and Mental Privacy' (2024) 112 *Neuron* 3017.

Marcello Ienca et al., 'Towards a Governance Framework for Brain Data' (2022) 15 (20) *Neuroethics* 20.

Vance Packard, *The Hidden Persuaders* (Longmans, Green & Co 1957).

Damien Dupré, et al. 'A Performance Comparison of Eight Commercially Available Automatic Classifiers for Facial Affect Recognition' (2020) 15(4) *PLoS One* e0231968.

John LaRocco, Minh Dong Le, and Dong-Guk Paeng, 'A Systemic Review of Available Low-Cost EEG Headsets Used for Drowsiness Detection' (2020) 14 *Front. Neuroinform* 553352.

Els J. Kindt, 'Biometric Data Processing: Is the Legislator Keeping Up or Just Keeping Up Appearances?', in Gloria González, Rosamunde Van Brakel, and Paul De Hert (eds) *Research Handbook on Privacy and Data Protection Law* (Edward Elgar 2022) 375.

Eline L. Leijten and Arno R. Lodder, 'On AI That Knows How We Feel, Without Knowing Who We Are: EU Law and the Processing of Soft Biometric Data by Emotional AI', in Rosa Ballardini, Rob van den Hoven van Genderen, and Sari Järvinen. *Emotional Data Applications and Regulation of Artificial Intelligence in Society* (Springer 2025) 93.

Jan Christoph Bublitz & Reinhard Merkel, 'Crimes against Minds: On Mental Manipulations, Harms and a Human Right to Mental Self-Determination' (2014) 8 *Crim L & Phil* 5.

Stephan Schleim, *Brain Development and the Law: Neurolaw in Theory and Practice* (Palgrave Macmillan 2025).

Jill Marshall, *Personal Freedom Through Human Rights Law?: Autonomy, Identity and Integrity under the European Convention on Human Rights* (Brill 2009).

Louis Henkin, 'Privacy and Autonomy' (1974) 74 *Columbia Law Review* 1410.

Ian Daly, 'Neural Decoding of Music from the EEG' (2023) 13 *Science Report* 624.

Tomoyasu Horikawa et al., 'Neural Decoding of Visual Imagery During Sleep' (2013) 340 (6132) *Science* 639.

Andrew McStay, *Emotional AI: The Rise of Empathic Media* (Sage 2018).

Jan Christoph Bublitz, 'Freedom of Thought in the Age of Neuroscience: A Plea and a Proposal for the Renaissance of a Forgotten Fundamental Right' (2014) 100(1) *Law and Social Philosophy* 1.

Nobuyoshi Ashibe, *Constitutional Law III Human Rights(1)* [芦部信喜『憲法学III人権各論(1)増補版』] (Additional edn, Yuhikaku 2000).

Masatoshi Kokubo, 'Cognitive Liberty Research Introduction: Neuroscience and Constitutional Law' [小久保智淳「『認知過程の自由』研究序説」:神経科学と憲法学] (2020) 126 *Hogaku Seijigaku Ronkyu* 375.

Keigo Komamura (ed), *Laws of the Internet-of-Brains: Basics and Case Studies in Neurolaw* [駒村圭吾『インターネット•オブ•ブレインズの法』] (Nippon Hyoronsha 2025).

Wayne Unger, 'Stay Out of My Head: Neurodata, Privacy, and the First Amendment' (2023a) 80(4) *Wash & Lee L Rev* 1439.

Mason Marks, 'Cognitive Content Moderation: Freedom of Thought and the First Amendment Right to Receive Subconscious Information' (2023) 76 *Fla L Rev* 469.

Eugene Volokh, 'The Law of Compelled Speech' (2018) 97(2) *Texas Law Review* 355.

Larry Alexander, 'Compelled Speech' (2006) 23(2) *Constitutional Commentary* 147.

Wayne Unger, 'The Constitutionality of Brain Searches' (2023b) 50(4) *Hastings Const LQ* 321.

Andrea Monti, *Lost in the Shell: Mind, Body, Identity and the Technological of Information* (Routledge 2025).

Reinhard Merkel, 'Neuroimaging and Criminal Law', in Jens Clausen and Neil Levy (eds) *Handbook of Neuroethics, vol.3* (Springer 2015) 1335.

Javier Escobar Veas, 'Brain-Reading Technologies and the Right Against Self-Incrimination: A Challenge for the Distinction Between Testimonial and Real Evidence' (2025) 26(4) *German Law Review* 1.

Sjors Ligthart, *Coercive Brain-Reading in Criminal Justice: An Analysis of European Human Rights Law* (CUP 2022).
Fenella M. W. Billing, *The Right to Silence in Transnational Criminal Proceedings* (Springer 2016).
Lynn Nadel and Walter P. Sinnott-Armstrong (eds), *Memory and Law* (OUP 2013).
Maria Chiara Errigo, 'Neuroenhancement and Law', in Antonio D'Aloia and Maria Chiara Errigo (eds), *Neuroscience and Law* (Springer 2020).
John Stuart Mill, Mark Philp and Frederick Rosen (eds), *On Liberty, Utilitarianism and Other Essays New edn* (OUP 2015).
René Descartes, *A Discourse on the Method* (Philosophical Library 2015).
Isaiah Berlin, Henry Hardy (ed), *Liberty* (2nd edn OUP 2002).
Richard Glen Boire, On Cognitive Liberty (Part 1) (2000) 1(1) *Journal of Cognitive Liberties* 7.
Jan-Christoph Bublitz, 'My Mind Is Mine!? Cognitive Liberty as a Legal Concept', in Elisabeth Hildt and Andreas G. Franke (eds), *Cognitive Enhancement: An Interdisciplinary Perspective* (Springer 2013) 233.
Christoph Bublitz, 'Cognitive Liberty or the International Human Right to Freedom of Thought', in Jens Clausen and Neil Levy (eds) *Handbook of Neuroethics vol.3* (Springer 2015) 1309.
Neil Richards, *Intellectual Privacy: Rethinking Civil Liberties in the Digital Age* (OUP 2015).
Christoph Bublitz and Martin Dresler, 'A Duty to Remember, a Right to Forget? Memory Manipulations and the Law', in Jens Clausen and Neil Levy, *Handbook of Neuroethics vol.3* (Springer 2015)1279.
Louis Michael Seidman, *Silence & Freedom* (Stanford University Press 2007).
Michael S. Green, 'The Privilege's Last Sound: The Privilege against Self-Incrimination and the Right to Rebel against the State' (1999) 65(3) *Brook L Rev* 627.
R. Kent Greenawalt, 'The Right to Silence and Human Dignity', in Michael J. Meyer and W.A. Parent (eds), *The Constitution of Rights: Human Dignity and American Values* (Cornell University Press 1992) 192.
Joseph Raz, *The Morality of Freedom* (OUP 1988).
Yu Takagi and Shinji Nishimoto, 'High-Resolution Image Reconstruction with Latent Diffusion Models from Human Brain Activity' (2023) 2023 IEEE/CVF Conference on Computer Vision and Pattern Recognition (CVPR).
UK Information Commissioner's Office, 'ICO Tech Futures: Neurotechnology' (2023).
Eduardo Bertoni and Marcello Ienca, 'The Privacy and Data Protection Implication of the Use of Neurotechnology and Neural Data from the Perspective of Convention 108' (T-PD(2024)1) (2024).
Peggy Valcke, Damian Clifford and Viltė Kristina Dessers, 'Constitutional Challenges in the Emotional AI Era', in Hans-W. Micklitz, et.al. (eds), *Constitutional Challenges in the Algorithmic Society* (CUP 2021) 57.

# Chapter 6
# Legal Constraints on the Use of Bio Data for Research Purposes and the Introduction of a Dynamic Consent Model as a Solution

**Chung Wonjun**

## 6.1 Introduction

This study examines the legal constraints on bio data utilization in Korea and argues for the necessity of introducing a dynamic consent model as a solution. Korea's personal information regulations are widely regarded as highly stringent, and among these, the inflexible rigidity of the consent system operates as a legal constraint in fields fundamentally reliant on data utilization. A prime example of this is the research-purpose data utilization in the bio-data field addressed in this paper. Data-driven research inherently involves significant uncertainty regarding the scope of future research, the definition of similar research, and the specific data requirements, all of which can change during the research process. This fundamentally conflicts with the basis of personal information regulations, which are premised on obtaining prior consent. Therefore, this paper argues for the necessity of introducing a dynamic consent model to ensure information transparency for the substantive exercise of data subjects' rights and to accommodate the need for ongoing consent due to the variability inherent in the research process.

C. Wonjun (✉)
Lee&Ko Law Firm, Seoul, Korea

TMT, TMT, Sejong si, Republic of Korea
e-mail: jun1@leeko.com



H. Miyashita et al. (eds.), *The Evolution of Data Protection Laws in China, Japan, and Korea*, https://doi.org/10.1007/978-981-95-8609-7_6

## 6.2 Concept and Significance of the Dynamic Consent Model

### *6.2.1 Significance of the Dynamic Consent Model*

In open science research and open research projects, such as biobanks, the consent process typically involves obtaining broad consent. Participants generally consent to their data and samples potentially being used in future research projects. At the time of initial consent, the specific research project may not be explicitly designated. However, there is also a negative argument that consenting to future research content does not satisfy the requirements of informed consent. While respecting participant autonomy is crucial in patient-centered biotechnology research, on the other hand, participation based on sufficient understanding of the information is a fundamental principle of health and medical research, so this argument cannot be simply overlooked.

As an alternative to resolve these issues, discussions have been held regarding the introduction of a 'dynamic consent model'. Here, the dynamic consent model refers to a system where consent is not merely obtained once for research participation, but rather, after the initial consent, participants can continuously choose and control their consent status whenever the research content changes, via a website or mobile platform.[1] Its defining feature is that data subjects can continuously control and manage whether their information is used, including exercising the right to withdraw consent for specific changes or for part or all of the information.[2] This contrasts with the static nature of consent typically seen in the field of bioethics, where consent is generally given in writing or verbally after receiving an explanation on the spot for research purposes or the donation of human-derived materials.

This consent model is known to have originated from the "Ensuring Consent and Revocation (ECR)" project conducted from 2008 to 2012.[3] The project aimed to investigate the feasibility of implementing flexible, electronically enabled consent and personal data management across various environments, including biobanks.

This dynamic consent-based interface connects to the biobank storing the participant's donated human-derived resources and data. Through its interactive mechanism with participants, it enables continuous feedback, thereby driving the biobank's ongoing operations. The interface provides participants with messages of gratitude for their donation, results from specific studies relevant to them, and even findings of health-related anomalies.[4] Participants can also set their level of consent, the frequency and type of information they wish to receive from biobank studies they are participating in. This does not force ongoing participation; for example,

---

[1] Steinsbekk et al. 2013, pp. 897–902.

[2] Mikkelsen et al. 2019, p. 71.

[3] Whitley 2013, pp. 165–176.

[4] Kaye et al. 2012, pp. 371–376.

participants can choose to grant broad consent without needing additional requests for consent. However, this choice can be changed at any time due to the nature of the online system.

### 6.2.2 *Development Trends of the Dynamic Consent Model*

Following the ECR project, numerous countries have actively attempted to implement dynamic consent models both technically and as services. For instance, the UK introduced a dynamic consent model to build a partnership model for sharing rare disease experiences. The US patient organization Genetic Alliance, drawing on its long history of collaboration with patient groups, launched the Platform for Engaging Everyone Responsibly (PEER).[5] Furthermore, in implementing consent models, dynamic consent software can be integrated with existing clinical trial management tools to obtain consent decisions and extend new information and clinical trial participation rights to participants. Moreover, the NHS has also considered applying dynamic consent models to electronic health records.

### 6.2.3 *The Need for Introducing Dynamic Consent Models: The Conflict of Arguments for and Against*

As seen in the development trends of consent models discussed earlier, many studies demonstrate tangible research outcomes through the design of dynamic consent models. Beyond the mentioned projects, dynamic consent models can serve as an excellent alternative in various studies utilizing genomic information—strictly treated as sensitive data—where obtaining consent for every single experiment is difficult.

However, on the other hand, there are also negative views pointing out that the dynamic consent model is not a perfect solution. Concerns exist that because consent is obtained on an individual basis, the ethical review of the research at the group level may be neglected.[6] Furthermore, as a general criticism of consent systems, the negative impact of consent fatigue, which can be felt when faced with an overwhelming number of consent items, is also pointed out. Consequently, some argue that comprehensive consent, rather than dynamic consent, is a better model for longitudinal biobank research. Furthermore, while the advantage and disadvantage of digital interfaces is their ability to continuously and rapidly provide diverse

---

[5] Teare et al. 2021, p. 651.

[6] Williams et al. 2015.

information to research subjects, they may pose operational limitations for groups unfamiliar with online platforms.[7]

Nevertheless, dynamic consent offers significant advantages as an alternative that complements the rigidity of the existing pre-consent system, ensuring flexible utilization for specific purposes. In the same vein, it is reasonable to accept the view[8] that since no system or model can be flawless and perfect, an approach minimizing the shortcomings of each model is necessary.[9]

## 6.3 Limitations of the Current Consent System Regarding Secondary Use of Bio-Data

### *6.3.1 Exemption Provisions for Consent Under the Bioethics Act*

In Korea, the Bioethics Act is a special law governing personal information related to bioethics, taking precedence over the general Personal Information Protection Act. Article 16(1) of this Act specifies the information that must be explained when obtaining consent for human subject research, while Article 37(1) details the information required for consent in research using human-derived materials. However, the Bioethics Act stipulates the following conditions for consent exemption: "1. When obtaining the research subject's consent is deemed practically impossible during the research process or would seriously affect the validity of the research," and "2. When there is no reason to presume the research subject would refuse consent, and the risk to the research subject is extremely low even if consent is exempted." This approach ensures the ethical validity of consent exemptions by having the IRB review the ethical justification for waiving the consent procedure itself, and it is undoubtedly an established method within the field of bioethics. However, even in this case, considerable interpretative debate remains regarding what constitutes the phrased "practically impossible." An approach that clarifies the scope of IRB discretion is necessary.

[7] Mikkelsen et al. 2019, p. 71.

[8] Won-bok 2024, p. 37.

[9] Mikkelsen et al. 2019, p. 71.

**Article 16 (Consent for Human Subject Research)**
① Before conducting human subject research, the researcher must obtain written consent (including electronic documents; the same applies hereafter) from the research subject that includes the following items:

1. The purpose of the human subject research
2. The duration, procedures, and methods of the research subject's participation
3. The risks and benefits anticipated for the research subject
4. Matters concerning the protection of personal information
5. Compensation for losses incurred due to research participation
6. Matters concerning the provision of personal information
7. Matters concerning the withdrawal of consent
8. Other matters deemed necessary by the Institutional Review Board

② Notwithstanding Paragraph 1, in the case of research involving research subjects who lack or have incomplete capacity to consent, as specified by Ministry of Health and Welfare regulations, written consent from the agent specified in the following subparagraphs must be obtained. In such cases, the agent's consent must not be contrary to the research subject's will.

1. Legal representative
2. If there is no legal representative, the order of priority shall be spouse, lineal ascendant, and lineal descendant. If there are multiple lineal ascendants or descendants, they shall be determined by mutual agreement; if no agreement is reached, the eldest shall act as the representative.

③ Notwithstanding Paragraph 1, written consent from the research subject may be exempted with the approval of the Institutional Review Board if all of the following conditions are met. In such cases, the written consent of the representative under Paragraph 2 shall not be exempted.

1. When obtaining the research subject's consent is deemed practically impossible during the research process or would seriously affect the validity of the research.
2. When there are no grounds to presume the research subject would refuse consent, and exempting consent poses an extremely low risk to the research subject.

④ Before obtaining written consent under Paragraphs 1 and 2, the human subject researcher must fully explain to the consenting party the matters listed in each item of Paragraph 1.

**Article 37 (Consent for Research Using Human-Derived Materials)**
① Before conducting research using human-derived materials, the researcher must obtain written consent from the donor of the human-derived materials, which includes the following matters:

1. The purpose of the research using human-derived materials
2. Matters concerning the protection and processing of personal information
3. Matters concerning the preservation and disposal of human-derived materials
4. Matters concerning the provision of human-derived materials and genetic information obtained therefrom (hereinafter referred to as "human-derived materials, etc.")
5. Matters concerning withdrawal of consent, disposal of human-derived materials, etc. upon withdrawal of consent, rights of the donor of human-derived materials, changes in research purpose, and other matters prescribed by Ministry of Health and Welfare Ordinance

② With regard to consent by a representative in cases where the donor of human-derived materials lacks or has incomplete capacity to consent, Article 16 (2) shall apply mutatis mutandis. In such cases, "research subject" shall be deemed to mean "human-derived material donor."

③ Notwithstanding Paragraphs 1 and 2, in the case of a human-derived material researcher who receives human-derived materials from a collector who is not a human-derived material researcher and conducts research using such materials, if the collector is a human-derived material donor(including an agent pursuant to Article 16(2) as applied mutatis mutandis under Paragraph 2; the same applies hereinafter in this Article and Article 38), it shall be deemed that written consent as required under Paragraph 1 has been obtained.

④ With regard to the exemption from written consent for human-derived material research, Article 16 (3)shall apply mutatis mutandis. In this case, "research subject" shall be deemed to mean "human-derived material donor."

⑤ Before obtaining written consent pursuant to Paragraphs 1 and 2, the human-derived material researcher shall fully explain to the human-derived material donor the matters listed in each item of Paragraph 1.

⑥ Necessary matters concerning the format of the consent form for written consent under Paragraphs 1 and 2 shall be prescribed by Ministry of Health and Welfare Ordinance.

③ Notwithstanding Paragraph 1, written consent from the research subject may be exempted with the approval of the Institutional Review Board if all of the following requirements are met. In such cases, written consent from the representative under Paragraph 2 shall not be exempted.

1. When obtaining the research subject's consent is deemed practically impossible during the research process or would seriously affect the validity of the research.
2. When there are no grounds to presume the research subject would refuse consent, and the risk to the research subject from waiving consent is extremely low.

This approach is also consistent with the EU GDPR. Recital 40 of the GDPR sets forth the following principle. However, obtaining consent from the data subject is not always feasible. Therefore, in human research, a method exists whereby the Institutional Review Board (IRB) or Research Ethics Committee (REC) (hereinafter collectively referred to as 'IRB') may grant exemptions from obtaining consent. This method is already outlined in the Declaration of Helsinki. The Declaration of Helsinki proclaims the principle of written consent and states that consent is required even for research using personal data or human biological samples. However, it also specifies the requirement for research to proceed through review by a research ethics committee in situations where obtaining consent is difficult.

GDPR recital (40) For the lawful processing of personal data, it must be based on the data subject's consent or on another lawful basis set out in this Regulation or in Union or Member State law as specified in this Regulation.

Helsinki Declaration 25. (Omitted) There may be situations where obtaining consent in research is impossible or impractical, or where seeking consent would threaten the validity of the research. In such situations, research may only be conducted after review and approval by an ethics committee.

### *6.3.2 Can Sensitive Information be Subject to Pseudonymization Under the Personal Information Protection Act?*

Article 28-2 of the Personal Information Protection Act stipulates that pseudonymized information may be processed without the data subject's consent when used for scientific research purposes. However, there may be differing opinions on whether this pseudonymization provision applies to sensitive information, such as genetic information. Regarding this, the "Healthcare Utilization Guidelines"[10] announced by the Ministry of Health and Welfare in December 2024 states that health information, which is sensitive information, can be subject to pseudonymization.[11] However, it also notes that due to the diverse nature of unstructured data in the healthcare field, it is difficult to prescribe uniform pseudonymization methods

[10] Ministry of Health and Welfare and Personal Information Protection Commission, "Guidelines for Utilizing Healthcare Data", 2024, p. 15.

[11] The guidelines explicitly state: "Sensitive information under Article 23 of the Personal Information Protection Act, specifically health-related information, is presented in detail according to data type." This point is clearly articulated. Ministry of Health and Welfare·Personal Information Protection Commission, "Guidelines for Utilizing Healthcare Data," December 2024, p. 2.

and levels. Accordingly, among health information, the following types of information require the data subject's consent for use: "mental illness information, acquired immunodeficiency syndrome (AIDS) information, sexually transmitted infectious disease information as defined in Article 2, Item 10 of the Infectious Disease Control and Prevention Act, rare disease information as defined in Article 2, Item 1 of the Rare Disease Management Act, and information related to abuse and abortion (based on disease classification codes T74, O04, and other information deemed necessary by medical professionals)."

A system specifically regulated in the healthcare field in Korea is the Data Review Board (DRB) presented in the aforementioned guidelines. The DRB is described as a review committee established to perform tasks such as adequacy reviews, in accordance with the internal management plan stipulating the pseudonymized information processing procedures of the pseudonymized information holding institution.[12] The DRB can be composed of five or more members, including both internal and external members (with at least two external members), and allows for review by other committees such as the Institutional Bioethics Committee. However, unlike IRBs, this committee is merely a recommendation regulated by guidelines, not law. It does not specifically define exemption requirements for secondary use during pseudonymized information processing. Furthermore, it creates overlapping regulations with IRBs, hindering the speed of information processing. These factors indicate a need for institutional improvement. Particularly in practice, numerous research projects handling data are currently operated to undergo both IRB and DRB review simultaneously. Therefore, there is a need to establish a legislative basis allowing the pseudonymization and utilization of medical data through the DRB without requiring prior IRB deliberation.

### 6.3.3 *Key Provisions of Recent U.S. Amendments*

The 2017 amendment to Section 116 of the U.S. HIPAA Act (45 CFR 46 §116) warrants attention. This provision establishes 'General Requirements for Informed Consent,' with subsection (a) covering general matters and subsection (b) specifying essential elements that must be explained when obtaining consent. Subsection (b)(9) mandates that "any research involving the collection of identifiable private information or identifiable biospecimens must provide one of the following statements" to "each research subject or their legally authorized representative." One such statement is as follows:

(i) A statement that identifiers may be removed from identifiable personal information or identifiable biospecimens, and that after such removal, the information or biospecimens may be used for future research or provided to another researcher for future research, if possible, without obtaining additional informed consent from the research subject or their legally authorized representative.

[12] Id. p. 29.

(ii) The subject's information or specimens collected as part of this study will not be used or provided for future research, even if identifiers are removed.

The intent of this provision is likely to ensure that consent is obtained with the sentence in (i) when secondary use is anticipated at the time of consent acquisition, and with the sentence in (ii) when it is not anticipated. This regulation can be seen as requiring detailed informed consent even for the processing of de-identified information.

The point where this U.S. legislation differs from Korea's Bioethics Act is that the U.S. has lower institutional restrictions on processing pseudonymized information. In the U.S., secondary use of de-identified information is permitted without special restrictions if 18 identifiers are removed or if it is approved through expert verification methods. Accordingly, this regulation can be evaluated as an approach contributing to ensuring transparency under the right to self-determination of personal information by requiring compliance with disclosure requirements.

### *6.3.4 Issues with Restrictions on Reuse of Bio-Data under Korean Law*

In Korea, third-party utilization of data without consent for secondary use is fundamentally impossible. While data construction is complete within each institution, the transfer of data resources between institutions remains inactive. This is because the legally prescribed research consent form (Form No. 34 of the Enforcement Rules) and the donation consent form (Form No. 41 of the Enforcement Rules of the Bioethics Act) obtained from the data subject (research participant) when donating to a human-derived material bank do not include consent items regarding third-party transfer or utilization.

The problem lies in Korea's personal information consent system, which prohibits blanket consent and requires separate, individual consent. Consequently, obtaining consent solely for the research purpose makes it difficult to meet the legal requirements for data transfer and sharing. Furthermore, since the consent form must specify the subject of consent, enumerating data that may become necessary during additional research or experimental processes on the consent form is extremely difficult.

Another contentious issue is how to define the scope of the research when obtaining consent. The general interpretation is that consent for research purposes typically allows use within the scope of the specific research or similar research. However, in data-based research, the boundaries of what constitutes similar or comprehensive research are highly ambiguous, and predicting these research categories at the time consent is obtained is impossible. Consequently, research subjects face the problem of having to consent without knowing the specific scope of research in which their information will be used. In light of this, this paper argues that a dynamic consent model could serve as a practical alternative.

## 6.4 Legal Challenges for Institutionalizing Dynamic Consent

### *6.4.1 Comparison with MyData Services Based on the Right to Request Transfer*

Article 35-2 of Korea's Personal Information Protection Act stipulates the right to request transfer, similar to the GDPR's Right to Data Portability. This right allows individuals to demand that a personal information processor transfer their information to themselves or to a third party. However, requiring all businesses to transfer personal information could impose excessive burdens and costs. Therefore, the law designates personal information processors meeting certain statutory requirements as the entities responsible for compliance. It also specifically defines, by statute, the information subject to transfer and the businesses capable of receiving such information to provide MyData services, such as various data analysis services or recommendation services. This provision was introduced into the Personal Information Protection Act in 2023, following the introduction of the right to request credit information transfer under the Credit Information Act applicable to the financial sector and the right to request administrative information provision under the Electronic Government Act.

Moreover, MyData services can also be considered a legal basis enabling consent and withdrawal to be implemented through a digital interface, ensuring the substantive rights of data subjects. When establishing the legal basis for MyData, no special provisions were designed specifically for digital interfaces. The reason is that the transmission right was added to enable transmission and sharing under the existing rights of consent and withdrawal; thus, the digital interface exists as the mediating environment where the act of transmission occurs. In other words, the exercise of the transmission right inevitably must occur through a digital interface.

What about the dynamic consent model? The dynamic consent model refers not to utilizing a digital interface to exercise the content or capacity of a specific right, but rather to the method and mechanism of obtaining consent. Therefore, the written consent method strictly required under current bioethics laws clearly needs improvement. Specifically, the Bioethics Act details the necessary elements for implementing written consent at the statutory level, such as prescribing the format of research consent forms and donation consent forms in its enforcement rules. Consequently, to implement the dynamic consent model, explicit legal grounds stating that consent can be obtained either through written consent or via a digital interface are considered necessary.

### *6.4.2 Recognition of Exceptions to Written Consent Requirements*

To implement the dynamic consent model, it is necessary to consider either recognizing exceptions to written consent or deleting existing legal provisions requiring written consent. This rationale stems from the model's intent to overcome the limitations of written consent entirely and leverage the advantages of electronic interfaces to utilize data effectively. In the same vein, some argue that electronic consent via digital interfaces is essential to enable researchers to swiftly filter and utilize demand data from collected datasets according to their research objectives.

However, Article 16(1) of the Bioethics Act stipulates that consent must be obtained through written consent, necessitating amendment. While the provision includes electronic documents, this was intended to allow electronic signatures when obtaining consent in person. Therefore, adding a phrase such as "including electronic signatures obtained non-face-to-face" is desirable.

### *6.4.3 Flexible Modification of Consent*

One of the core features of the dynamic consent model is the flexibility to modify consent content at any time and the ease of exercising the right to withdraw consent for individual items. However, the Bioethics Act does not contain provisions allowing research subjects or human-derived material donors to modify or change their consent. Furthermore, Article 24 of the Act stipulates that written consent must be obtained from the egg donor, sperm donor, in vitro fertilization (IVF) procedure recipient, and, if applicable, the spouse of the donor or recipient (hereinafter referred to as the "consent holder") for embryo creation. Item 5 specifically lists matters concerning the modification and withdrawal of consent as detailed items. However, even without such explicit wording, under the interpretation of the general Personal Information Protection Act, modifying or changing consent can be understood as inherently permissible by obtaining new consent.

The issue lies in the fact that existing consent only supports a binary decision of either selection or non-selection. This makes partial modification or change of consent impossible, ultimately requiring re-consent. Therefore, in implementing the dynamic consent model, it is necessary to secure a legal basis that allows for the systematic implementation of consent modification and withdrawal. Furthermore, amendments are needed to explicitly include "modification of consent" in provisions like Article 16 (Consent for Human Subject Research), Article 37 (Consent for Research Using Human-Derived Materials), and Article 42 (Consent for Collection of Human-Derived Materials) of the Bioethics Act, which currently only mention withdrawal.

### *6.4.4 The Issue of Relaxing Requirements for Re-Review Following Consent Modification*

It is also necessary to examine whether public management and oversight are required when, while operating the dynamic consent model, the content of consent, the scope of the consented research, or the scope of collected data changes. Under current law, conducting new research requires obtaining new consent, leading to inefficiency as re-consent necessitates repeated IRB review. Potential solutions include enabling comprehensive research design during initial review and, for re-consent, allowing notification instead of review for studies falling within the same broad category, thereby easing implementation obligations.

Personally, I believe allowing comprehensive research to be subject to IRB review could make the review process more difficult or, due to legal ambiguity, lead to an expansion of the non-permissible categories. Ultimately, this could result in a practical operation where specific research designs are required to pass IRB review, making it difficult to actually benefit from the intended system improvements. Therefore, for studies involving multiple subjects with the same purpose, I believe the system should be operated from a post-hoc management perspective. This would involve retaining documentation of the renewed consent obtained during the process, regularly notifying the IRB of this, and, if problems arise, halting the research through subsequent review.

## References

Steinsbekk KS, Kåre Myskja B and Solberg B (2013), Broad consent versus dynamic consent in biobank research: Is passive participation an ethical problem?, European Journal of Human Genetics 21(9), pp. 897–902.

Mikkelsen RB, Gjerris M, Waldemar G, et al. (2019), Broad consent for biobanks is best Provided it is also deep, BMC Medical Ethics 20(1), p. 71.

Whitley EA. Towards effective (2013), consent based control of personal data. In: O'Hara K, Hildebrandt M and Waidner M (eds) Digital enlightenment forum yearbook. Amsterdam: IOS Press, pp. 165–176.

Kaye J, Curren L, Anderson N, et al. (2012), From patients to partners: participant-centric initiatives in biomedical research, Nat Rev Genet 13, pp. 371–376.

Teare, H.J.A., Prictor, M. & Kaye, J. (2021), Reflections on dynamic consent in biomedical research: the story so far, Eur J Hum Genet 29, p. 651

Williams H, Spencer K, Sanders C, Lund D, Whitley EA, Kaye J, et al. (2015), Dynamic consent: a possible solution to improve patient confidence and trust in how electronic patient.

Lee Won-bok, "Understanding Dynamic Consent and Establishing Its Legal Basis," Bioethics Policy Research, Vol. 17, No. 2, 2024, p. 37.

# Part III
# Data Protection Law and Artificial Intelligence

# Chapter 7
# China Approach to Data Protection Practices in Context of Artificial Intelligence

**Hui Yuan**

In 2017, the State Council issued the 2017 New Generation Artificial Intelligence Development Plan (2017 Plan),[1] inaugurating a systematic phase for the healthy development of artificial intelligence (AI). In the years that followed, while striving to become a leading global power in AI, China has progressively established a multi-layered AI governance framework aimed at balancing AI development and safety. Within this framework, data protection laws have assumed a central role in regulating AI—a pattern also observed in jurisdictions such as Japan and South Korea—given that both model training and AI application phases involve extensive data processing, including that of personal data. This article examines how China navigates data protection in the AI context while striking a balance between AI development and safety in practice. Overall, China has adopted a relatively stringent approach to regulating harms to individuals with regards to personal data when arising from provision of AI services to the public, while maintaining a more lenient stance on the regulation of model training.

This chapter is supported by Tianjin Municipal Education Commission on the project "Systematization of Personal Information Protection Legislation (个人信息保护法体系融合研究)"(2022SK186). The author declares that there are no conflicts of interest relevant to this study.

[1] Official text published on Website of State Council (8 July 2017) <www.gov.cn/zhengce/content/2017-07/20/content_5211996.htm> accessed 25 November 2025; Unauthorized English translation (DigiChina, Stanford University, 20 July 2017) <https://digichina.stanford.edu/work/full-translation-chinas-new-generation-artificial-intelligence-development-plan-2017/> accessed 25 November 2025.

H. Yuan (✉)
Law School, Tianjin University of Finance and Economics, Tianjin, China
e-mail: yuanhui2022@tjufe.edu.cn



H. Miyashita et al. (eds.), *The Evolution of Data Protection Laws in China, Japan, and Korea*, https://doi.org/10.1007/978-981-95-8609-7_7

The discussion proceeds in four parts. Section 7.1 outlines feature of emerging AI governance framework. Section 7.2 examines the general interplay between AI and data protection. Section 7.3 analyses the stringent protective approach to data protection enforcement in three categories of AI applications that have attracted disproportionate attention from judicial and administrative authorities: automated decision-making, facial recognition, and deep synthesis AI. Section 7.4 describes the pro-AI mechanisms within data protection law and their application in practice.

## 7.1 The Emerging AI Governance Framework in China

In the context of the global race for AI leadership and the uncertain risks posed by disruptive AI technologies, China has not yet enacted an omnibus AI law equivalent to that of the EU, nor has it adopted targeted pro-AI statutes similar to those in Japan or South Korea. Instead, it has pursued a fragmentary and vertical approach, establishing to date a multi-layered governance structure composed of strategic policies and diverse normative instruments, including soft law such as ethical principles and standards, and hard law in the form of statutes and ministerial regulations.

Several English-language scholarly works have highlighted distinctive features of China's AI governance. Bradford characterises China's response to AI development as 'state-driven', contrasting it with the 'rights-driven' approach of the EU and the 'market-driven' model of the US, noting the central government's dominant role in planning and implementing the AI agenda.[2] Responding to the international perception that China has adopted stringent AI regulation based on a series of targeted AI rules, Zhang contends that China's AI governance framework is in fact pro-innovation, revealing the expressive function underlying those specific norms.[3] Although AI governance in China appears vertically structured, Xiao points out that the bureaucratic expertise and iterative regulatory tools embedded across different sectoral regulations reflect certain horizontal elements, such as a service-provider-centred regulatory focus, registration requirements, and risk assessment mechanisms.[4] Zhu outlined legislation proposal made by scholars which aimed to bring certainty to AI future.[5] Beyond these observations, two further points are relevant to situating data protection law within China's emerging AI governance system, particularly where personal information processing is involved.

[2] Bradford 2023.

[3] Zhang 2025, p. 1.

[4] Xiao 2025, p. 106183.

[5] Zhu et al. 2025.

### *7.1.1 The Underlying Shift from Governance By Soft Law Toward Hard Law*

The AI governance system was formally introduced in 2017 Plan, which outlined China's strategic agenda to become a leading global competitor in the AI era by 2030. The Plan positioned the AI governance system as a mechanism to promote the healthy development of AI and set out a three-stage roadmap for its establishment. In the first stage (by 2020), China aimed to initially establish ethical norms, policies, and regulatory frameworks for AI in selected areas. In the second stage (by 2025), it sought to preliminarily build a system of AI laws, regulations, ethical standards, and policies, along with corresponding security assessment and governance capabilities. In the third stage (by 2030), China is expected to realise a comprehensive framework integrating AI legislation, ethical norms, and policy systems. To date, China has advanced the construction of AI governance system broadly in line with these stages, coming to shifting gradually from an ethics-based approach to a law-based governance approach.

The governance framework initially took shape through soft law instruments, particularly ethical norms. The Ministry of Science and Technology (MST) has played a leading role in designing an ethics-based governance mechanism. It convened the National New Generation AI Governance Expert Committee, which was tasked with formulating ethical guidelines for AI governance. The Committee endorsed the concept of 'Responsible AI' and, in 2019, issued Governance Principles for a New Generation of Artificial Intelligence: Developing Responsible Artificial Intelligence,[6] which sets out eight governance principles including fairness and justice, respect for privacy, and agile governance. Subsequently, in 2021, the Committee further refined these principles into more concrete ethical standards through the publication of Ethical Norms for a New Generation of Artificial Intelligence.[7] By 2022, these expert-drafted guidelines were formally endorsed by China's central leadership—the Central Committee of the Chinese Communist Party and the State Council—and elevated to national policy status with the issuance of the Guiding Opinions on Strengthening the Ethical Governance of Science and Technology.[8] Although these ethical norms are not legally binding, the Committee has emphasised

[6] (发展负责任的人工智能:新一代人工智能治理原则)(MST, 17 June 2019) <www.most.gov.cn/kjbgz/201906/t20190617_147107.html> accessed 25 November 2025; unofficial English translation (DigiChina, Stanford University, 17 June 2019) <https://digichina.stanford.edu/work/translation-chinese-expert-group-offers-governance-principles-for-responsible-ai/> accessed 25 November 2025.

[7] (新一代人工智能伦理规范)(MST, 26 September 2021) <https://www.most.gov.cn/kjbgz/202109/t20210926_177063.html> accessed 25 November 2025; unofficial English translation (Center for Security and Emerging Technology, 21 October 2021) <https://cset.georgetown.edu/publication/ethical-norms-for-new-generation-artificial-intelligence-released/> accessed 25 November 2025.

[8] (关于加强科技伦理治理的意见)(State Council, 20 March 2022) <www.gov.cn/gongbao/content/2022/content_5683838.htm> accessed 25 November 2025; unofficial English translation (Center for Security and Emerging Technology, 21 October 2021) <https://cset.georgetown.edu/publication/china-science-ethics-opinions/> accessed 25 November 2025.

that they are intended to instil a culture of safety awareness among AI stakeholders throughout the AI system lifecycle, thereby helping to ensure the healthy development of AI technologies.

In light of abstract nature of ethical governance and the legislature's cautious stance toward legal intervention, technical standards have played a nuanced and guiding role in steering AI development in practice. To date, the National Standardization Administration (NSA) has issued 22 recommended technical standards related to AI and one compulsory standard entitled Cybersecurity Technology—Method for Identifying Synthetic Content Generated by Artificial Intelligence. Although these standards are not legally binding, they are widely regarded as industry norms and have even been cited by courts in determining whether enterprises have taken reasonable compliance measures.[9] China's governance framework demonstrates an iterative approach that has been adaptive to the evolution of AI, incorporating not only ethical norms but also national standardisation.

As AI applications have been deployed at scale and made accessible to the public, China is now transitioning from an ethics-dominated model toward a law-based governance model. In 2023, the State Council—the central administrative authority—for the first time listed the preparation of drafted '*AI law*' within its legislative priorities in the State Council Legislative Agenda for 2023. Since then, scholars and policymakers have actively engaged in deliberating the appropriate regulatory approach for AI in China.[10] Subsequently, the Standing Committee of the National People's Congress—the national legislative body—included a legislative initiative '*legislation for healthy AI development*' in the preliminary review category of its *Legislative Agenda for 2024*.[11] Notably, the legislative branch adopted a different framing '*legislation for healthy AI development*' from the administrative branch's '*AI law*'. In response, the State Council aligned its terminology with that of the Standing Committee in its Legislative Agenda for 2025.

Although revisions to legislative agendas are not uncommon in specialised policy areas, the shift in terminology from '*AI law*' to '*legislation for the healthy AI development*' reflects the government's hesitancy regarding both the substantive focus and the legislative form of AI regulation. Key questions, such as whether it is appropriate to introduce an omnibus AI law at this stage, and whether such a law should be designed to promote AI innovation or to regulate its risks, continue to occupy central authorities' heads. Given the inherent uncertainties of AI technology

---

[9] *Guangzhou VIPs E-commerce Ltd. (广州唯品会电子商务有限公司) v Zhou (周)* [2022] Guangzhou Intermediate Court Appellate Decision Civil 01-3937 (粤*01*民终*3937*号).

[10] Linghan 2024, p. 3; Hanhua 2024, p. 17；Ke 2025, p. 59; Xiaodong 2024, p. 51.

[11] NPC Standing Committee 2024 Legislation Plan (全国人大常委会*2024*年度立法工作计划) (8 May 2024) <http://www.npc.gov.cn/npc/c2/c30834/202405/t20240508_436982.html> accessed 25 November 2025.

and ongoing geopolitical tensions, these issues are likely to remain unresolved for the foreseeable future. Instead of merely wait-and-see, China has adopted a characteristically '*small, fast, and flexible*' approach to AI-related rule-making, enabling it to maintain adaptability in the face of technological evolution.

### *7.1.2 The Interim* **'Small, Fast, and Flexible'** *(***xiao小kuai快 ling灵***) Approach to AI-Related Law-Making*

In the absence of a comprehensive AI law, China's regulatory strategy has been characterised by what is domestically termed a '*small, fast, and flexible*' approach. It prioritises the introduction of agile, targeted regulations, to address urgent concern out of specific AI applications. It functions as a provisional governance mechanism, enabling regulators to accumulate practical experience and respond adaptively to technological shifts without being prematurely constrained by a rigid, overarching comprehensive statute. As a result, this iterative rule-making process helps to bridge the immediate regulatory gap while simultaneously informing the broader, ongoing debate concerning the future form and substance of AI legislation in China.

The distinctive '*small, fast, and flexibl*e' approach is not unique to the AI domain but represents a well-established method for regulating emerging sectors, aimed at reconciling development and safety in contexts of uncertainty. China systematised this approach in 2020 and has since promoted its application across a range of nascent industries.[12] Here, 's*mall*' denotes a narrow focus: rather than addressing all challenges within an emerging field, regulators may concentrate on specific issues of pressing public concern. '*Fast*' relates to the legislative timeline, emphasising the need to respond swiftly to urgent problems by streamlining ordinarily protracted rule-making procedures. These objectives are facilitated by the adoption of 'flexible' regulatory instruments, which are not limited to formal statutes and allow for adaptive implementation.

In accordance with this approach, China has established a vertically-oriented regulatory framework for AI, characterised by the targeted regulation of specific categories of AI technologies or publicly available services. Regulatory bodies have responded with agility by jointly enacting flexible ministerial-level rules. Among the various regulators involved, the Cyberspace Administration of China (CAC) has assumed a leading role in formulating such instruments. The AI categories subject to these targeted regulations are typically those associated with high risks, which have already caused tangible public harm and are closely linked to information

---

[12] President Xi Jinping in 2020 put forward a new legislative approach as 'small-fast -flexible model' to enhance the specificity, applicability and operability of legislation.

generation and dissemination, as those areas fall squarely within the CAC's core mandate as the authority responsible for online content governance. To date, four key regulations have been promulgated, addressing respectively: Algorithmic Recommendation Services Provisions (2021),[13] Deep Synthesis Provisions (2022),[14] Generative AI Measures (2023),[15] and Facial Recognition Technology Measures (2025)[16]. In addition, as Zhang's research indicates, local governments (provincial or municipal) have also actively participated in creating AI-targeted rules.[17] These local norms are predominantly designed to facilitate and promote AI innovation, rather than to impose restrictive regulatory constraints.

However, both ministerial agencies like CAC and local governments can only exercise rule-making power in align with and for implementating the Constitution and statutes made by the central legislature.[18] Although these ministerial rules or local provisions target specific AI technologies, their lower status in China's hierarchy of legal norms restricts them from depriving rights or imposing new obligations on legal entities. Such targeted AI rules remain constrained by indirectly relevant statutes—notably Cybersecurity Law (2017, amended in 2025), the Data Security Law (2021), and the Personal Information Protection Law (2022, hereinafter 'PIPL'). Those statutes regulate AI constituent elements, such as data and infrastructure and serve not only as a legal basis for AI governance but also supply specific regulatory tools applicable in the AI context. In practice, personal data-related law has assumed a central role in regulating AI in China, given the inherent data-processing dimensions of AI systems. A similar practical reliance on data law as a proxy for AI regulation can be observed in Japan and South Korea.

---

[13] Provisions on the Management of Algorithmic Recommendations in Internet Information Services (*互联网信息服务算法推荐管理规定*) (2022) <www.cac.gov.cn/2022-01/04/c_1642894606258238.htm> accessed 25 November 2025；unofficially translated in English <www.chinalawtranslate.com/en/algorithms/> accessed 25 November 2025.

[14] Provisions on the Administration of Deep Synthesis Internet Information Services (*互联网信息服务深度合成管理规定*) *(2022)* <www.cac.gov.cn/2022-12/11/c_1672221949354811.htm>; unofficially translated in English <www.chinalawtranslate.com/en/deep-synthesis/> accessed 25 November 2025.

[15] Interim Measures for the Management of Generative Artificial Intelligence Service (生成式人工智能服务管理暂行办法) (2023) <www.gov.cn/zhengce/zhengceku/202307/content_6891752.htm> accessed 25 November 2025.

[16] Measures for the Administration of the Security of the Application of Facial Recognition Technology (*人脸识别技术应用安全管理办法*) (2025) <https://www.cac.gov.cn/2025-03/21/c_1744174262156096.htm> accessed 25 November 2025.

[17] Zhang 2025, p. 1.

[18] Law of Legislation (立法法) Chapter 4 Section 1 and 2.

## 7.2 Interplay of China Data Protection Laws with AI in General

### *7.2.1 Features of Inherent Data Processing in AI Context*

Artificial intelligence is fundamentally a data-driven technology. Data processing permeates the entire AI lifecycle—from development and deployment to the application stage, through which AI services are delivered to the public. The processing of personal data is indispensable not only during model training and deployment but also in the application phase.

On the one hand, personal data serves as a foundational input for the development of AI models. In the case of decision-making AI systems, un-anonymised personal data is often necessary to generate predictions about individuals. Even for certain generative AI models, access to personal data may be required. For instance, Meta has acknowledged training its models using personal data, noting that the anonymisation of such data would be insufficient to complete the training process effectively.[19] On the other hand, AI applications frequently process personal information during user interactions. Such applications may pose direct risks or harms to individuals, as they not only collect users' personal data for further model training but also generate predictions or content that may incorporate or reveal personal data relating to others. Consequently, policymakers in China and elsewhere have generally sought to facilitate the use of personal data to promote AI development during the model training and deployment phases, while advocating stronger individual protections at the application stage.

Data processing in the AI context may be categorised into two types: individual-based and collective-based. In most scenarios, the model training phase involves collective data processing, as the principal focus lies in the statistical properties of datasets rather than individual data entries. Raw personal data are typically anonymised—particularly in generative AI applications—or pseudonymised where re-identification remains necessary, such as in decision-making AI systems. The value derived by the model stems from patterns identified across the dataset, not from specific personal data. By contrast, data processing during the application stage is predominantly individual-based. The processing of personal information is a prerequisite for providing automated decision-making services, wherein an AI system compares a specific individual's behavioural data against patterns generated through machine learning or statistical models to produce predictions or recommendations.[20] Even in the context of generative AI, service providers are incentivised to collect users' personal data during interactions, both to refine models through further training and for other commercial applications. Each of these processing activities may involve identifiable users.

---

[19] Ireland Data Protection Commission, 'Statement on Meta AI' (21 May 2025) <www.dataprotection.ie/en/news-media/latest-news/dpc-statement-meta-ai> accessed 25 November 2025.

[20] Muhlhoff 2023, p. 1.

### 7.2.2 *Adaptability of China Data Protection Law to AI Governance*

Due to the inherent power asymmetry in data processing, China PIPL adopts a protective architecture similar to that of the EU GDPR,[21] consisting of core processing principles and a dual-approach enforcement mechanism. The first approach is individual-right-based, endowing data subjects with a suite of due-process rights, such as the right to information, access, objection, explanation, and erasure.[22] Those rights enable them to maintain a degree of control over the processing of their personal data throughout its lifecycle. Alongside these individual rights, PIPL establishes a dual administrative and judicial redress mechanism, allowing data subjects to seek remedies through either avenue.[23] Furthermore, to address harms arising from collective data processing, PIPL introduces a form of public-interest litigation, under which procuratorates, consumer protection organisations, and other bodies approved by CAC may initiate legal proceedings on behalf of affected individuals.[24]

The second enforcement track under the PIPL is a collective-based or accountability approach. The law designates competent regulatory authorities to adopt a more proactive role in supervising data processing activities. These authorities are empowered to ensure that data controllers fulfil their accountability obligations. Controllers must implement proactive measures to guarantee compliance with statutory responsibilities and must be prepared to demonstrate such compliance upon request. Failure to do so may result in the imposition of penalties. Where processing involves large-scale personal data, additional statutory responsibilities are imposed, such as the appointment of a dedicated data protection officer[25] and the conduct of a data protection impact assessment.[26] Regulatory agencies are vested with investigative and sanctioning powers, enabling them to intervene flexibly and proactively in high-risk data processing operations.

These two enforcement mechanisms are not mutually exclusive but operate in a complementary manner, calibrated to balance data protection with processing. In the AI context where collective forms of data processing are predominant and individual data subjects often occupy a structurally vulnerable position, the collective-based or accountability approach assumes greater significance. It is through empowering regulators to take proactive and leading protective measures that the inherent power asymmetries in AI-related data processing can be most effectively counterbalanced.

[21] Ausloos 2020; Kaminski 2019, p. 1529.

[22] PIPL Chapter 4.

[23] PIPL Article 50.

[24] PIPL Article 70.

[25] PIPL Article 52.

[26] PIPL Article 55.

These modern data protection mechanisms are further supplemented by other conventional legal remedies, including tort and criminal law, which help address data protection challenges arising from AI. Individuals have frequently brought claims before the courts based on the actionable right to personality or general tort basis, often invoking specific provisions of PIPL given its overlap with the Civil Code in the field of data protection. According to empirical research, the enactment of the PIPL has substantially strengthened the level of protection.[27] Prior to the introduction of the PIPL, the plaintiff compensation rate in personal information infringement cases remained around 20%. Following the law's implementation, this rate rose significantly, reaching 29.79% in 2022 and 41.67% in 2023. Nevertheless, even after the PIPL came into effect, Chinese courts have continued to rely primarily on the Civil Code as the legal basis for deciding such disputes, including those stemming from AI applications.[28]

China's data protection legal system has been consciously infused with AI-specific considerations. PIPL was formulated after the 2017 Plan, and during the legislative process, careful attention was paid to the development and security needs of AI technology. On one hand, the legislature not only established a '*right to object to solely automated decision-making*' but also specifically addressed characteristic AI-related issues such as discriminatory pricing, information cocoons, and the application of facial recognition technology.[29] On the other hand, the PIPL incorporates provisions designed to unlock the value of data to empower AI development. Although scholars debate whether it constitutes a full equivalent to the GDPR's right to data portability, the law helps reduce unnecessary obstacles to the free flow of personal information, thereby unleashing data value by a more diverse range of actors.[30] Most significantly, the PIPL also establishes an explicit lawful basis for processing publicly available personal information as a substitute for obtaining individual consent.[31]

## 7.3 Navigating Data Protection Practices Against AI in Context

The over-reliance of AI on massive datasets and the inherent black-box nature of algorithmic models have compounded the challenges on practical implementation of existing data protection mechanisms. In particular, the informed consent is often rendered ineffective in practice; rights to information and erasure become significantly more difficult to exercise; and requirements such as purpose limitation and

[27] Yao 2025, p. 80.

[28] See Part 3.

[29] PIPL Article 24.

[30] Xin 2025, p. 29.

[31] See Part 4.

data minimisation appear increasingly at odds with the data-intensive demands of AI development. These long-standing tensions within data protection law not only persist but are substantially amplified in the AI context. Although scholars have proposed amendments to better tailor data protection rules to AI,[32] judicial and regulatory authorities have generally refrained from moving far beyond a textual interpretation of existing provisions. They continue to grapple with recalibrating the balance between protection and technological development.

This section therefore undertakes a scenario-based analysis of three high-risk categories of AI applications involving personal information processing: automated decision-making, facial recognition, and deep synthesis. Two principal considerations inform this selection. First, the majority of judicial decisions concerning AI and personal protection relate to these specific scenarios. Second, regulatory authorities have disproportionately dedicated resources to their governance, through both rule-making and enforcement actions. Drawing on relevant judgments and regulatory measures, the analysis that follows will identify the key legal and practical issues arising in each context. While these three categories are not mutually exclusive in theoretical terms, they are usefully distinguished by the distinct regulatory challenges posed in each scenario.

### *7.3.1 Automated Decision-Making AI*

Under Article 73(2) of PIPL, automated decision-making (ADM) is defined as the activity of automatically '*analysing and evaluating an individual's behavioural habits, interests, or economic, health, and credit conditions through computer programs, and making decisions based on the results*'. Analysis of enforcement practice reveals three significant observations.

Firstly, the PIPL creates ambiguity regarding whether profiling alone constitutes a distinct form of automated decision-making subject to the right to object under Article 24. ADM typically comprises two stages: profiling and the subsequent decision. Article 22 of the GDPR explicitly includes profiling within the scope of automated decision-making, a position later affirmed by the Court of Justice of the European Union in *OQ v Land Hessen*, which recognised credit scoring itself as a definitive ADM activity.[33] In contrast, the PIPL provides no statutory definition for either automated decision-making or profiling, nor does it clarify the relationship between them. Given that *Information Security Technology—Personal Information Security Specification*—a national standard issued by the Standardization Administration—defines profiling as '*the process of collecting, aggregating and analysing personal information to analyse or predict the personal characteristics of*

[32] Daoqin 2024, p. 16; Teng 2024, p. 116.

[33] Case C-634/21 *OQ v Land Hessen* [2023] ECLI-957.

*a specific natural person...and forming a personal characteristic model*',[34] Chinese policymakers appear to have conceptually excluded the final decision-making based on profiling from the profiling process itself.

In the *Mai* case, the Guangzhou Internet Court found that the defendant's creation and its subsequent disclosing of Mr. Mai's profiling for assisting users on the defendant's platform to find matching legal services constituted automated decision-making (ADM).[35] This reasoning implies that profiling alone is a constituent element of, but does not by itself amount to, ADM. The *Mai* decision was subsequently selected into the Supreme People's Court's Case Database in 2025, thus enhancing its persuasive authority.[36] The Supreme People's Court only highlighted the judgment's persuasive relevance for determining the lawfulness of processing publicly available personal information, without providing explicit guidance for finding whether profiling per se qualifies as ADM under Article 24 of the PIPL. Therefore, the issue remains legally ambiguous. Nevertheless, the fact that both judicial and policy preference appear to treat profiling as an ordinary processing activity rather than a distinct form of ADM will be further referred by courts in later cases.

Secondly, the most pertinent right in the context of ADM under the PIPL—the right to object to solely automated decision-making—demonstrates a notable differentiation from its counterpart under the GDPR. Whereas the GDPR situates its provisions on automated decision-making (Article 22) within the chapter concerning data subject rights, the PIPL places this right (Article 24) within Chapter 2 of General Processing Rules, rather than in Chapter 4 of Individual Rights. From the perspective of contextual interpretation, this structural distinction reflects a differing legislative intent. The Chinese legislature appears to have conceptualised this type of processing more as a specific scenario governed by special rules, rather than as a right functionally equivalent to the individual entitlements enumerated in Chapter 4. Therefore, Article 24 of PIPL imposes dual tracks: placing a responsibility on processors (functionally equivalent to controllers under the GDPR) to ensure that automated decision-making is transparent, fair, and equitable, and concurrently conferring on individuals the rights to an explanation and to object to a decision based solely on automated processing.

Furthermore, the nature of the right to object to solely automated decision making under the PIPL is not equivalent to its counterpart in GDPR, prescribed as the '*right not to be subject to a decision based solely on automated processing*'. The Court of Justice of the European Union has interpreted the latter as constituting, in effect, a general prohibition on decisions producing legal or similarly significant

[34] Information Security technology-Personal Information Security Specification (信息安全技术个人信息安全规范), Article 3.8 (2020).

[35] *Mai (麦某某) v Beijing Fa Technology Ltd. (北京某法科技有限公司) and Beijing Lv Technology Ltd. (北京某律科技有限公司)* [2022] Guanzhou Internet Court Civil 0192-20966 (粤*0192*民初*20966*号).

[36] Case 2025-07-2-369-003 (selected in 2025) <www.court.gov.cn/zixun/xiangqing/471161.html> accessed 25 November 2025.

effects that are based exclusively on automated processing.[37] In contrast, the textual formulation of the PIPL favours the interpretion as a genuine right that can be exercised by the individual or not, rather than as a general prohibition.[38] Such an distinction represents that unlike the GDPR's default restriction, the PIPL permits automated decision-making by default, unless specifically prohibited or restricted by laws or regulations.

Thirdly, Chinese courts have demonstrated a more lenient approach to ADM technologies when deployed for socially beneficial purposes. The Beijing Internet Court adjudicated the first case concerning tort liability arising from an algorithmic risk control system.[39] The defendant, a match-making platform, employed such a system to comply with the Anti-Fraud Telecommunication Law by flagging keywords associated with fraud, such as investment, fund, and pig-butchering scam (a hybrid fraud combining fictitious romantic relationships with financial traps). The plaintiff, a financial sector professional, frequently used these terms in platform communications, leading the system to classify him automatically as a high-risk fraudster. Consequently, the platform suspended his account and issued alerts to other users. Although the plaintiff's account was restored following a human review after his initial complaint, he subsequently filed a tort claim for reputational infringement. The court ruled that the platform, acting in compliance with legal mandates and public interest objectives, had employed an impartial algorithmic system for behavioural risk screening. While acknowledging that technical constraints could result in erroneous profiling, the court found that the platform had fulfilled its proportionate duty of care and implemented reasonable safeguards. The plaintiff's claims were rejected.

### 7.3.2 Facial Recognition AI

Facial recognition technology (FRT) has been widely deployed for identity verification across both private and public sectors in China, particularly in security, healthcare, and the marketing of products and services. While the technology has brought considerable convenience to individuals and society, it has also sparked considerable public concern and debate regarding its appropriate application in daily life. For instance, real estate agencies have installed FRT devices to document the identity of prospective home buyers. The purpose is to determine whether the initial contact with a buyer was made by the agency itself or through a collaborating

[37] *OQ* (n 32).

[38] Yuan 2022, p. 72.

[39] *Li* (李某) *v Beijing X Technology Ltd.*(北京某科技公司), Ten Typical Cases on Data and Algorithm of Beijing Internet Court (Beijing Internet Public Account, 2023) <https://mp.weixin.qq.com/s/XRB3TqJs-VL67FjKkO-IMw> accessed 25 November 2025.

broker, so as to allocate sales commissions accordingly upon transaction completion.[40] Such use of FRT has triggered privacy concerns and attracted widespread attention on social media. Relevant cases have fuelled ongoing public debate about whether current personal information protection frameworks are adequate to address the risks posed by pervasive deployment of FRT.

To effectively address public concerns arising from the application of FRT, the Supreme People's Court issued the Provisions on Certain Issues Concerning the Application of Law in Civil Cases Involving the Processing of Personal Information through Facial Recognition Technology to guide lower courts in adjudicating FRT-related personal information disputes.[41] Subsequently, the legislature incorporated a specific provision addressing the use of FRT in public spaces into PIPL. Article 26 of the PIPL stipulates that the installation of FRT equipments in public places must be necessary for the purpose of maintaining public security, and clear warning signs must be prominently displayed. Personal images and identification information collected in such settings may only be used for maintaining public security and must not be used for other purposes without obtaining separate individual consent.

Chinese law distinguishes facial biometric data from simple portrait data. Facial recognition information constitutes the biological digital features abstracted from facial images, falling within the category of biological identification information under Article 1035 of the Civil Code and qualifying as sensitive personal information under Article 28 of the PIPL. In general, the processing of personal information via FRT must comply with the general principles of the PIPL. Furthermore, Article 62(2) of the PIPL authorises CAC, in coordination with other relevant authorities, to formulate specific regulations or technical standards for FRT.[42] In March 2025, the CAC, jointly with the Ministry of Public Security, issued the Facial Recognition Technology Measures (FTR Measures). Additionally, the National Standardization Administration has thus far promulgated five related national standards governing the technical and security aspects of FRT systems.[43]

A primary public concern relates to the compulsory collection of facial biometrics recognition. In the first landmark civil litigation concerning facial recognition

[40] Yu Jing, 'China's Home Buyers Find Their Moment of Facial Recognition Reckoning' (CGTN, 2 December 2020) <https://news.cgtn.com/news/2020-12-02/China-s-home-buyers-find-their-moment-of-facial-recognition-reckoning%2D%2DVSXeqfB51C/index.html> accessed 25 November 2025.

[41] Judicial Interpretation (2021) <www.court.gov.cn/zixun/xiangqing/315851.html> accessed 25 November 2025.

[42] PIPL Article 62 (2).

[43] GB/T 44248-2024 Information technology— Biometrics—Face recognition system application requirements (信息技术 生物特征识别 人脸识别系统应用要求) ; GB/T 42981-202 Information technology—Biometrics—Test methods for face recognition system (信息技术 生物特征识别 人脸识别系统测试方法) ; GB/T 41987-2022 Public security—Face recognition applications—Test methods for presentation attack detection with fake face9(公共安全 人脸识别应用 防假体呈现攻击测试方法); GB/T 41819-2022 Information security technology—Security requirements of face recognition data (信息安全技术 人脸识别数据安全要求).

data in 2019,[44] the plaintiff had purchased an annual membership card from a wildlife park and initially selected fingerprint verification for entry. Subsequently, the park introduced a facial recognition system at its entrances and made this the mandatory verification method. Using a photograph previously submitted by the plaintiff during his membership application, the park generated a facial recognition template without obtaining fresh consent, notified him of the change, and requested that he activate facial recognition access. Upon his refusal, the plaintiff brought an action against the park for breach of contract and infringement of personal rights, including privacy. The court held that processing his photograph to create facial biometric data exceeded the original purpose of collection and violated the principles of lawfulness and legitimacy under personal information protection norms. It ordered the defendant to delete the facial recognition information it had processed.

Furthermore, the FRT Measures stipulate several provisions addressing typical issues in the FRT context. First, they explicitly prohibit the practice of 'compulsory facial scanning'.[45] Personal information processors are required to provide alternative methods of identity verification that fulfil the same purpose or achieve equivalent business requirements. Second, the installation of facial recognition devices is forbidden in private areas within public venues, such as hotel rooms, public bathrooms, changing rooms, and toilets.[46] Third, the Measures address the needs of vulnerable groups. Certain judicial case[47] sparked online controversy concerning potential discrimination against elderly and disabled individuals, whose physical characteristics may make FRT verification more difficult. The FTR Measures thus stipulates that when processing the facial information of persons with disabilities and the elderly, processors must also comply with relevant state regulations on the construction of barrier-free environments.[48] Fourth, data security obligations are reinforced. Facial recognition information should be stored locally within the recognition device and must not be transmitted over the internet, unless separate individual consent is obtained or where otherwise provided by law.[49] Finally, for processing activities involving the facial information of more than 100,000 individuals, processors are required to register their FRT systems with the provincial-level CAC.[50]

---

[44] *Guo Bing (郭兵) v Hangzhou Wild Zoo (杭州野生动物世界)* [2022] Hangzhou Intermediate Court Civil Case 01-10940 (浙*01*民终*10940*号).

[45] FTR Measure (n 15) Article 10.

[46] Ibid Article 13.

[47] *He (何某) v X Technology Ltd. (某科技公司)* [2022] Beijing Internet Court Civil Case 0491-9526 (京*0491*民初*9526*号).

[48] FTR Measures (n 15) Article 5.

[49] Ibid Article 8.

[50] Ibid Article 15.

### 7.3.3 Deep Synthesis AI

Deep synthesis (DS) technology refers to the use of techniques such as deep learning and virtual reality to generate or synthesize text, images, audio, video, and virtual scenes.[51] While such technology has driven innovation across sectors such as entertainment, marketing, and education, it has also introduced significant risks of harm to individual, public, and national interests. Consequently, it attracted regulatory attention at a relatively early stage of its application. The Civil Code, enacted in 2020, explicitly prohibits the use of information technology to fabricate or manipulate another individual's likeness in a manner that infringes upon their portrait rights.[52] Following the adoption of PIPL, regulators issued a series of implementing rules targeting DS, including Deep Synthesis Provisions. Data protection issues frequently arise when such technology is used to process personal information. In judicial practice, cases decided by the courts have predominantly involved the unauthorized manipulation of facial and vocal data, commonly referred to as 'AI face-swapping' or 'AI voice-swapping'.

Prior to the enactment of PIPL, data protection issues arising from DS technology were adjudicated primarily under the legal cause of action for the right to personality. A landmark judicial decision concerned AI companion services, which was subsequently selected by the Supreme People's Court as a typical case concerning the infringement of personal rights.[53] The plaintiff, a well-known celebrity with a substantial fan base, brought a claim against the developer and operator of an application providing AI companion services. The software enabled users to create personalised 'AI companions' by configuring names, avatars, and designated relationships (such as boyfriend, sister, or mother-son dynamics), and to interact with these virtual entities. The defendant had collected the plaintiff's name, portrait, and personality traits, and enabled fans to create a virtual likeness of the plaintiff. Using a clustering algorithm, the platform then recommended this virtual character to other user-fans. The court found that the defendant's actions constituted an infringement of the plaintiff's right to name, right to portrait, and the general right to personality, awarding damages to the plaintiff accordingly.

Following the enactment of PIPL and alongside the rapid advancement of deep synthesis services, a key issue before the courts has been whether information involved in such cases qualifies as personal information. Courts have applied the 'identifiability test' as stipulated in Article 4(1) of the PIPL. It is well-established that an operator providing an individual's facial image without consent for users to

[51] Deep Synthesis Provisions (n 13) Article 23.

[52] Civil Code Article 1019(1).

[53] Supreme People's Court Selected Typical Cases confer the judicial decision more persuasive effect on later similar cases but less than the Supreme Court Selected Guiding Cases which provide a quasi-law guiding effect. Supreme Court Selected Cases concerning Using Internet and Information Technology to infringe on Right to Personality Rights (最高法发布利用网络、信息技术侵害人格权典型案例) (Supreme People's Court, 12 June 2025) <www.court.gov.cn/zixun/xiangqing/467631.html> accessed 25 November 2025.

generate content infringes upon personal information interests.[54] However, a face-swap template created by removing facial features from a natural person should receive legal protection has been treated differently across jurisdictions. Three cases shared substantially similar facts that the defendants used DS technology to process a video of the plaintiff's image for creating a face-swapping video template, uploaded the template onto a face-swapping application, and made it available for users's access, through which the defendants gained economic profit. Two of these cases were adjudicated by the Beijing Internet Court and one by the Hangzhou Internet Court. While both courts found for individual plaintiffs, they adopted differing legal rationales to achieve this end.

The Beijing Internet Court has shown a preference for categorising AI-generated face-swap templates as general personal information eligible for protection under the PIPL or 1035 of Civil Code, rather than as the object of a right to portrait under 1018 of Civil Code.[55] The court adopted a narrow interpretation of the right to portrait, requiring a high threshold for identifiability. It reasoned that while the right to portrait was not strictly limited to facial images, the face was the primary component for identifying an individual in a video. Other elements such as makeup, hairstyle, and clothing are easily replicated or fabricated and thus cannot, by themselves, constitute identifiable features of the plaintiff.[56] The removal of the plaintiff's facial image was therefore held to render the video template unidentifiable, thus not subject to protection of right to portrait.

However, in the *Liao* case, where the plaintiff sought remedies for infringement of both personal information interests and a violation of right to portrait, the Beijing Internet Court held that the defendant using the plaintiff's image in the video to generate AI templates constituted unlawful processing, in despite of not violation of right to portrait.[57] The court distinguished between the identifiability standards for the right to portrait and for personal information: the former requires that the relevant public within a given context can recognise a specific natural person, whereas identifiability under personal information law is assessed from the perspective of the data processor. That is, if the information being processed can identify or be linked to a specific natural person, it qualifies as personal information.

In contrast, the Hangzhou Internet Court held that the disputed face-swap video template constituted an object of the right to portrait.[58] Adopting a more protective stance, the Court interpreted the right to portrait in a broader sense. It reasoned that even absent facial image, distinctive features such as makeup, body movements, and other contextual elements could still enable the relevant public to identify the specific individual. Therefore, both the original and the face-swapped video were

[54] Ibid. *Peng (彭某某) v X Software Operation Technology Corporation (某软件运营公司).*

[55] *Lin (林某某) v Beijing X Technology Co (北京某科技有限公司)* [2023] Beijing Internet Court Civil Case 0491-12766 (京0491民初12766号); *Liao (廖某) v X Culture Co (某文化公司)* [2023] Beijing Internet Court Civil Case 0491-3820 (京*0491*民初*3820*号).

[56] Ibid *Lin v Beijing X Technology Co.*

[57] *Liao (n 54).*

[58] *Lou (楼某某) v X Information Technology Co (某信息科技公司)* [2022] Hangzhou Internet Court Civil Case 0192-6186 (浙*0192*民初*6186*号).

deemed worthy of protection under the right to portrait. The two courts highlights a clear jurisprudential division: the Hangzhou Internet Court appears inclined to lower the identifiability threshold for the right to portrait to adapt to new technological realities, whereas the Beijing Internet Court prefers to maintain the traditional, high threshold for this specific personality right, opting instead to regulate the proliferation of face-swap services through the more general framework of personal information interests under the PIPL. This conflicting interpretation underscores the need for further clarification, ideally from the Supreme People's Court, to provide a guiding case.

A further issue arising in judicial practices is the determination of who qualifies as a personal information processor (equivalent as controllers in GDPR) and is therefore subject to corresponding liabilities. In accordance with Article 73(1) of the PIPL, a processor is defined as an entity that autonomously determines the purposes and methods of processing. This is particularly complex in cases where the DS-generated templates are created by one entity, while the services utilising these templates are provided to users by another.

The Beijing Internet Court has adopted a broad interpretation of 'processor', holding that any operation performed on personal information constitutes 'processing' and that any entity contributing to the determination of the processing purposes may also be classified as a processor. In an AI voice-related case,[59] the plaintiff, a professional voice actor, had accepted commission from the second defendant to produce voice recordings. The second defendant sold these recordings to the third defendant, accompanied by a forged authorisation letter purportedly from the plaintiff. The third defendant then utilised AI technology to process the voice data and create AI-generated audio products replicating the plaintiff's voice. These synthetic products were made available for sale on the fourth defendant's platform. Separately, the first defendant providing an AI voice-conversion service transforming text into audio, procured the third defendant's AI voice products through the fifth defendant and integrated them into its service, enabling its users to generate audio output in the plaintiff's voice. The court determined that the voice data was identifiable with the plaintiff and thus constituted personal information protected under the PIPL. It held that all defendants were processors. The court appears to broadly construe processors defined in Article 73(1), which requires the entity to determine the purposes and means of the processing. Although the first defendant was reasonably considered a processor as it autonomously determined the purposes and means of its text-to-audio service, the fourth and fifth defendants were not found to have determined the processing purposes. This expansive interpretation suggests a tendency towards recognising joint-processor relationships in complex technological service arrangements, thereby widening the scope of potential liability under the PIPL.

In the *Wu* case,[60] Beijing Internet Court decided the processor from the user's perception of whom provides those services. The defendant operated a face-swap

[59] *Yin (殷某某) v Bejing X Smart Technology Co (北京某智能科技公司)* [2023] Beijing Internet Court Civil Case 0491-12142 (京*0491*民初*12142*号).

[60] *Wu (吴某) v X Co* (某公司) [2023] Beijing Internet Court Civil Case 0491-3821 (京*0491*民初*3821*号).

video generation application. The service involved replacing the face of an individual appearing in a video with another person's facial features, creating a template that enabled users to generate their own face-swapped videos. The defendant sought to avoid liability by contending that the actual operator of the service was a separate developer company. However, the court noted that published Privacy Policy explicitly identified the defendant as the service operator. The Court held that a private contractual arrangement between the defendant and another entity could not be invoked to exempt the defendant from liability towards the plaintiff for the unauthorised processing of personal information.

Furthermore, competent regulatory authorities have specified additional obligations for providers of deep synthesis services through Deep Synthesis Provisions later reaffirmed by Generative AI Measures. First, personal information processors are subject to reinforced consent obligations. When processing biometric identification information, service providers must remind their users to inform the affected individuals and obtain separate consent.[61] Second, service providers are required to conduct periodical reviews, evaluations, and verifications of their algorithmic mechanisms.[62] Third, providers offering services that generate or edit biometric identification information, such as facial or vocal data, are obliged to carry out security assessments.[63] Fourth, providers must ensure appropriate labelling where generated or edited content involves voice or facial features.[64]

## 7.4 Navigating Publicly Available Personal Information (PAPI) Processing for AI Model Training

### *7.4.1 Pro-Innovation Context in China*

China has demonstrated a clear policy inclination to harness the power of data to accelerate artificial intelligence development, particularly following the global impact of ChatGPT's release in late 2022. Against the backdrop of a perceived technological gap with the United States in the AI field, a growing number of Chinese scholars have shifted from a predominantly protection-oriented stance toward advocating an AI-driven data governance framework that operates within legal boundaries.[65] Building an AI-facilitated data governance system has increasingly become a consensus among both policymakers and academic experts. This consensus has been further reinforced by the transformative impact of subsequent domestic AI advancements, such as the emergence of DeepSeek, on the global AI landscape.

[61] Deep Synthesis Provisions (n 13) Article 14 (2).

[62] Ibid Article 15 (1).

[63] Ibid Article 15 (2).

[64] Generative AI Measures (n 14) Article 12.

[65] Xiaodong 2023, p. 175; Xinbao 2024, p. 86.

In contrast to the protective stance adopted in regulating AI applications accessible to the public, China has embraced a pro-innovation approach towards AI model training. The advancement of AI technology relies heavily on large-scale, high-quality datasets. Although China possesses substantial data reserves, such data are often fragmented or otherwise unavailable for AI training purposes. To better leverage data for AI development, China has recently implemented measures to increase access to and improve the quality of public data through authorised operational mechanisms.[66] According to statistics from the National Data Administration, the proportion of Chinese-language data used in training datasets for most domestic AI models has reportedly increased to approximately 60%.[67] Significantly, the FRT Measures explicitly exclude from their scope facial recognition technology research and development activities, along with algorithm training that utilises facial information.[68] Concurrently, the National Data Administration has launched trustworthy data space initiatives, including personal data spaces, to facilitate secure data utilisation.[69]

With regard to personal data, data protection law also provides lawful grounds for processing personal information to advance AI development. In current model training practices, data corpora are predominantly sourced from publicly available personal information (PAPI), direct collection from individuals, or acquisition from third-party suppliers. Among these sources, publicly available personal data constitute the largest portion of training material. How to harness their potential for AI development remains subject to the framework of data protection law, closely tied to the interpretation and application of provisions governing the processing of publicly available personal information under the PIPL.

### *7.4.2 The Independent and Restraint Lawful Ground for Promoting Data Processing in Model Training*

Under Article 13 of the PIPL, personal information processors must satisfy one of lawful grounds to process personal information. In practice, AI developers in China commonly rely on either the data subject's consent under Article 13(1) or the

[66] Chen 2025, p. 106; National Development and Reform Commission and National Data Administration, *Implementation Specification for Authorized Operation of Public Data Resources (Trial)* (January 8, 2025) <www.gov.cn/gongbao/2025/issue_11886/202502/content_7007129.html> accessed on 25 November 2025.

[67] China Youth, 'Chinese Data Now Accounts for Over 60% of the Training Datasets Used in Most Domestic AI Models' (17 August 2025) <www.nda.gov.cn/sjj/swdt/mtsy/0817/20250817132616087099878_pc.html> accessed 25 November 2025.

[68] FTR Measures (n 15) Article 2(2).

[69] National Data Administration, *Action Plan for Trustworthy Data Spaces Development (2024–2028)* (2024) <https://www.gov.cn/zhengce/zhengceku/202411/content_6996363.htm> accessed 25 November 2025.

processing of '*personal information that has been legally made public*' under Article 13(6).

In the context of AI model training, the processing of PAPI similarly serves as a viable substitute for consent. Article 14 of the PIPL stipulates that consent must be informed, freely given, and explicit. However, when processing personal information on a massive scale for AI training purposes, obtaining legally valid consent from each data subject is often impractical, if not impossible. This is particularly evident where data is acquired from third-party sources, making it difficult to contact the relevant individuals. Furthermore, due to the technical complexity of most AI models—often characterised as black boxes—providing meaningful transparency is technically unattainable. Even developers may be unable to fully trace how personal data is processed within the model, thereby rendering the fulfilment of informed consent requirements unfeasible. The informed-consent mechanism has consequently faced sustained criticism within China in relation to AI development. Some scholars have proposed lowering the transparency requirements specifically for the model training phase,[70] while others have advocated more radical reforms, such as creating a new, bespoke lawful ground for AI-related data processing.[71] Although such a proposal is theoretically feasible under the open clause in Article 13(7), which permits additional lawful grounds to be established by other laws or administrative regulations, policymakers have thus far been reluctant to activate this clause.

The PIPL also lacks a direct equivalent to the GDPR's 'legitimate interests' clause, which permits processing necessary for the purposes of the legitimate interests pursued by the controller or a third party, except where such interests are overridden by the data subject's interests or fundamental rights.[72] Within China's current legal framework, the most pertinent substitute for consent in this context is the provision for processing PAPI under Article 13(6). This approach positions China on a distinctive intermediate path. Unlike the EU, which subjects publicly available personal data to the same stringent protection as other personal data, or the United States, where many state-level privacy laws exclude such data from the definition of personal information altogether, China has established an explicit, standalone lawful basis specifically for processing publicly available personal data.

The processing of PAPI is primarily governed by Article 13(6)[73] and Article 27[74] of the PIPL. These provisions establish that processing such information is lawful provided specific conditions are met. First, the personal information in question

[70] Xiaodong 2023, p. 175.

[71] Pei 2025, p. 23.

[72] GDPR Article 5(1)(f).

[73] Article 13(6), 'The personal information disclosed by the individual himself or other legally disclosed personal information of the individual is reasonably processed in accordance with this Law.'

[74] Article 27, 'A personal information processor may reasonably process the personal information disclosed by an individual himself or other legally disclosed personal information, except where the individual expressly objection. Where the processing of disclosed personal information may

must have been lawfully disclosed to the public at large, not merely to specific individuals. Lawful disclosure arises in two scenarios: information voluntarily disclosed by the data subject themselves, or information legally disclosed by others in accordance with statutes or regulations. Second, the subsequent processing must remain within a reasonable scope. Third, the processing must not have a significant impact on the individual's rights and interests. Finally, the individual has not demonstrated any objection for further processing.

Among all the above conditions, debates have been ongoing concerning how to interpret 'reasonable scope' of processing among Chinese legal scholars even since the drafting of PIPL. The drafter initially attempted to provide a more specific provisions in the first and second drafts of PIPL. The second draft stated that '*[p]ersonal data processors must process publicly disclosed personal data in accordance with the purpose for which it was disclosed... if the purpose of the disclosure is unclear, the processor should process reasonably and cautiously*'.[75] However, the legislature simplified the provision without any elaboration on 'reasonable scope'. Some scholars explained that such deletion may be attributed to the difficulty and impossibility in identifying initial disclosure purpose,[76] or incoherence with the Civil Code,[77] or an intent to maintain ambiguity for further contextual interpretation.[78] Whether the reasonable scope means 'with the initial purpose of disclosing' as the second draft's prescription is not ambiguous. Some argued that the deletion of initial purpose demonstrated the legislative did not constrain the processing only within initial purpose,[79] while some others advocated for those with clear initial purpose shall refrain from processing beyond.[80] In the following PAPI-related case, the court interpreted the reasonable scope beyond initial purpose and in combination of the third condition 'no significant impact on individual'.

In the 2022 *Mai* case, the Guangzhou Internet Court adopted an impact assessment to determine the reasonable scope of processing under Article 27 of the PIPL.[81] The plaintiff, Mr. Mai, was a lawyer. The defendant had scraped his personal data from publicly accessible online sources and processed it to create a professional

---

have a significant impact on an individual's rights and interests, the personal information processors shall first obtain the individual's consent in accordance with the provisions of this Law.'

[75] Article 28 of the Second Draft of Personal Information Protection Law, full text referenced to <www.caict.ac.cn/xwdt/ynxw/202108/P020210820840956111496.pdf> accessed 25 November 2025.

[76] Daoqin 2025, p. 47.

[77] Constitution and Law Commission of Standing Committee of NPC, 'Deliberation Report on Personal Information Protection Law Draft' (20 August 2021) <www.npc.gov.cn/npc/c2/c30834/202108/t20210820_313090.html> accessed November 25 2025.

[78] Jingwu 2024, p. 144.

[79] Xiaochun 2022, p. 52.

[80] Xiao 2022, p. 82.

[81] *Mai (麦某某) v Beijing Fa Technology Co (北京某法科技有限公司) and Beijing Lv Technology Co (北京某律科技有限公司)* [2022] Guanzhou Internet Court Civil 0192-20966 (粤*0192*民初*20966*号).

profile, which was then displayed on the defendant's platform for potential clients seeking legal services. However, no contractual relationship existed between Mr. Mai and the defendant, and the generated profile contained inaccuracies that resulted in misleading advertising and potential fraud. The court ruled that the processing was highly intrusive, its purpose was purely commercial, and its consequences—false advertising and fraud—demonstrated that it fell outside the reasonable scope permitted by law. The underlying legal rationale is that the assessment of reasonableness must consider the purpose and means of the processing alongside its negative impact on the individual. Although this is a first-instance decision, its subsequent selection by the Supreme People's Court as a typical case imbues it with significant persuasive authority, offering lower courts substantive guidance for adjudicating similar disputes.

## 7.5 Conclusion

China is currently navigating the tension between protection-oriented and innovation-facilitating approaches to the data protection challenges posed by artificial intelligence. While the establishment of a comprehensive AI legal framework is the ultimate objective, its specific timeline and legislative form remain uncertain in light of both the inherent unpredictability of technological advancement and the ongoing global competition in AI development. What remains evident is that data protection law will continue to serve as a primary and effective regulatory instrument for governing AI technologies in China. In the interim, it is anticipated that a growing body of judicial decisions and implementing regulations will emerge to address the current gaps in applying existing data protection norms to the evolving AI context.

## References

Anu Bradford, Digital Empires: The Global Battle to Regulate Technology (OUP 2023).
Angela Huyue Zhang, 'The Promise and Perils of China's Regulation of Artificial Intelligence' (2025) 63 Columbia Journal of Transnational Law 1.
Baiyang Xiao, 'Agile and iterative governance: China's regulatory response to AI' (2025) 58 Computer Law & Security Review 106183
Yue Zhu et al., 'China's Emerging Regulation toward an Open Future For AI' (9 October 2025) Science
Zhang Linghan, 'What Kind of Artificial Intelligence Law Does China Need? The Fundamental Logic and Institutional Framework of China's AI Legislation '(中国需要一部怎样的《人工智能法》?——中国人工智能立法的基本逻辑与制度架构) (2024) 42(3) Law Science (法律科学) 3
Zhou Hanhua, 'On the Orientation of China's Artificial Intelligence Legislation' (论我国人工智能立法的定位) (2024) 46 Modern Law Science (现代法学) 17

Xu Ke, 'The Third Way for the Legal Regulation of Artificial Intelligence' (人工智能法律规制的第三条道路) (2025) 43 Law Science (法律科学) 59
Ding Xiaodong, 'China's Artificial Intelligence Legislation from a Global Comparative Perspective' (全球比较下的我国人工智能立法) (2024) Journal of Comparative Law (比较法研究) 51
Rainer Muhlhoff, 'Predictive Privacy: Collective Datea Protection in the Context of Artificial Intelligence and Big Data' (2023) 10 Big Data & Society 1
Jef Ausloos, *The Right to Erasure in EU Data Protection Law: From Individual Rights to Effective Protection* (Oxford University Press 2020)
Margot E Kaminski, 'Binary Governance: Lessons from the GDPR's Approach to Algorithmic Accountability' (2019) 92 Southern California Law Review 1529
Jin Yao, 'Judicial Dilemmas and Regulatory Responses in Personal Information Protection: An Empirical Study Based on 331 Personal Information Judgments'(个人信息保护的司法困境与规则应对——基于*331*例个人信息案件的实证考察) (2025) 4 Jiaoda Law Journal (交大法学) 80
Fu Xin, 'Development, Challenges and Reflections of the Right to Data Portability in China' (2025) 13 China Legal Science 29
Ding Daoqin, 'Data Legal Issues and Legislative Recommendations in the Training Phase of Generative Artificial Intelligence' (生成式人工智能训练阶段的数据法律问题及其立法建议) (2024) 6 Administrative Law Review (行政法研究)16
Wu Teng, 'The Dilemma and Path of Personal Data Protection in the Artificial Intelligence Era' (人工智能时代个人数据保护的困境与出路) (2024) 46 Modern Law Science (现代法学) 116
Wang Yuan, 'The Justification and Implementation Path of the Right to Object to Solely Automated Decision-Making: Centred on Article 24(3) of China's Personal Information Protection Law' (完全自动化决策拒绝权之正当性及其实现路径——以《个人信息保护法》第*24*条第*3*款为中心) (2022) Jurists Review (法学家) 72
Ding Xiaodong, 'On the AI-Facilitated Data Regime' (论人工智能促进型的数据制度) (2023) 6 China Law Review (中国法律评论) 175
Zhang Xinbao, 'A Study on Personal Information Protection in Training Corpora for Generative Artificial Intelligence' (生成式人工智能训练语料的个人信息保护研究) (2024) 6 China Legal Science (中国法学) 86
Jingxian Chen, 'Public Data Authorised Operation and the Rise of Data Finance in China: Origins, Risks, and Prospects' (2025) 57 Computer Law & Security Review 106
Huang Pei, 'Risk Types and Legal Regulation of Training Data for Large Artificial Intelligence' (人工智能大模型训练数据的风险类型与法律规制) (2025) 1 Political Science and Law Forum (政法论丛) 23
Ding Daoqin, 'Processing Rules for Publicly Available Personal Information and Their Reconstruction' (已公开个人信息处理规则及其重构) (2025) 43 Political Science and Law Review (政法论坛) 47
Zhao Jingwu, 'The Interpretation and Judicial Determination of the Reasonable Use of Publicly Available Personal Information: Using Automated Decision-Making Scenarios as an Example' (已公开个人信息合理使用的解释方式与司法认定——以自动化决策应用场景为例) (2024) 3 China Review of Applied Jurisprudence (中国应用法学) 144
Liu Xiaochun, 'The Construction of Rules for the Protection and Utilisation of Publicly Available Personal Information' (已公开个人信息保护和利用的规则建构) (2022) 44 Global Law Review (环球法律评论) 52
Cheng Xiao, 'On the Legal Regulation of Publicly Available Personal Information Processing' (论公开的个人信息处理的法律规制) (2022) China Legal Science (中国法学) 82

# Chapter 8
# Artificial Intelligence and Data Protection from a Japanese Perspective

**Yoichiro Itakura**

## 8.1 What Is AI and What Is Generative AI?

This paper discusses AI and data protection in Japan. As a premise for the discussion, we examine the definitions of "AI" and "generative AI" under Japanese law.

While Japanese statutes do not directly define "AI" or "artificial intelligence," the Basic Act on Promotion of Utilization of Public and Private Data (Act No. 103 of 2016, hereinafter referred to as the "Public-Private Data Act") defines "artificial intelligence-related technology" in Article 2, Paragraph 2 as "technology related to the realization of intellectual functions such as learning, inference, and judgment through artificial means, and the utilization of such functions realized through artificial means." The Act on Promotion of Research and Development and Utilization of Artificial Intelligence-Related Technologies (Act No. 53 of 2025, hereinafter referred to as the "AI Act") similarly defines "artificial intelligence-related technology" in Article 2 as "technology necessary to realize functions that substitute for human cognitive, reasoning, and judgment capabilities through artificial means, and technology related to information processing systems that realize functions to process input information using such technology and output the results." The AI Act's definition encompasses technologies necessary to realize functions that substitute human capabilities, containing elements distinct from the Public-Private Data Act. However, as discussed later, neither the Public-Private Data Act nor the AI Act are statutes that establish and enforce specific obligations; thus, scenarios where these subtle differences become problematic are unlikely.

The definition of "AI" is provided in the 'AI Operator Guidelines (Version 1.1)'. It states that "it is difficult to strictly define the broad scope of artificial intelligence," and specifies that "AI in these guidelines refers to the abstract concept of an

Y. Itakura (✉)
Hikari Sogoh Law Offices, Tokyo, Japan
e-mail: itakura@hikari-law.com



H. Miyashita et al. (eds.), *The Evolution of Data Protection Laws in China, Japan, and Korea*, https://doi.org/10.1007/978-981-95-8609-7_8

'AI system (defined below)' itself or software/programs that perform machine learning."[1] (Page 9).

Regarding "Generative AI," the 'AI Operator Guidelines (Version 1.1)' adopts a broad definition, stating it "refers to the collective term for AI based on AI models capable of generating text, images, programs, etc." (p. 10). Generative AI is developed using a base model pre-trained on large datasets and a model fine-tuned to optimize it for specific tasks or domains. Applications and services with functions to generate text, images, sound, etc., using such models (hereinafter referred to as 'Generative AI Products') are provided.[2]

## 8.2 Data Protection and AI Legislation in Japan

### *8.2.1 Compare with Europe for Reference*

When discussing Japan's data protection and AI legislation, it is useful to explain their structure by comparing them with the European legislation that is widely referenced internationally.

The European data protection law is, of course, the General Data Protection Regulation (GDPR).[3] It is a comprehensive regulation covering both the private and public sectors, with supervision and enforcement carried out by independent data protection authorities. It requires a legal basis for processing personal data and international transfers, mandates compliance with principles and responsiveness to data subjects' rights, and establishes substantial fines. Regarding AI, it particularly emphasizes the obligation to ensure transparency (Articles 13 and 14) and the right concerning automated decision-making (Article 22). Article 22, in particular, is explicitly expected to be applied to regulating AI.

The European AI regulation is referred to as the AI Regulation or AI Act (hereinafter "European AI Law").[4] Building upon GDPR regulations, it mandates risk-based handling for AI, characterized by strict regulations on prohibited AI practices (Article 5) and high-risk AI systems (Article 6). The core focus is on regulating

[1] Ministry of Internal Affairs and Communications and Ministry of Economy, Trade and Industry, 'AI Operator Guidelines (Version 1.1)' (March 28, 2025). https://www.meti.go.jp/shingikai/mono_info_service/ai_shakai_jisso/20240419_report.html.

[2] Fair Trade Commission, 'Competition over Generating AI (Discussion Paper)' (October 2024). https://www.jftc.go.jp/houdou/pressrelease/2024/oct/241002_generativeai_02.pdf.

[3] Regulation (EU) 2016/679 of the European Parliament and of the Council of 27 April 2016 on the protection of natural persons with regard to the processing of personal data and on the free movement of such data, and repealing Directive 95/46/EC. https://eur-lex.europa.eu/eli/reg/2016/679/oj/eng.

[4] Regulation (EU) 2024/1689 of the European Parliament and of the Council of 13 June 2024 laying down harmonized rules on artificial intelligence and amending Regulations (EC) No 300/2008, (EU) No 167/2013, (EU) No 168/2013, (EU) 2018/858, (EU) 2018/1139 and (EU) 2019/2144 and Directives 2014/90/EU, (EU) 2016/797 and (EU) 2020/1828 (Artificial Intelligence Act), https://eur-lex.europa.eu/eli/reg/2024/1689/oj/eng.

high-risk AI systems, requiring compliance with requirements established from perspectives such as "risk management systems," "data governance," "technical documentation and log management," "transparency," "human oversight," and "cybersecurity." Fines exceeding those under the GDPR may also be imposed. It also establishes regulations for General-Purpose AI (presumably referring to generative AI services).

The core of Japan's data protection legislation is the Act on the Protection of Personal Information (Act No. 57 of 2003, hereinafter "APPI"). Like the GDPR, it establishes comprehensive regulations and is supervised and enforced by the Personal Information Protection Commission, but it lacks provisions for fines. Japan has a close relationship with the GDPR, being subject to adequacy decisions by the EU and the UK,[5,6] while Japan has also received adequacy decisions from the EU and the UK regarding the equivalence of its system.[7] On the other hand, Japan's AI Act, as described later, is a type of promotion law. It lacks the stringent regulations found in European AI legislation and contains no enforcement provisions such as fines.

Thus, while Japan's data protection laws align with European frameworks, its AI legislation fundamentally differs in nature. Below, we outline Japan's AI Act and the AI-related provisions within its Personal Information Protection Act.

## 8.2.2 *AI Regime*

### 8.2.2.1 AI Act in Japan

As mentioned earlier, Japan's "AI Act" is formally titled the "Act on Promotion of Research and Development and Utilization of Artificial Intelligence-Related Technologies (Act No. 53 of 2025)." It is a new law enacted during the 2025 ordinary session of the Diet. This short law consists of 4 chapters and 28 articles. True to its title, it is a type of promotion law and does not intend to impose specific obligations on businesses or other entities.

Its main provisions are the establishment of an Artificial Intelligence Strategy Headquarters within the Cabinet to serve as the central command for AI-related

[5] Commission Implementing Decision (EU) 2019/419 of 23 January 2019 pursuant to Regulation (EU) 2016/679 of the European Parliament and of the Council on the adequate protection of personal data by Japan under the Act on the Protection of Personal Information. https://eur-lex.europa.eu/legal-content/EN/TXT/?uri=uriserv:OJ.L_.2019.076.01.0001.01.ENG&toc=OJ:L:2019:076:TOC.

[6] Guidance UK-Japan data adequacy: joint statement, Published 23 April 2025. https://www.gov.uk/government/publications/uk-japan-data-adequacy-joint-statement/uk-japan-data-adequacy-joint-statement.

[7] "Foreign countries, etc., deemed to have a system for protecting personal information equivalent to that of Japan in terms of protecting the rights and interests of individuals" (Personal Information Protection Commission Notification No. 1 of 2019), https://www.ppc.go.jp/files/pdf/h31kokuji1_rev2023April18.pdf.

policies (Article 19) and the obligation for the government to formulate a Basic Plan for Artificial Intelligence (Article 18). This will enable the formulation of an integrated administrative plan for AI, led by the Artificial Intelligence Strategy Headquarters. The first Artificial Intelligence Plan was formulated on December 23, 2025:[8]

The AI Act stipulates the responsibilities of the national government (Article 4) and local governments (Article 5) regarding the "promotion of research, development, and utilization of artificial intelligence-related technologies." While the Act imposes an obligation on research and development institutions (such as universities and research and development corporations) (Article 7) and entities that develop products utilizing AI-related technologies (referred to as "utilizing businesses") (Article 8) to cooperate with the policies of the national government and local governments (with research and development institutions having a best-efforts obligation), these provisions are largely conceptual in nature and do not include any sanctions. In the process of deliberating the AI Act, it is assumed that specific obligations will be addressed through "measures under other laws and regulations," with examples cited including "the Penal Code, the Act on the Personal Information Protection, the Copyright Act, etc." and "various industry-specific laws and regulations, laws and regulations concerning product safety, etc."[9] Specific obligations are established by these "other laws and regulations." For example, medical devices that utilize AI are already subject to review under the "Act on Securing the Quality, Efficacy, and Safety of Pharmaceuticals, Medical Devices, and Other Products" (Act No. 145 of 1960) (Approval of Medical Devices (Article 23-2-5)). This has the force of law as enforceable hard law.[10] This is similar to how the European AI Act requires the individual laws listed in ANNEX I (List of Union harmonisation legislation) to reflect the obligations for high-risk AI in their standards.

#### 8.2.2.2 AI Principles and Guidelines in Japan

Previously, Japan's AI policy has been guided by the 'Principles for a Human-Centred AI Society' (decision of March 29, 2019, Integrated Innovation Strategy Promotion Council). Within the Basic Plan for Artificial Intelligence, these principles were positioned under the first of three principles: ① "Balancing Innovation Promotion and Risk Management." The other two principles are ② "Agile Response" and ③ "Domestic and International Policy Promotion." Additionally, four fundamental policies were outlined: ① Accelerating the Utilization of AI ("Using AI"), ② Strategically Strengthening AI Development Capabilities ("Creating AI"), ③ Leading AI Governance ("Enhancing AI Reliability"), and ④ Continuous

---

[8] "Basic Plan for Artificial Intelligence: 'Japan's Revival through Trustworthy AI'" (Cabinet Decision, December 23, 2025), https://www8.cao.go.jp/cstp/ai/ai_plan/aiplan_20251223.pdf.

[9] Cabinet Office, Science and Technology Innovation Promotion Office, "Current Status and Institutional Challenges of AI Policy" (August 2, 2024), p. 10, https://www8.cao.go.jp/cstp/ai/ai_senryaku/11kai/shiryo1.pdf.

[10] Subcommittee on Software as a Medical Device Utilizing AI and Machine Learning of the Science Board, "Report on AI-based Software as a Medical Device (SaMD)," Aug. 28, 2023. https://www.pmda.go.jp/files/000266099.pdf.

Transformation Toward an AI Society ("Collaborating with AI"). Previously, specific regulations for businesses were set forth in the guidelines issued by the Ministry of Internal Affairs and Communications and the Ministry of Economy, Trade and Industry, titled "Guidelines for AI Operators (Version 1.01)" (November 22, 2024). These guidelines have been formally recognized under the AI Act, as stated in the Basic Plan on Artificial Intelligence (p. 11): "While encouraging voluntary initiatives by businesses and other entities to ensure the appropriateness of AI research, development, and utilization, we will establish guidelines based on Article 13 of the AI Act and other relevant guidelines to facilitate the smooth and appropriate utilization of AI in government administration, and ensure thorough dissemination of this information to all stakeholders."

Furthermore, numerous guidelines have been established for specific fields in addition to the "Guidelines for AI Operators (Version 1.01)".

## *8.2.3 Data Protection Regime*

### 8.2.3.1 Data Protection Legislation in Japan

The official name of Japan's Personal Information Protection Act is the Act on the Protection of Personal Information (Act No. 57 of 2003). Subordinate regulations include government ordinances, regulations, guidelines (basic ones such as the General Rules Part), and guidelines by business sector.

A key feature is that legal obligations are tiered based on the subject matter being either "Personal Information," "Personal Data," or "Retained Personal Data" (GDPR generally imposes obligations uniformly on "personal data").

Furthermore, the Act itself employs an omnibus approach, establishing obligations across both the private and public sectors. The subjects of these obligations are "Businesses Handling Personal Information" (Private Sector) and "Public Authorities" (Public Sector). In both cases, the Personal Information Protection Commission is responsible for monitoring, supervision, and enforcement.

Under the Personal Information Protection Act, obligations that personal information handling businesses must comply with include: proper acquisition and use of personal information (Articles 19, 20), specification of purpose of use and prohibition of use beyond that purpose, notification and disclosure obligations (Articles 17, 18, 21), obligations for security management measures for personal data (including supervision obligations for employees and contractors, Articles 23–25), prohibition of third-party provision of personal data (Articles 27 and 28 for provision to third parties located abroad), and obligations regarding responses to requests for disclosure by the data subject concerning retained personal data (Articles 32–39). Following the 2021 amendments, there is no comprehensive exemption for use by academic research institutions for academic research purposes; therefore, individual verification is required.

As a basis for providing data to third parties located abroad, Japan is focusing on the APEC-CBPR and Global-CBPR systems, which are in operation (in relation to this joint research, Korea has also obtained CBPR certification).

Furthermore, a so-called triennial review system (reviewed every 3 years after entry into force) exists, as described later. The bill regarding the second so-called triennial review was scheduled to be submitted to the 2026 Regular Session of the Diet; however, since that session was dissolved shortly after it began, the bill is expected to be submitted during a special session of the Diet following the House of Representatives election.

#### 8.2.3.2 References to AI in the Act on the Protection of Personal Information

The current Personal Information Protection Act contains no direct provisions concerning AI. Furthermore, there are no direct provisions akin to Article 22 of the GDPR concerning profiling. The application of the prohibition on improper use (Article 19) and, based on this, requests for suspension of use, etc., under Article 35, Paragraphs 1 and 5, when "there is a risk that the rights or legitimate interests of the individual concerned may be harmed by the handling of retained personal data that identifies the individual concerned," is anticipated. However, its use is not particularly active, not only in relation to AI.

Furthermore, while no AI-specific APPI guidelines exist, some information is provided in Q&A. Specifically, see Personal Data Protection Commission, 'Q&A on "Guidelines on the Act on the Protection of Personal Information"' (1 July 2025). In Q&A 1-8, it states: "Trained parameters (weight coefficients) generated using the personal information of several individuals as a machine learning training dataset are processing and calculation coefficients adjusted to produce a specific output in the trained model. As long as the correspondence between such parameters and a specific individual is excluded, they are not considered to be 'personal information' as they do not fall under the category of 'information on individuals'." (Additional question, June 2021) It is assumed that AI models themselves do not constitute personal data. However, as this is a question added in 2021, verification is needed to determine if it consistently applies to generative AI models.

## 8.3 Development of AI and Data Protection Regime

### *8.3.1 PIPC's Alert on AI and Implementation*

The Personal Information Protection Commission published 'Alerts and other information on the use of generated AI services' and 'Summary of Alerts to OpenAI' on 2 June 2023. This is considered the second-fastest guidance example globally concerning generative AI (the fastest being enforcement by Italy's data protection authority[11]). The content is as follows.

[11] Artificial intelligence: Italian SA halts ChatGPT Personal data collected unlawfully, no age verification system for children March 31, 2023 https://www.garanteprivacy.it/web/guest/home/docweb/-/docweb-display/docweb/9870847#english.

### 8.3.2 *'Summary of Alerts to OpenAI' (June 2, 2023), Annex 1, 'Alerts, etc. on the Use of Generated AI Services'*

**(1) Points of caution for businesses handling personal data**

(i) **When prompts containing personal information are entered into the AI service generated by a business operator handling personal information, it shall be sufficiently confirmed that the prompts are within the scope necessary to achieve the purpose of use of the relevant personal information specified**.

If a business operator handling personal information inputs a prompt containing personal data to a generated AI service **without obtaining the prior consent of the individual**, and **the personal data is handled for purposes other than outputting the response results to the prompt**, the business operator handling personal information may be **in breach of the provisions of the Act on the Protection of Personal Information**. Therefore, when entering such prompts, the business operator providing the generated AI service shall sufficiently confirm that the personal data in question will not be used for machine learning, etc.

**(2) Points to note in administrative bodies, etc.**

(i) When prompts containing personal information are entered into AI services generated by administrative agencies, etc., it shall be sufficiently confirmed that the use or provision of such personal information is the minimum necessary for the specified purpose of use of such information.

(ii) If an administrative agency, etc. inputs a prompt containing retained personal information to a generative AI service, and the retained personal information is handled for purposes other than outputting the response results to the prompt, the administrative agency, etc. may be in violation of the provisions of the Personal Information Protection Law. Therefore, when inputting such a prompt, the entity providing the generated AI service shall sufficiently confirm that the retained personal information concerned will not be used for machine learning, etc.

**(3) Points to note for general users**

(i) **Personal information entered into a generative AI service may be used for machine learning of the AI**. **There is a risk that this information could be output from the generative AI service after being statistically linked to other information, potentially with accurate or inaccurate content**. Therefore, when entering personal information into a generative AI service, appropriate decisions should be made based on these risks.

(ii) Generative AI services may produce responses containing inaccurate content. For example, some services generate natural sentences as responses, but since these sentences are based on probabilistic correlations, there is a risk that responses may contain inaccurate personal information. Therefore, when using a generative AI service to handle personal information, appropriate decisions should be made based on these risks.

(iii) Users of generative AI services should thoroughly review the terms of use and privacy policies of the service providers. They should make appropriate decisions regarding the use of generative AI services based on the content of the information to be input.

When a personal information handler uses a generative AI service, the key points under the APPI are summarized as follows:

- When using personal information held by the personal information handler in a generative AI service, notification or public disclosure of the purpose of use to the individual concerned is required.
- If the generated AI service learns personal data, this constitutes a third-party provision of personal data, requiring the individual's consent.
- If the generative AI service does not learn personal data, it is considered an outsourcing of personal data handling. Therefore, consent from the data subject is not required unless the third party is located overseas. If the third party is located overseas, consent from the data subject is generally required, even if the provision is part of outsourcing personal data handling.

### 8.3.3 *'Summary of Alerts to OpenAI' (June 2, 2023), Annex 2, 'Summary of Alerts to OpenAI'*

1 Acquisition of Sensitive Personal Information

Without obtaining the consent of the individual in advance, ChatGPT users (hereinafter referred to as "users") and other individuals **shall not acquire sensitive personal information that identifies the individual** (except in cases that fall under each item of Article 20, Paragraph 2 of the Act).

In particular, the following must be observed

**(1) The following four points should be implemented with regard to collecting information for machine learning**

(i) Necessary efforts shall be made to ensure that the collected information **does not contain Sensitive Personal Information**.

(ii) As soon as possible after collecting the information, **take measures to reduce as much as possible the sensitive personal information that may be included in the collected information**.

(iii) If it is discovered that the collected information contains sensitive personal information even after implementing the measures in (i) and (ii) above, measures shall be taken to **delete such sensitive personal information or to make it impossible to identify specific individuals, as soon as possible and before processing it into a dataset for learning purposes**.

(iv) If the individual or PIPC requests or instructs not to collect the personal information required from a specific site or third party, comply with the request or instruction unless there are justifiable reasons for refusal.

**(2) Sensitive Personal Information that the user has chosen not to have used for machine learning and entered in the prompt shall not be handled unless there are justifiable reasons to do so.**

(2) Notification of purpose of use, etc.

2 Notification of Purpose of Use, etc.

Notification or publication, using the Japanese language, to both users and individuals other than users, of the purpose of use of personal data concerning the user and individuals other than the user as the principal.

The APPI norms that generative AI services such as OpenAI should comply with are summarized as follows:

- When collecting information, appropriate measures must be taken to prevent the collection of sensitive personal information.
- If sensitive personal information is collected, the sensitive portions must be deleted as much as possible before handling it.
- If sensitive information is inadvertently included, it must be rendered unidentifiable to specific individuals before handling.
- If an individual or the PIPC requests that personal information not be collected from a particular site or third party, this request must be complied with.

This is a somewhat peculiar norm. The "acquisition" (Article 20, Paragraph 2) of sensitive personal information is illegal without the individual's consent. The idea that there is a buffer between "collection" and "acquisition" or "handling," where removing sensitive parts or making specific individuals unidentifiable renders it legal, does not arise in other contexts under the APPI. This can be evaluated as a special legal interpretation made to ensure guidance to OpenAI is actionable.

### 8.3.4 February 2025, 'Informative on DeepSeek'

To DeepSeek's (Hangzhou DeepSeek Artificial Intelligence Co., Ltd., Beijing DeepSeek Artificial Intelligence Co., Ltd. and affiliates) published privacy policy. Information provided.

(i) Data, including personal information, obtained by DeepSeek in connection with the use of such services will be stored on servers located in **the People's Republic of China**.

(ii) **The laws and regulations of the People's Republic of China shall apply to such data**.

(Reference.)

Regarding point (ii) above, the following legislation will apply to the data concerned, for example

Personal Data Protection Act of the People's Republic of China

Cybersecurity Act

Data Security Act

State Information Act of the People's Republic of China, etc.

* The personal data protection system of the People's Republic of China is introduced on the website of the Personal Data Protection Commission.

https://www.ppc.go.jp/enforcement/infoprovision/laws/offshore_report_china/

This serves as a cautionary notice regarding DeepSeek, China's generative AI, particularly focusing on the existence of laws such as the Cybersecurity Act and Data Security Act within China that permit public access.

### 8.3.5 Triennial Review System

As described above, the relationship between the Personal Information Protection Act and AI training is not necessarily clear, but the Second Triennial Review includes provisions aiming to legalize this practice.

Here, an overview of the APPI amendments is as follows: Established the Act in 2003. Established PIPC (for Private Sector) and started the Triennial Review System in 2015. Conducted the 1st Triennial Review in 2020. Key items included Strict International Transfer, Data Breach Notifications, etc. In 2021: Omnibus Legislation Amendment, Expansion of PIPC Jurisdiction (for Public Sector). The second triennial review should have been conducted during the 2025 regular Diet session if the schedule had been followed correctly. However, due to various circumstances, it will be submitted to the 2026 regular Diet session. Moreover, according to reports, a dissolution of the Diet at the outset is anticipated. It would not be surprising if it were delayed until the 2026 extraordinary Diet session.

### 8.3.6 Statistical (Including AI Models) Purposes Exemption

The document "Approaches to Institutional Challenges of the Personal Information Protection Act.", published by the Personal Information Protection Commission on March 5, 2025, for the second triennial review, titled  It states: "The nature of consent required when processing personal data solely for the purpose of obtaining and using general or generic analytical results that exclude any correspondence with specific individuals, such as for statistical compilation" (Section 1.1(1)) is clearly influenced by GDPR Art. 89(1) and recital 50.

Specifically, the anticipated scenarios can be categorized as: ① AI development, etc., involving the creation of statistics, etc., using secret computation or similar methods, which entails matching personal data across multiple businesses, and ② AI development, etc., involving the creation of statistics, etc., using website crawling, which entails acquiring sensitive personal information. Regarding the former, while "processing into statistical data" by a single business operator is not subject to purpose limitation regulations,[12] this provision aims to permit the creation of statistics after matching personal data using so-called privacy-enhancing technologies (PETs)

[12] Personal Information Protection Commission, "Q&A Regarding the 'Guidelines Concerning the Act on the Protection of Personal Information'," July 1, 2025, QA2-5.

like confidential computation, under certain conditions, as it constitutes a provision of personal data to a third party. This also addresses the significant expectations for PETs in data utilization.[13] The latter can be seen as a retroactive measure addressing the fact that, despite certain provisions in the Copyright Act (e.g., Article 30-4), the Personal Information Protection Act did not necessarily provide reasonable norms (as mentioned in Sect. 8.3.1 above). This section, while details are expected to be delegated to Personal Information Protection Commission regulations, presents numerous items requiring consideration—such as "written agreements" with recipients and disclosure requirements—and necessitates further discussion.

### *8.3.7 AI Legislation Related to Copyright*

Regarding generative AI, copyright law frequently becomes an issue. The Subcommittee on Legal Systems of the Copyright Subcommittee of the Cultural Affairs Council published "Considerations on AI and Copyright" (March 15, 2024). Japan's Copyright Act broadly permits exceptions for uses not aimed at enjoying the ideas or emotions expressed in a work (non-enjoyment-purpose use) even without the copyright holder's permission (Article 30-4). This has sometimes led to Japan being called a "machine learning paradise." Similarly, the Personal Information Protection Act permits the acquisition of sensitive personal information for AI development purposes that can be categorized as statistical compilation, aligning with copyright policy.

## 8.4 Conclusion

Japan addresses AI primarily through its existing legal framework, favoring flexibility over comprehensive regulation. However, given the rapid expansion of generative AI, more concrete governance on transparency, accountability, cross-border transfers, and research exemptions will be increasingly necessary.

## References

Ministry of Internal Affairs and Communications and Ministry of Economy, Trade and Industry, 'AI Operator Guidelines (Version 1.1)'(March 28, 2025). https://www.meti.go.jp/shingikai/mono_info_service/ai_shakai_jisso/20240419_report.html

[13] Liberal Democratic Party Policy Research Council Digital Society Promotion Headquarters, "Digital Nippon 2025: Launching 'Digital Policy 2.0' Toward the 'Next 100 Years'," May 15, 2025, p. 4.

Fair Trade Commission, 'Competition over Generating AI (Discussion Paper)' (October 2024). https://www.jftc.go.jp/houdou/pressrelease/2024/oct/241002_generativeai_02.pdf
Regulation (EU) 2016/679 of the European Parliament and of the Council of 27 April 2016 on the protection of natural persons with regard to the processing of personal data and on the free movement of such data, and repealing Directive 95/46/EC. https://eurlex.europa.eu/eli/reg/2016/679/oj/eng
Regulation (EU) 2024/1689 of the European Parliament and of the Council of 13 June 2024 laying down harmonized rules on artificial intelligence and amending Regulations (EC) No 300/2008, (EU) No 167/2013, (EU) No 168/2013, (EU) 2018/858, (EU) 2018/1139 and (EU) 2019/2144 and Directives 2014/90/EU, (EU) 2016/797 and (EU) 2020/1828 (Artificial Intelligence Act), https://eurlex.europa.eu/eli/reg/2024/1689/oj/eng
Commission Implementing Decision (EU) 2019/419 of 23 January 2019 pursuant to Regulation (EU) 2016/679 of the European Parliament and of the Council on the adequate protection of personal data by Japan under the Act on the Protection of Personal Information. https://eur-lex.europa.eu/legalcontent/EN/TXT/?uri=uriserv:OJ.L_.2019.076.01.0001.01.ENG&toc=OJ:L:2019:076:TOC
Guidance UK-Japan data adequacy: joint statement, Published 23 April 2025. https://www.gov.uk/government/publications/uk-japandata-adequacy-joint-statement/uk-japan-data-adequacy-joint-statement
Personal Information Protection Commission Notification No. 1 of 2019), https://www.ppc.go.jp/files/pdf/h31kokuji1_rev2023April18.pdf
"Basic Plan for Artificial Intelligence: 'Japan's Revival through Trustworthy AI'" (Cabinet Decision, December 23, 2025), https://www8.cao.go.jp/cstp/ai/ai_plan/aiplan_20251223.pdf
Cabinet Office, Science and Technology Innovation Promotion Office, "Current Status and Institutional Challenges of AI Policy" (August 2, 2024), p. 10, https://www8.cao.go.jp/cstp/ai/ai_senryaku/11kai/shiryo1.pdf
Subcommittee on Software as a Medical Device Utilizing AI and Machine Learning of the Science Board, "Report on AI-based Software as a Medical Device (SaMD)," Aug. 28, 2023. https://www.pmda.go.jp/files/000266099.pdf
Artificial intelligence: Italian SA halts ChatGPT Personal data collected unlawfully, no age verification system for children March 31, 2023 https://www.garanteprivacy.it/web/guest/home/docweb/-/docweb-display/docweb/9870847#english
Personal Information Protection Commission, "Q&A Regarding the 'Guidelines Concerning the Act on the Protection of Personal Information'," July 1, 2025, QA2-5.
Liberal Democratic Party Policy Research Council Digital Society Promotion Headquarters, "Digital Nippon 2025: Launching 'Digital Policy 2.0' Toward the 'Next 100 Years'," May 15, 2025, p. 4.

# Chapter 9
# Data Protection Within the AI Context in Korea

**Nohyoung Park**

## 9.1 The AI Basic Act

### *9.1.1 Adoption and Scope*

The AI Basic Act was passed by the National Assembly on December 14, 2024, promulgated on January 21, 2025, and is to take effect on January 22, 2026. Managed by the AI Policy Bureau of the Ministry of Science and ICT, the Act's stated purpose is "to contribute to the protection of the rights and dignity of the people, the improvement of their quality of life, and the enhancement of national competitiveness by prescribing the basic matters necessary for the sound development of artificial intelligence and the establishment of a foundation of trust."[1]

### *9.1.2 Status as a Framework*

While claimed to position Korea as a global leader in comprehensive AI governance, the AI Basic Act establishes itself as the primary legislation governing AI in Korea. Unless otherwise provided for in other laws, matters concerning AI, AI technology, the AI industry, and an AI-based society are to be governed by this Act.[2]

[1] AI Basic Act Art. 1.

[2] AI Basic Act Art. 5(1).

N. Park (✉)
Korea University Law School, Seoul, Korea
e-mail: wtopark@korea.ac.kr



H. Miyashita et al. (eds.), *The Evolution of Data Protection Laws in China, Japan, and Korea*, https://doi.org/10.1007/978-981-95-8609-7_9

Furthermore, in enacting or amending other laws pertaining to AI, the purpose of this Act is to be duly reflected.[3]

### 9.1.3 Relationship Between the AI Basic Act and the PIPA

Unlike the EU AI Act,[4] Korea's AI Basic Act is primarily focused on promoting the AI industry,[5] and does not include direct clauses concerning data protection in AI particular context. Data protection issues continue to be governed principally by the PIPA.

Article 6 of the PIPA provides that "unless otherwise provided for in other Acts with respect to the processing and protection of personal information, matters shall be governed by this Act." This establishes the PIPA as a general law, where other laws take precedence only when they contain special provisions expressly governing personal information protection.

The key question is whether the "principle of prior permission" (*i.e.*, allow-first) under the AI Basic Act constitutes such a special provision that displaces the regulatory framework of the PIPA. The conclusion is that it does not. The AI Basic Act is a framework statute intended to promote the AI industry and ensure technological safety. It cannot be interpreted as a special law that overrides the PIPA regarding personal information processing. Even if an AI service provider freely develops services under the AI Basic Act, any collection or processing of personal information in the course of such activities must still comply with PIPA requirements, such as obtaining data subjects' consent or establishing legitimate interests, or applying pseudonymization, etc. The AI Basic Act cannot serve as a free pass for the unauthorized use of personal information.

---

[3] AI Basic Act Art. 5(2).

[4] Regulation (EU) 2024/1689 of the European Parliament and of the Council of 13 June 2024 laying down harmonised rules on artificial intelligence and amending Regulations (EC) No 300/2008, (EU) No 167/2013, (EU) No 168/2013, (EU) 2018/858, (EU) 2018/1139 and (EU) 2019/2144 and Directives 2014/90/EU, (EU) 2016/797 and (EU) 2020/1828, OJ L, 2024/1689, 12.7.2024, ELI: http://data.europa.eu/eli/reg/2024/1689/oj. See generally Nohyoung Park, *An Introduction to the EU AI Act* (in Korean), Oct. 2025.

[5] The AI Basic Act's principal chapter with 14 articles is Chapter 3 on Development of AI Technology and Promotion of the AI Industry, consisting of Section 1 on Establishment of the Foundation for the AI Industry and Section 2 on Development of AI Technology and the AI Industry. And the accompanied chapter with 10 articles is Chapter 4 on AI Ethics and Ensuring Trustworthiness.

## 9.2 Fully Automated Decisions

### 9.2.1 *Overview of the Provisions*

The PIPA specifically addresses decisions made through AI by introducing Article 37-2 on fully automated decisions on March 14, 2023, which became enforceable on March 15, 2024. This reform was prompted by the growing recognition that AI-driven decisions can significantly impact an individual's rights and obligations. The provision establishes the data subject's rights concerning decisions made by processing personal information without substantial human involvement.

### 9.2.2 *Scope of the Provisions*

Article 37-2 applies when a fully automated system, including a system applying AI technology, processes personal information to make a final decision that has a significant impact on the data subject's rights or obligations.[6] It grants data subjects three key rights regarding automated decisions.

First, if the decision has a significant impact on his or her rights or obligations, the data subject can refuse the decision.[7] Upon refusal, the controller must suspend the application or re-process it with human intervention.[8] Second, the data subject can request an explanation or relevant information regarding the decision.[9] Upon request, the controller must provide an explanation.[10] Third, the data subject may request from the controller any of the following explanations or reviews with respect to the automated decision:[11] (1) an explanation of the criteria and processing procedures underlying the automated decision, and (2) a review as to whether the controller can reflect the data subject's opinions, such as by submitting additional personal information in the automated decision.

---

[6] See generally PIPC, *Guide to Data Subjects' Rights Regarding Automated Decision-Making*, September 2024.

[7] PIPA Art. 37-2(1).

[8] PIPA Art. 37-2(3). The term "개인정보 처리자(個人情報 處理者)" under the PIPA corresponds to the concept of a "controller" under the GDPR. A literal translation that includes the term "processor" corresponding to "처리자" could cause confusion with the GDPR's separate notion of a "processor." For this reason, "개인정보 처리자" should be rendered in English as "controller."

[9] PIPA Art. 37-2(2).

[10] PIPA Art. 37-2(3).

[11] Presidential Decree Art. 44-2(2).

## 9.3 Prior Adequacy Review Mechanism

### 9.3.1 *Mechanism and Purpose*

The PIPC launched the Prior Adequacy Review Mechanism (PARM) officially on March 27, 2024, following a pilot operation that began in October 2023. This initiative addresses the perceived shortcomings regarding AI in the existing legislation. This mechanism allows businesses to collaborate with the PIPC in developing AI services to establish compliance plans that align with rapidly changing privacy landscapes. It helps bridge gaps where existing legal interpretations and precedents under the PIPA are insufficient for new technologies and services.

Once plans are properly devised and deployed, businesses are exempted from future administrative sanctions.[12] Companies can voluntarily apply for a prior adequacy review of their compliance with the PIPA. If they faithfully execute the compliance measures jointly formulated with the PIPC, they are granted prior exemption from administrative sanctions under the PIPA regarding that specific activity. This pragmatic approach by the PIPC aims to support AI development and balance innovation with regulatory compliance.

### 9.3.2 *Nature and Case Examples*

Although the PARM resembles regulatory sandboxes, it differs because it requires adherence to the existing law, i.e., the PIPA, through proactive legal interpretation rather than temporary regulatory suspension. The PARM positions the PIPC as both a regulator and a partner in AI development, showcasing Korea's effort to reconcile industrial policy goals with fundamental rights protection.

A review of 15 cases as of October 2025 shows that a wide range of organizations such as public institutions, large corporations, overseas companies have used the PARM.[13] For example, the mechanism has been applied to a financial institution–telecom company voice phishing detection service and Kakao's AI assistant service, producing preventive privacy protection effects broadly felt by the public. Additionally, by examining services from foreign companies, such as Meta's SNS impersonation detection, the PARM has strengthened the protection of users' personal information in the global service environment.

---

[12] PIPC, "The PIPC Concludes Deliberations on Prior Adequacy Review Results of Kanana, Kakao's AI Assistant Service", Press Release, March 13, 2025.

[13] PIPC, "Before launching your service, ensure 'Privacy by Design (PbD)' through the PARM!", Press Release, September 25, 2025. Of the 15 services that underwent the PRAM, 7 have been launched or are scheduled to be launched.

## 9.4 PIPC Guidelines

The PIPC has issued guidelines which, while not legally binding, function as *de facto* regulatory standards to clarify how the PIPA applies to the AI context.

### *9.4.1 Guidelines on Processing Publicly Available Personal Information for AI Development and Services*

Issued in July 2024, the *Guidelines on Processing Publicly Available Personal Information for AI Development and Services* (hereinafter "Publicly Available Personal Information Guidelines") enable the lawful and safe processing of publicly available personal information, a key ingredient for AI development.

Publicly available personal information refers to personal information, as defined in Article 2(1) of the PIPA, that is lawfully accessible to anyone.[14] This primarily contemplates situations in which personal information is included in datasets collected for AI training from publicly accessible sources using web-scraping technologies. However, publicly available personal information is not limited to personal information disclosed by the data subjects themselves.[15]

The legitimate interests provision under Article 15(1)(6) of the PIPA serves as the substantive legal basis for collecting and using publicly available personal information for AI training or AI services.[16] The legitimate interests of a controller refer to lawful interests related to the processing of personal information, and may encompass not only the business interests of AI developers and service providers, but also various layers of interests such as the broader social benefits arising therefrom.[17]

Unlike other legal bases under Article 15(1) such as data subject's consent (subparagraph 1), compliance with a statutory obligation (subparagraph 2), or performance of a contract (subparagraph 4), which have clearly defined scopes of application, the legitimate interests provision allows for a balancing of the controller's interests against the rights of the data subject, taking into account the specific context of AI development.

As to the Requirements to justify processing under legitimate interest basis, three criteria must be met:[18] (1) the controller must have a legitimate interest; (2) the processing of personal information must be necessary for achieving that legitimate interest and must demonstrate reasonable and substantial relevance; and (3) the legitimate interests of the controller must clearly outweigh the rights of the data

[14] Publicly Available Personal Information Guidelines, p. 2.
[15] Publicly Available Personal Information Guidelines, p. 2.
[16] Publicly Available Personal Information Guidelines, p. 6.
[17] Publicly Available Personal Information Guidelines, p. 7.
[18] PIPA Art. 15(1)(6).

subject. Where AI developers or service providers find it difficult to determine whether their legitimate interests clearly outweigh the rights of data subjects, it is advisable that they implement sufficient security and safeguarding measures to prevent or mitigate any restriction or infringement of data subjects' rights.[19]

### 9.4.2 Guidelines on Personal Information Processing for Generative AI

On August 6, 2025, the PIPC issued the *Guidelines on Personal Information Processing for Generative AI* (hereinafter "Generative AI Guidelines") to reduce uncertainty regarding the application of the PIPA throughout the generative AI lifecycle. These guidelines are expected to benefit companies using LLM-as-a-Service and developers fine-tuning open-source models.

If the personal information of an AI user is used for AI training and development and that has a reasonable correlation with the original collection purpose, the additional use clause of the PIPA, Article 15(3), may apply.[20] Article 15(3) was inserted on Feb. 4, 2020 and effective on Aug. 5, 2020.[21] This requires considering predictability, the possibility of undue infringement of the data subject's interests, and safety measures such as pseudonymization and encryption.

### 9.4.3 Guidelines on the Protection and Use of Personal Video Information for Mobile Video Processing Devices

Released on October 14, 2024, the *Guidelines on the Protection and Use of Personal Video Information for Mobile Video Processing Devices* (hereinafter "Mobile Video Guidelines") reflect the specific applicability criteria of Article 25-2 on mobile video processing devices, newly inserted in the PIPA on March 14, 2023 and enforceable on September 15, 2023. They demonstrate a balance between public interests of safety and innovation and individual rights to data protection.

For example, operators of video devices used in autonomous vehicles and similar systems should delete all footage after the completion of driving, except for video that is strictly necessary for business purposes, excluding footage related to incidents or accidents.[22] Footage required for the development of autonomous driving

[19] Publicly Available Personal Information Guidelines, p. 14.

[20] Generative AI Guidelines, pp. 12–13.

[21] It provides: "A controller may use personal information without the data subject's consent, as prescribed by Presidential Decree, where the use falls within a scope reasonably correlated to the original purpose of collection, taking into account whether the use causes any negative effect to the data subject and whether necessary security measures, such as encryption, have been implemented."

[22] Mobile Video Guidelines, p. 56.

systems should be anonymized or pseudonymized so that individuals cannot be identified.[23] This approach helps minimize the likelihood that data subjects will seek to exercise rights such as access or deletion, and strengthens public trust in the protection of personal information.

When autonomous vehicles, robots, or similar devices capture video footage for the purpose of safe operation and an abnormal event such as a collision with an obstacle, a traffic accident, or intentional damage occurs, the use of such footage to identify the cause of the incident or to provide it to an insurance company for insurance claims may be regarded as falling within a scope reasonably related to, or foreseeable from, the original purpose of collection.[24]

Even in such cases, however, it is desirable to minimize any infringement of data subjects' rights by anonymizing or pseudonymizing personal video information that is not relevant to handling the incident, or by ensuring the secure use and provision of such information through measures such as password protection or access restrictions for unauthorized persons.[25]

In contrast, when footage captured in public places by autonomous vehicles or robots during pilot operations is separately stored and used for AI training in a manner that allows individuals to be identified, although such use may be related to the original purpose of collection to some degree, data subjects in public settings cannot reasonably anticipate that their video will be used for AI training in an identifiable form. Accordingly, such additional use or provision of personal video information cannot be considered foreseeable.[26]

## 9.5 DeepSeek Case

On January 15, 2025, Chinese AI company Hangzhou DeepSeek Artificial Intelligence Co., Ltd. (DeepSeek) launched its R1 Large Language Model chatbot service in Korea. Immediate concerns were raised regarding the cross-border transfer of user prompt inputs and device data, as well as opaque privacy policies. DeepSeek provided privacy policies only in Chinese and English and failed to obtain separate consent from users for transferring device and user input data to Beijing Volcano Engine Technology Co., Ltd. (Volcano).[27]

DeepSeek used publicly available personal information, such as open-source data, data collected by web-scraping, and user-entered data for its AI development and training. But it failed to provide users with features to opt-out of providing user input for AI development and training.

[23] Mobile Video Guidelines, p. 56.

[24] Mobile Video Guidelines, p. 60.

[25] Mobile Video Guidelines, p. 60.

[26] Mobile Video Guidelines, p. 60.

[27] DeepSeek claimed that Volcano is a subsidiary of ByteDance, but it is an independent corporation.

The PIPC immediately launched a prior status examination under Article 63-2 on January 31, 2025.[28] Article 63-2 was inserted in the PIPA on March 14, 2023, and was effective on September 15, 2023. This marked the first use of this tool in the context of AI. DeepSeek suspended new domestic downloads of its chatbot service on Apple's App Store and Google Play on February 15, 2025, and admitted to partial compliance failures. By April 10, 2025, it had blocked the transfer of user prompt data to a specific Chinese affiliate.

On Apr. 24, 2025, the PIPC officially issued a Corrective Recommendation.[29] Following updates to the Korean version of its privacy policy and the introduction of opt-out functionality associated with providing user-entered data for AI development and training, DeepSeek resumed service on April 28, 2025. This incident illustrates the PIPC's proactive supervision and effective utilization of new enforcement tools against foreign operators regarding AI-related risks, cross-border data transfer, and transparency issues.

## 9.6 Proposed Amendments to the PIPA

### *9.6.1 Key Contents*

In line with the PIPC's policy declaration of innovation issued in January 2025, a significant amendment to the PIPA was proposed to the National Assembly on January 31, 2025.[30] The main purpose of this proposal is to ensure that training data should be secured and utilized in a manner that can flexibly accommodate evolving data-processing practices and emerging societal needs to support the advancement of AI technologies. This proposal stems from the recognition that the current legal framework does not adequately accommodate the needs of AI development.

The core innovation of the proposed amendment is the expansion of the permitted scope for processing personal information beyond the original collection purpose for the development and performance improvement of AI technology. The proposed new Article 28-12(1) will allow this under specific conditions: (1) where pseudonymization or anonymization is impractical due to the nature of the data, (2) where appropriate safety measures (technical, organizational, and physical) are in place, and (3) where the PIPC approves.

---

[28] The technical analysis with the Korea Internet & Security Agency (KISA) found out traffic generated by third-party data transfer and insufficient transparency in DeepSeek's privacy policy.

[29] PIPC, "The PIPC Announces Status Examination Results of DeepSeek Service", Press Release, April 24, 2025.

[30] [Bill No. 2207858] Partial Amendment to the Personal Information Protection Act (Proposed by Representative Min Byung-Deok and 9 Others).

### *9.6.2 Legislative Paradigm Shift*

This proposed amendment signals a transition from a protection-centric to a utilization-oriented governance model for data protection in relation to AI in Korea. While critics argue this may weaken constitutional guarantees like the right to informational self-determination, proponents deem it essential for maintaining industrial competitiveness in the AI sector.

## 9.7 Observation

Data protection within Korea's AI regulation context unfolds via a dual-track system involving the AI Basic Act and the PIPA. The AI Basic Act establishes the general legal foundation for AI policy, prioritizing industrial promotion, while the PIPA functions as the primary safeguard against AI-related risks through its automated decision provisions and the introduction of the Prior Adequacy Review Mechanism (PARM) by the PIPC.

The PIPC's guidelines, recently issued, flexibly interpret legal grounds of legitimate interests for AI training and clarify safety measures for generative AI throughout its lifecycle. The DeepSeek case also affirmed the PIPC's proactive enforcement capacity, including over foreign operators, concerning cross-border data transfer and transparency. Furthermore, autonomous driving video data guidelines prove a practical equilibrium between data protection and innovation.

Ultimately, the pending PIPA amendments indicate a structural shift toward a utilization-oriented governance model. The legislative proposal briefly mentioned above in particular explicitly supports AI development by allowing the processing of personal information beyond its original purpose, provided it adheres to strict safety conditions and the PIPC supervision. This model, relying on layered general AI law and evolving data protection statutes, may contrast with the EU's integrated approach, opting instead for flexibility to ensure fundamental rights protection alongside sustained industrial competitiveness. The PIPC appears to support the development of AI and data ecosystems by laying a legal foundation for safely utilizing personal information to develop AI models that are conducive to society.

## References

1. Nohyoung Park, *An Introduction to the EU AI Act* (in Korean, 2025.10.31.).
2. PIPC, "Before launching your service, ensure 'Privacy by Design (PbD)' through the PARM!", Press Release, https://www.pipc.go.kr/np/cop/bbs/selectBoardArticle.do?bbsId=BS074&mCode=C020010000&nttId=11508#LINK (2025.9.25).
3. PIPC, *Guidelines on Personal Information Processing for Generative AI*, https://www.pipc.go.kr/eng/user/ltn/new/noticeDetail.do?bbsId=BBSMSTR_000000000001&nttId=2875 (2025.8.6.).

4. PIPC, "PIPC Announces Status Examination Results of DeepSeek Service", Press Release, https://www.pipc.go.kr/eng/user/ltn/new/noticeDetail.do?bbsId=BBSMSTR_000000000001&nttId=2819 (2025.4.24.).
5. PIPC, "The PIPC Concludes Deliberations on Prior Adequacy Review Results of Kanana, Kakao's AI Assistant Service", Press Release, https://www.pipc.go.kr/eng/user/ltn/new/noticeDetail.do?bbsId=BBSMSTR_000000000001&nttId=2806 (2025.3.13.).
6. [Bill No. 2207858] Partial Amendment to the Personal Information Protection Act (Proposed by Representative Min Byung-Deok and 9 Others), https://likms.assembly.go.kr/bill/bi/billDetailPage.do?billId=PRC_Y2Z5Y0Y1G2G2E1D0E5C3C1L3L0J4K5&currMenuNo=2600044 (2025.1.31.).
7. PIPC, "PIPC's Policy Vision and Tasks for 2025: Trustworthy AI Era Backed by Safe Use of Personal Information", Press Release, https://www.pipc.go.kr/eng/user/ltn/new/noticeDetail.do?bbsId=BBSMSTR_000000000001&nttId=2763 (2025.1.13.)
8. PIPC, *Guidelines on the Protection and Use of Personal Video Information for Mobile Video Processing Devices, https://www.pipc.go.kr/np/cop/bbs/selectBoardArticle.do?bbsId=BS074&mCode=C020010000&nttId=10678#LINK* (2024.10.14.).
9. PIPC, *Criteria for Controllers' Actions Regarding Automated Decisions* (PIPC Notice No. 2024-9, 2024.9.26.).
10. PIPC, *Guide to Data Subjects' Rights Regarding Automated Decision-Making* (2024.9.).
11. PIPC, *Guidelines on Processing Publicly Available Personal Information for AI Development and Services,* https://www.pipc.go.kr/eng/user/ltn/new/noticeDetail.do?bbsId=BBSMSTR_000000000001&nttId=2591 *(2024.7.).*
12. PIPC, *Regulation on the Operation of the Prior Adequacy Review Mechanism* (PIPC Notice No. 2024-6, 2024.4.2.).

# Part IV
# Data Transfer Regulations

# Chapter 10
# Compliance Mechanisms of China's Cross-Border Data Transfer Regime

Jie Meng

## 10.1 The Evolution of China's Cross-Border Data Transfer Regulatory Regime

The emergence of China's cross-border data transfer regulatory regime has gone through four stages: exploratory inception, framework establishment, institutional improvement, and mechanism optimization.

### *10.1.1 Exploratory Inception: Targeting Critical Information Infrastructure Operators*

The legal framework for cross-border data transfer originates from the CSL which came into effect on June 1, 2017. It first proposed a security assessment mechanism for cross-border data transfer, clearly stipulating that critical information infrastructure operators (CIIO) must apply to the national Cyberspace Administration of China (CAC) to conduct a security assessment in accordance with rules developed by the CAC in conjunction with relevant departments of the State Council, when providing personal information and key data overseas for business purposes.[1] The National Cybersecurity Standardization Technical Committee (TC260) later issued the Information Security Technology—Guidelines on Security Assessment for

[1] Cybersecurity Law, Article 37.

J. Meng (✉)
Global Law Office, Beijing, China
e-mail: mengjie@glo.com.cn



H. Miyashita et al. (eds.), *The Evolution of Data Protection Laws in China, Japan, and Korea*, https://doi.org/10.1007/978-981-95-8609-7_10

Cross-border Data Transfer (Draft for Comment), which provided guidance on the processes, methods, and key points of security assessment before formal rules were enacted.[2] This marked China's initial construction of a data outbound regulatory framework, balancing data security with cross-border data transfer.

### *10.1.2 Establishment Phase: Comprehensive Cross-Border Data Transfer Regime*

The DSL enacted in 2021, not only reaffirms the requirement that CIIOs conduct a security assessment before cross-border data transfer of key data but also establishes the legal basis for regulating the outbound transfer of key data by non-CIIO data processors.[3] Additionally, it imposes restrictions on transferring data to foreign judicial and law enforcement agencies, requiring domestic entities and individuals to obtain approval from competent authorities before transferring data stored within mainland China to overseas agencies.[4]

On November 1, 2021, the PIPL came into effect, strengthening compliance requirements for cross-border transfer of personal information. In the same month, the CAC released the Regulation on Network Data Security Management (Draft for Comment), which specifically stipulates 'Cross-border Security Management of Data' in a dedicated chapter.[5] Article 38 of the PIPL clarifies three main compliance routes for data export: (a) passing the security assessment conducted by the CAC, (b) obtaining personal information protection certification by accredited agencies, and (c) concluding and performing standard contracts with overseas recipients as prescribed by the CAC, which stipulate the rights and obligations of both parties, and submitting such contracts to the CAC at the provincial level where the data exporter is located for filing (collectively referred to as the 'data export mechanisms').[6] These three routes constitute the core of China's cross-border data transfer regime.

[2] Information security technology - Guidelines for data cross-border transfer security assessment (信息安全技术　数据出境安全评估指南) <https://std.samr.gov.cn/gb/search/gbDetailed?id=E116673EB1EBA3B7E05397BE0A0AC6BF> accessed 30 November 2025.

[3] Data Security Law, Article 31.

[4] Data Security Law, Article 36.

[5] CAC, 'Soliciting Public Opinion on the "Regulation on Network Data Security Management" (Draft for Public Comment)' (国家互联网信息办公室关于《网络数据安全管理条例(征求意见稿)》公开征求意见的通知) <https://www.cac.gov.cn/2021-11/14/c_1638501991577898.htm> accessed 30 November 2025.

[6] Personal Information Protection Law, Article 38.

### *10.1.3 Improvement Phase: Specification for Implementation*

To promote the practical implementation of data outbound rules, relevant authorities introduced multiple interim policies and standards for specifying the statutory mechanism.

CAC, as the leading competent authority regulating cross-border data transfer, officially released the Measures for the Security Assessment of Cross-Border Data Transfer (the Assessment Measures),[7] which came into effect on September 1, 2022. The Measures reaffirm statutory objectives, such as regulating cross-border data transfer activities, protecting the rights and interests of personal information, safeguarding national security and public interests, and promoting the safe and free flow of cross-border data. In February 2023, the CAC also issued the Measures for the Standard Contract for the Cross-Border Transfer of Personal Information (the Measures for the Standard Contract)[8], which provide a contract template to facilitate lawful and compliant cross-border data transfer.

The standardization organizations have engaged actively in developing technical standards. In 2022, TC260 released the first Guidelines on Cybersecurity Standards-Specification on Security Authentication for Cross-Border Personal Information Processing Activities (V1.0)[9] in June and later revised them in December, detailing certification requirements and responsibilities.[10] On November 21, 2024, the Guidelines on Cybersecurity Standards—Requirements for the Protection of Cross-border Personal Information Processing in the Guangdong-Hong Kong-Macao Greater Bay Area were officially issued to facilitate free data transfer across jurisdictions.[11]

[7] Measures for the Security Assessment of Cross-Border Data Transfer (数据出境安全评估办法) <https://www.gov.cn/zhengce/zhengceku/2022-07/08/content_5699851.htm> accessed 30 November 2025.

[8] Measures for the Standard Contract for the Cross-Border Transfer of Personal Information (个人信息出境标准合同办法) <https://www.gov.cn/zhengce/202311/content_6917770.htm> accessed 30 November 2025.

[9] Notice on the Release of 'Cybersecurity Standards Practice Guidelines - Security Certification Specifications for Cross-border Processing of Personal Information' (关于发布《网络安全标准实践指南—个人信息跨境处理活动安全认证规范》的通知) <https://www.tc260.org.cn/portal/article/2/20220624175016> accessed 30 November 2025.

[10] Notice on the Release of 'Cybersecurity Standards Practice Guidelines - Security Certification Specifications for Cross-border Processing of Personal Information (V 2.0)' (关于发布《网络安全标准实践指南—个人信息跨境处理活动安全认证规范V2.0》的通知) <https://www.tc260.org.cn/portal/article/2/20221216161852> accessed 30 November 2025.

[11] Notice on the Release of 'Cybersecurity Standards Practice Guidelines - Protection Requirements for Cross-border Processing of Personal Information in the Guangdong-Hong Kong-Macao Greater Bay Area (Mainland, Hong Kong)' (关于发布《网络安全标准实践指南——粤港澳大湾区(内地、香港)个人信息跨境处理保护要求》的通知) <https://www.tc260.org.cn/portal/article/2/20241121082051> accessed 30 November 2025.

Until then, the cross-border data transfer regime had been characterized by a protection-oriented policy approach. Such an approach shifted toward facilitating cross-border data transfer in 2024, marking the transition of the regulatory regime into the optimization phase.

### *10.1.4 Optimization Phase: A Policy Shift from Restriction to Facilitation*

China's policies on cross-border data transfer have always revolved around 'security', with regulations repeatedly emphasizing that '*key data shall not be transferred abroad at will*' and '*transfers require security assessment*'.[12] It has raised the compliance threshold for cross-border data transfer for enterprises to a certain extent, affecting the free flow of data elements and the operational efficiency of enterprises on a global scale.[13] Recognizing the significance of cross-border data transfer in reinforcing China's opening-up policy, the CAC issued the Provisions on Promoting and Regulating Cross-Border Data Flow (2024 Cross-border Provisions) on March 22, 2024.[14]

This reflects a major policy shift in China's cross-border data governance, optimizing existing frameworks and signaling a clear directional transition—from a 'security-centered' approach to a 'balanced security and development' approach—thereby building a more pragmatic and flexible governance mechanism. Scholarship has already noted this shift.[15] The Provisions explicitly promote the lawful and orderly free flow of data, strengthens full-process regulation across the stages before, during, and after transmission, and lower the compliance thresholds to encourage digital trade and international cooperation. It defines several exemption scenarios, including: the cross-border transfer of personal information collected and processed entirely outside China without incorporating domestic data; outbound transfers deemed necessary for human resource management or contract performance; cross-border sharing of personal information in emergencies to protect life, health, or property safety; and general business activities such as international trade, cross-border transport, academic cooperation, production, and marketing.

[12] Cybersecurity Law, Article 37; Data Security Law, Article 31; Personal Information Protection Law, Articles 36 and 40; The Measures for the Security Assessment of Cross-Border Data Transfer, Article 4; 2024 Cross-border Provisions, Article 7; Cyberspace Data Security Management Regulation, Articles 29 and Article 37.

[13] Jingwu 2022, p. 148.

[14] 2024 Cross-border Provisions (促进和规范数据跨境流动规定) <https://www.gov.cn/gongbao/2024/issue_11366/202405/content_6954192.html> accessed 30 November 2025. Informal English Version: https://appinchina.co/government-documents/provisions-on-promoting-and-regulating-cross-border-data-flows/.

[15] Guo and Li 2025, p. 1.

It establishes a graded governance principle emphasizing supervision focused on high-risk activities and low-risk activities eligible for default exemption, replacing the prior one-size-fits-all high-threshold mode, enabling the precise allocation of regulatory resources. Enterprises can adopt differentiated management strategies for different risk levels arising out of data transfer, thereby reducing the operational costs and institutional friction. For high risks, enterprises should follow the principle of "prevention first", multi-faceted control, strengthened supervision, and flexible response to ensure proper risk management.[16] For low risks, enterprises can implement risk monitoring and early warning, improve mechanisms and norms, and enhance communication and coordination.[17]

The State Council reinforced this stance in the Regulation on the Administration of Cyber Data Security and thus elevated the legal status of those requirements.[18] Chapter 5 provides detailed provisions on the security management requirements for cross-border data transfer, covering multiple compliance routes for protecting personal information and key data. It integrates previous mechanisms for security assessment, certification, and standard contract, and adds special mechanisms for data processing based on international treaties. Data processors must strictly abide by the assessment results and contractual agreements when conducting cross-border data transfer activities to effectively prevent and respond to security risks, ensure data security, and avoid violations.

### *10.1.5 Overall Trend of China's Cross-Border Data Transfer Regulatory Regime*

This four-stage evolution reveals the policy shift from 'restriction-oriented' to 'promotion-oriented'. The new regulation explicitly foregrounds 'promotion' in its title and content, stating the goal to '*promote lawful, orderly, and free data transfer*' based on ensuring national security, public interests, and personal information protection.[19] It reflects the policy shift in China, optimizing the framework and signaling a clear directional transition—from a 'security-centered' approach to a 'balanced security and development' approach.

Furthermore, in terms of the enforcement mechanism, the 2024 Cross-border Provisions introduce a governance concept mainly based on 'mid-process and post-process supervision', promoting the transformation of the government's role from

[16] 2024 Cross-border Provisions, Article 7.

[17] 2024 Cross-border Provisions, Article 3 and Article 6.

[18] Cyberspace Data Security Management Regulation (网络数据安全管理条例) <https://www.gov.cn/zhengce/zhengceku/202409/content_6977767.htm> accessed 30 November 2025. Informal English Version: https://appinchina.co/government-documents/regulation-on-network-data-security-management/.

[19] 2024 Cross-border Provisions, Article 1.

an 'approver' to a 'rule-setter and supervisor'. Especially in the standard contract filing and certification process, the government no longer 'examines each item', but rather relies more on enterprises' compliance commitments, information disclosure, and post-process spot checks for dynamic supervision.

At the same time, the regulations also strengthen the credit mechanism and penalties for violations, forming a policy logic of 'lenient entry and strict management': increasing tolerance in the entry stage and intensifying punishment at the violation stage. This shift in regulatory strategy not only enhances the operational efficiency of the mechanism but also helps to cultivate enterprises' intrinsic compliance motivation, thereby achieving structural optimization of governance outcomes.

## 10.2 The Substantive Regime for Cross-Border Data Transfer

Unlike the EU's adequacy decision which relied heavily on the protection effect of the data-receiving jurisdiction's legal framework,[20] China imposed responsibility on domestic data exporters, and has adopted three main routes to regulate cross-border data transfer, that is data outbound security assessment, standard contract, and certification. The three routes are conferred with distinct legal effects. Data security assessment is mandatory for obtaining approval for cross-border data transfer with high risks of data security. Standard contract and certification functions as self-regulatory tools and are optional for those that do not fall into the specific list of data security assessment. Data exporters can choose either one based on their actual circumstances and legal regulations requirements.

### *10.2.1 Data Outbound Security Assessment*

The data outbound security assessment is a crucial compliance requirement in China's current cross-border data regulatory framework. Whether a data security assessment is requested depends on the legal identity of data processors and the nature of the data. According to the newly issued 2024 Cross-border Provisions and the 2025 *Guidelines on Submission of Security Assessment for Cross-Border Data Transfer,*[21] processors in two scenarios must acquire a permit from the CAC.

The first scenario involves processors that are regarded as CIIO. The legal subject of CIIO was first established under the CSL and later defined in the Critical

---

[20] Si 2021, p. 261.

[21] The CAC has released the 'Data Export Security Assessment Declaration Guidelines (Third Edition)' (国家互联网信息办公室发布《数据出境安全评估申报指南(第三版)》) <https://www.cac.gov.cn/2025-06/27/c_1752652339765002.htm> accessed 30 November 2025.

Information Infrastructure Security Protection Regulations issued by the State Council in 2021 as those operating '*information infrastructures that are in such important industries and fields as public communication and information services, energy, transport, water conservancy, finance, public services, e-government, defense science, technology and industry, as well as those that, in the event of damage, loss of function or data leakage, may seriously endanger national security, national welfare, the people's livelihood or the public interest.*'[22] When exporting data containing personal information or key data, a mandatory data security assessment is required before obtaining a permit. The other scenario involves non-CIIO data processors who export special categories of data including key data or sensitive personal information of more than 10,000 individuals or non-sensitive personal information of more than 100,000 individuals since January 1 of the current year.

The two scenarios may both involve key data. Key data is defined in Article 62(4) of the DSL as '*data in specific sectors, pertaining to specific groups or regions, or reaching a certain level of precision and scale, which, if tampered with, destroyed, leaked, illegally obtained, or illegally used, may directly endanger national security, economic operations, social stability, public health, and safety*'. Given the abstract definition, the standardization organizations have issued a list of key data in Data Classification and Grading Rules as a reference.[23]

The declaration process for the data outbound security assessment may be conducted online or offline. Non-CIIO data processors generally submit declarations through the 'Data Outbound Declaration System' operated by the CAC. Required materials—such as the unified social credit code certificate, identification documents of the legal representative and the responsible person, a power of attorney, the declaration form, relevant contracts, and a self-assessment risk report—must be prepared, and account registration, system configuration, and document uploading must be completed in accordance with platform requirements. For CIIOs and other cases where online declaration is unsuitable, an offline procedure applies, whereby materials are compiled and submitted to the provincial-level CAC, which forwards them to the national CAC.

Provincial-level CAC branches must review the completeness of materials and provide feedback within 5 business days. The CAC must decide whether to accept the application within 7 business days of receiving the declaration materials. Once accepted, the security assessment shall be completed within 45 business days. This period may be extended in complex circumstances or where supplementary materials are required. Results are notified in writing to the data processor, which may apply for a re-assessment within 15 business days. The result of the re-assessment is final.

[22] Critical Information Infrastructure Security Protection Regulations (关键信息基础设施安全保护条例) <https://www.gov.cn/gongbao/content/2021/content_5636138.htm> accessed 30 November 2025.

[23] GB/T 43697–2024 Data Security Technology—Rules for Data Classification and Grading (数据安全技术 数据分类分级规则) (2025) <https://openstd.samr.gov.cn/bzgk/gb/newGbInfo?hcno=F0C385EDC38CBF277AEC021F23126ADE> accessed 30 November 2025.

### 10.2.2 Standard Contract

Personal information processors may opt to legally carry out cross-border data transfer activities by signing and filing a standard contract for the cross-border transfer of personal information between data exporters and overseas recipients, when the following circumstances are met: (1) non-CIIO data processors cumulatively provide non-sensitive personal information of more than 100,000 but less than 1 million individuals to overseas recipients since January 1 of the current year; or (2) non-CIIO data processors cumulatively provide sensitive personal information of less than 10,000 individuals to overseas recipients since January 1 of the current year and do not fall under statutory exemptions.

However, according to the 2024 Cross-border Provisions, for personal information identified as key data, a security assessment must be conducted and the standard contract filing path alone is not permitted. The specific operational procedures are as follows: First, the personal information processor must conduct a Personal Information Protection Impact Assessment (PIPIA), which comprehensively covers: (a) risks associated with outbound transfers, and (b) corresponding mitigation measures. Then, a personal information outbound standard contract that complies with the CAC's standard contract template must be signed with the overseas recipient. Once the contract is signed, the personal information processor shall submit an online filing application through the 'Data Outbound Declaration System' provided by the CAC within 10 business days of the effective date of the contract.

Materials to be submitted for the filing application include the unified social credit code certificate, identity certificates of the legal representative and the person in charge, the power of attorney, the signed and sealed commitment letter, the standard contract text, and the PIPIA report. After submission, the filing process enters the material verification stage by the CAC at the provincial level, which must be completed within 15 business days. After the materials are reviewed and found to be complete, the CAC will issue a filing number to the applicant. If the materials are incomplete or need to be supplemented, the applicant must complete the supplementary submission within 10 business days; otherwise, the filing process will be terminated. Once the filing is successful, the personal information processor can lawfully conduct outbound personal information processing activities based on the filed standard contract.

Overall, this filing path effectively ensures compliance and risk control of cross-border transfers of personal information, promoting the safe and lawful transfer of data.

### 10.2.3 Personal Information Protection Certification

Personal information protection certification mechanism provides a compliance alternative for personal information processors that are of a relatively large scale yet do not meet the criteria of CIIOs. This enables them to fulfill data security and compliance requirements for cross-border data transfer. The applicable conditions mainly include the following aspects: not falling under any of the six exemption categories stipulated by law, not being a CIIO, the data being exported not falling under the category of key data; the cumulative number of individuals whose personal information has been provided to overseas recipients since January 1 of the current year exceeding 100,000 but less than 1 million; or the number of individuals whose sensitive personal information has been provided is less than 10,000.

The certification path and the standard contract filing path can be chosen concurrently. They differ significantly in terms of the following aspects. First, the certification mechanism allows both domestic and overseas processors to apply; the standard contract filing path is only available for domestic signatories. Second, the certificate is valid for 3 years, while the validity period of the standard contract is determined by the contract parties. Third, personal information processors shall file a record with the CAC at the provincial level where they are located within 10 business days of the effective date of the standard contract. Fourth, certification is conducted by officially approved professional certification bodies, while the standard contract filing requires review by the CAC at the provincial level. Fifth, certification bodies need to report significant impacts on rights and interests and accept spot checks by the Market Supervision and CAC, while the standard contract mechanism relies on the performance obligations of both parties and filing management.

The certification process is structured into several key stages. It commences with the certification application stage, where the applicant, after completing a self-assessment and confirming compliance, submits the required materials for the certification body to review in detail, determining whether to accept the application and confirm the certification plan. This is followed by the technical verification phase, in which the certification body commissions a specialized technical institution to perform tests and issue a corresponding verification report. An on-site review is then conducted by the certification body, leading to the issuance of an audit report. Based on all compiled review materials, the certification body evaluates and decides whether to approve and issue the certificate, with approved results reported to the national certification information platform. Throughout the three-year validity period, post-certification supervision is carried out to ensure ongoing compliance. For certificate extension or modification, relevant applications must be submitted and undergo necessary verification and review during the validity term. Finally, in cases of identified non-compliance, the certification body may suspend, cancel, or revoke the certificate and issue a public announcement.

Overall, the personal information protection certification system provides eligible personal information processors with a path to have their cross-border data transfer security and compliance verified by an authoritative third-party institution. This is particularly applicable to enterprises and organizations that aim to enhance their compliance credibility through a comprehensive and rigorous certification process.

### 10.2.4 Core Regulatory Features

From the regulatory structure explained above, three core regulatory features can be summarized.

First, full-process regulation of 'before, during, and after' led by the CAC. China's cross-border data transfer regulatory mechanism, with the CAC as the core regulatory body, has formed a three-in-one institutional mechanism covering 'pre-event review, in-event management, and post-event supervision'.

In the 'pre-event' stage, enterprises should select a compliance path according to data type, volume, and sensitivity, complete a PIPIA, and either submit a standard contract for filing, initiate a data outbound security assessment procedure, or apply for the corresponding certification mechanism. In the 'during-event' stage, enterprises need to establish a record-keeping mechanism for data outbound activities, including transmission content, time, recipient identification, encryption mechanisms, and records of abnormal situations. Meanwhile, some regions are piloting a 'Real-time Supervision Platform for Cross-border Data Transfer' to establish behavioral pattern recognition models for high-frequency activities and identify compliance risks. In the 'post-event' supervision stage, national and local CAC authorities will review enterprises that have submitted standard contracts based on a random inspection mechanism. According to Article 11 of the Measures for the Standard Contract, if data leakage occurs, the recipient violates contract terms, or data re-transfer is uncontrollable, the enterprise should activate the emergency response process and report to the CAC.

Second, coordinated governance between local CAC authorities and industry regulatory authorities. Within China's multi-level governance structure, local CAC offices play a key role in conducting initial reviews of standard contract filings, verifying submitted materials, forwarding documents for security assessments, and issuing filing numbers. Many local CAC offices have established 'cross-border data service windows', such as those in Shanghai, Shenzhen, and Hangzhou, which offer dual-track (online and offline) processing channels, enhancing compliance accessibility for enterprises. Sectoral regulators, such as the healthcare and financial sectors, also play an irreplaceable role in supervising specific types of data.

Third, a multi-level regulatory basis established by laws, regulations, standards, and guidelines. China's regulatory mechanism for cross-border data transfer has formed a multi-layered compliance structure based on laws and regulations, supported by technical standards, and supplemented by practical guidelines.

At the law level, the CSL imposes mandatory security assessments for data exports by CIIOs. The DSL establishes the principle of data classification and graded protection and grants the CAC comprehensive enforcement coordination functions. The PIPL establishes three lawful paths for cross-border transfer of personal information, namely conducting a security assessment, filing a standard contract, or applying for certification.

At the administrative regulation level, the Assessment Measures, the Measures for the Standard Contract, and the 2024 Cross-border Provisions constitute the core operational basis for cross-border data management. As mentioned earlier, especially the 2024 Cross-border Provisions provide clear boundary definitions for the cross-border data exemption mechanism, the implementation triggers of security assessment, and related pilot policies.

In terms of the standardization mechanisms, although GB/T 35273-2020 Information Security Technology-Personal Information Security Specification is a recommended standard rather than a mandatory one, it is commonly adopted as a key reference for evaluating the compliance of personal information processing activities. The standards applicable to the certification path include the Certification Specification V2.0, among others.

In addition, the CAC has issued various practical operation documents such as the Standard Contract Filing Guidelines, the Security Assessment Application Guidelines, the Guidelines on PIPIA Templates, the Negative List Sample (Pilot), providing enterprises with a clearer compliance roadmap. The state encourages industry associations and local cyberspace authorities to compile compliance operation manuals based on their own industry characteristics, thus building a three-tier compliance mechanism consisting of central guidance, local implementation, and industry standard adaptation.

In conclusion, this multi-tiered regulatory framework establishes a governance model that equally emphasizes both security and development. It effectively safeguards national security and data sovereignty while providing institutional assurance for the healthy growth of the digital economy. Through targeted, risk-tiered supervision, it has significantly lowered corporate compliance costs, offering a Chinese approach to global data governance that balances security and development.

## 10.3 Specific Compliance Requirements for Organizations in Cross-Border Data Transfer Practices

Cross-border transfers of personal information occupy an important position in China's data governance regime. China's regulations have constructed a multilayered compliance architecture that requires enterprises to conduct pre-transfer assessments, obtain separate and fully informed consent, implement technical and organizational safeguards, and maintain ongoing supervision throughout the data lifecycle. This part examines these core mechanisms in a systematic manner, clarifying their legal foundations, operational requirements, and regulatory logic, and offering a critical evaluation of their function within China's broader cross-border data governance model.

## *10.3.1 Implementing PIPIA*

Enterprises conducting cross-border transfers of personal information in China must complete a PIPIA before any data is exported, ensuring the legality, necessity, and security of all processing activities. They must issue formal assessment reports detailing data scope, transfer purposes, overseas recipient capabilities, rights-protection mechanisms, and emergency plans. These materials, along with corporate identity documents and signed agreements, must be submitted to the relevant authorities in the required formats and within strict timelines. Overall, this regulatory framework is comprehensive and highly structured, strengthening data protection but also imposing a compliance burden on enterprises, requiring careful planning, continuous updates, and substantial administrative capacity.

### 10.3.1.1 Conducting a Thorough Data Inventory Check

Generally speaking, the main contents of the standard contract are pre-set and compulsorily incorporated by the state. Public-law rights and obligations are fixed and standardized, restricting data exporters and importers, protecting third-party interests, and having dual attributes of public-law regulation and private-law autonomy. It is important for ensuring data security, protecting personal information rights, and promoting the orderly and legal flow of data.[24] According to the PIPL and related regulations, enterprises must conduct a PIPIA before cross-border data transfer, which is a legal compliance obligation to examine the legality of personal information processing, assess potential risks to individuals' rights, and ensure effective protection measures. As per Article 55 of the PIPL and Article 5 of the relevant Measures,[25] when providing personal information to overseas entities, enterprises must complete a PIPIA and prepare a formal report before data transfer.

The impact assessment of personal information protection (PIPIA) is a mandatory self-regulatory, pre-compliance, assessment and risk assessment procedure[26]. PIPIA mainly systematically assesses data export necessity, data types, transmission paths, recipient capabilities, data re-transfer control, and individual rights protection mechanisms. When conducting a PIPIA, the principles of legality, propriety, and necessity must be followed strictly, meaning personal information processing should have a clear legal purpose and proper methods limited to necessity. Enterprises should also adhere to the principles of transparency, security guarantee, responsibility, and minimum impact. In practice, enterprises should identify responsible parties, data formats, and transmission nodes at each stage, then use a

[24] Guangxi 2025, p. 108.

[25] 'The Measures on Standard Contracts for the Cross-Border Transfer of Personal Information' (个人信息出境标准合同办法) <https://www.moj.gov.cn/pub/sfbgw/flfggz/flfggzbmgz/202306/t20230620_481044.html> accessed 29 November 2025.

[26] Quan 2022, p. 39.

risk matrix evaluation model to classify risks as high, medium, or low and adopt effective prevention and mitigation measures for each level.

#### 10.3.1.2 Issuing the PIPIA Report and Providing Risk Control Recommendations

In August 2021, Article 38 of the PIPL introduced the standard contract for the cross-border transfer of personal information for the first time and made it one of the three major regulatory tools for cross-border data transfer, alongside security assessments and personal information protection certifications.[27] When an enterprise chooses to use standard contracts as the compliance route for cross-border transfers of personal information, it is necessary to issue a PIPIA report and a Data Export Risk Self-Assessment Report as part of the necessary preparatory work before filing. According to Article 7 of the Measures on Standard Contracts for the Cross-Border Transfer of Personal Information and the Guidelines for Standard Contract Filing for Cross-Border Transfer of Personal Information (Second Edition),[28] the PIPIA report must be completed within 3 months prior to the filing of the standard contract, and must ensure that no significant changes occur up to the filing date.

The PIPIA report should typically include the following core contents: (1) the scope, types, and volume of exported data, including whether sensitive personal information or biometric data are involved; (2) the purposes, methods, and legal basis of data processing activities; (3) basic information about the overseas recipients, their legal background, and data security capabilities; (4) the retention period, storage methods, and access control policies for data stored overseas; (5) mechanisms for protecting the rights of personal information subjects, including notification, consent, access, correction, and withdrawal; (6) early warning mechanisms and emergency response plans for potential security incidents; (7) whether the exported data may be further transferred, controls on such re-transfers, and allocation of responsibilities; and (8) a complete internal data security management mechanism, including access control, regular training programs, and the designation of a data protection officer.

The risk self-assessment report serves as an important supporting document for enterprises to demonstrate the comprehensive identification and control of risks in the data export process. It must include the following items: (1) an overview of the self-assessment process; (2) an overview of export activities, such as the basic profile of the data processor, including a brief introduction, information on the organizational structure and data security management institution, and overall business and data asset status; and (3) self-assessment results and conclusions of export

[27] Jingwu 2023, p. 78.

[28] 'The Guidelines for Standard Contract Filing for Cross-Border Transfer of Personal Information (Second Edition)' (个人信息出境标准合同备案指南(第二版)) <https://www.tjcac.gov.cn/wsfw/sjkj/grxxcjbzht/202408/t20240823_6705573.html> accessed 29 November 2025.

activities. To enhance compliance transparency and public trust, enterprises should establish mechanisms to update risk assessments and remediation reports, promptly reassessing and revising reports when there are significant changes in data transfer scale, scenarios, recipients, or legal environments. Additionally, enterprises are encouraged to proactively disclose parts of their assessment results and risk mitigation measures, under the premise of protecting trade secrets and information security, to accept social supervision.

This approach enhances the transparency and credibility of corporate data governance and contributes to the development of an accountable data export compliance mechanism.

#### 10.3.1.3 Submitting Application to the Competent Authorities

According to the requirements of the Assessment Measures, the Measures on Standard Contracts for the Cross-Border Transfer of Personal Information, and their supporting guidelines, enterprises must complete the PIPIA and issue its report before the data is officially transferred abroad. The PIPIA report is not only the fundamental risk control document for the enterprise itself but also an important document that must be submitted when applying for a security assessment or filing a standard contract with the competent authority.

First, enterprises should prepare entity identity and authorization information, which should include a stamped copy of the Unified Social Credit Code certificate. Moreover, identity documents for the legal representative and the responsible person are also necessary. In addition, they should prepare a written commitment from the data processor, which confirms the authenticity and compliance of the submitted materials.

Second, enterprises must submit a formally prepared PIPIA report, detailing the purpose, category, and scope of the exported data, as well as technical and organizational measures, potential risk assessments, and remediation suggestions. If the standard contract filing path is applied, the signed standard contract for cross-border transfer of personal information must be attached, along with any supplemental agreements or data protection addendum (DPA). If the security assessment path is chosen, an additional Data Export Security Assessment Declaration Form must be completed according to the template issued by the CAC and submitted simultaneously.

In terms of submission time, according to the Civil Code of the PRC and relevant legal requirements, enterprises must file declarations within 10 working days after the contract takes effect. The submitted PIPIA report should be prepared within 3 months before the filing date for timeliness and accuracy. If the security assessment path is applicable, all assessment materials must be submitted at least 45 working days in advance. During the assessment, the Guidelines on Submission of

Security Assessment for Cross-border Data Transfer (Third Edition)[29] require the CAC at the provincial level to complete the review of the completeness of the materials and provide feedback within 5 working days. For those that pass the check, the CAC at the provincial level will submit the declaration materials to the CAC; for those failing, the CAC at the provincial level will inform the data processor of the reasons. The CAC will determine whether to accept the application and notify the data processor in writing within 7 working days after receiving materials from the CAC at the provincial level. According to Article 12 of the Assessment Measures, the CAC will complete the security assessment within 45 working days after sending the written acceptance notice, and the period may be extended under special circumstances. Therefore, relevant enterprises should start project assessment and materials preparation in advance to avoid transfer delays due to extended review cycles.

### *10.3.2 Ongoing Compliance Review by Overseas Recipients*

This section explains the technical and organizational safeguards required for compliant cross-border data transfers, including thorough due diligence on overseas recipients' security capabilities, strict controls on onward transfers, and the establishment of a continuous supervision mechanism across the entire data lifecycle. After transfer, ongoing oversight—such as regular compliance reports, scheduled audits, anomaly detection, suspension mechanisms, and long-term archival—is essential to ensure sustained protection. This framework imposes multilayered controls that significantly strengthen cross-border data governance but also demands substantial technical capacity, contractual precision, and long-term monitoring resources from enterprises.

#### 10.3.2.1 Comprehensive Assessment in Line with Technical Safeguards and Organizational Measures

Before initiating cross-border transfers, data processors must conduct a comprehensive due diligence assessment of overseas recipients to ensure they have adequate technical and organizational data-protection capabilities. Specific review components include: (1) data encryption and transmission mechanisms such as TLS, HTTPS, and VPNs; (2) data storage and access control mechanisms such as audit logging and role-based controls; (3) data isolation measures like secure zones or data sandboxes; (4) incident response infrastructure including a 24/7 breach notification mechanism and emergency response teams; (5) security governance

[29] 'The Guidelines on Submission of Security Assessment for Cross-border Data Transfers (Third Edition)' (数据出境安全评估申报指南(第三版)) <https://www.cac.gov.cn/2025-06/27/c_1752652339765002.htm> accessed 29 November 2025.

structures, such as a DPO and the implementation of ISO/IEC 27001; and (6) training programs and staff awareness for data protection and regulatory compliance.

To support a systematic evaluation, enterprises are encouraged to establish a scoring model for assessing recipients' data protection capabilities. Based on the scoring outcome, enterprises should determine whether the recipients are qualified to receive personal information from China. The overseas entity must also sign a compliance undertaking, making written commitments regarding their technical capability, organizational safeguards, and legal obligations.

#### 10.3.2.2 Continuous Control over Subsequent Data Transfers and Ensuring Sustainability Throughout the Data Lifecycle

To prevent unauthorized onward transfers by overseas recipients, enterprises must implement an onward transfer control mechanism and a closed-loop accountability mechanism. Key contract clauses should specify: (1) the overseas recipient is prohibited from transferring data without the original data exporter's written consent; (2) if such a transfer is necessary, details of the new recipient, its use of the data, and the security measures should be provided and prior approval obtained; (3) the onward recipient must follow the same obligations and have equivalent data protection responsibilities; (4) the original recipient bears full legal liability for transfer-related breaches. Meanwhile, it is recommended to deploy an intelligent data transmission monitoring platform. This should use measures like audit logs, IP control, and usage records to track data transfer and conduct real-time surveillance to prevent unauthorized transfers. However, these safeguards increase operational complexity and may pose challenges to multinational enterprises relying on flexible data transfer.

#### 10.3.2.3 Establishment and Implementation of a 'Continuous Supervision' Mechanism

Completion of a data transfer does not signify the end of supervision but rather the initiation of a continuous review mechanism. Enterprises should clearly stipulate detailed supervision terms in the contract, and in accordance with the Provisions on the Scope of Archiving Enterprise Document Materials and the Preservation Period of Archives,[30] keep all reports, letters, and system records for at least 10 years for random checks.

In addition, enterprises are encouraged to utilize advanced technical platforms that provide visual dashboards of recipients' access frequency, data usage trends, and anomaly logs. These mechanisms should also feature alert modules for

[30] The Scope of Archiving Enterprise Document Materials and the Preservation Period of Archives (企业文件材料归档范围和档案保管期限规定) (2012) <https://www.gov.cn/gongbao/content/2013/content_2361577.htm> accessed 29 November 2025.

sensitive field access, thereby enhancing proactive governance of cross-border data transfer.

The incorporation of technical monitoring tools further signals a shift toward proactive, data-driven oversight rather than reliance on post-incident enforcement. Yet these requirements also impose administrative and technical burdens on enterprises, particularly in coordinating audits across jurisdictions and maintaining long-term documentation. As a result, while the mechanism significantly strengthens transparency and traceability, its practical success hinges on enterprises' capacity to operationalize these obligations in a sustainable and coherent manner.

### *10.3.3 Obtaining Separate Consent from Personal Information Subjects*

In China's cross-border data transfer regime, obtaining the separate consent of personal information subjects is a fundamental prerequisite and core mechanism for protecting individual rights and mitigating risks associated with data exports. According to Articles 13 and 39 of the PIPL, enterprises must fulfill their legal obligation to inform data subjects and obtain their explicit authorization specifically for this matter before transferring personal information abroad, ensuring that 'informed consent' is genuine, specific, and verifiable. The following three aspects constitute the core compliance requirements of the separate consent mechanism.

While this consent-centered model strengthens user autonomy and transparency, it also places a heavy procedural burden on enterprises, because it requires meticulous disclosure, precise documentation, and continuous coordination with overseas recipients. The regime is protective, but its effectiveness ultimately depends on whether enterprises can operationalize these requirements without compromising user experience or business efficiency.

#### 10.3.3.1 The Legal and Valid Form

According to Article 14 of the PIPL, the processing of personal information must be based on the premise of 'informed and voluntary consent'. In particular, when handling personal information for cross-border purposes, 'separate consent' or other legally binding authorization bases should be obtained. The Measures for the Certification of Personal Information Protection for Cross-border Transfer of Personal Information (Draft for Comment)[31] (the Certification Measures (Draft)) further require that, if the certification path is adopted, enterprises shall provide

[31] 'The Measures for the Certification of Personal Information Protection for Cross-border Transfer of Personal Information (Draft for Comments)' (2025) (个人信息出境个人信息保护认证办法(征求意见稿)) <https://www.cac.gov.cn/2025-01/03/c_1737600915141373.htm> accessed 29 November 2025.

clear justification for the legality of cross-border activities. The legally valid forms of obtaining personal consent mainly include written and electronic forms.

It is noteworthy that in recruitment scenarios, when enterprises collect candidates' résumé information, the employment relationship has generally not yet been established, and thus Paragraph 2 of Article 13 of the PIPL (human resource management) cannot be used as the legal basis. In such cases, data processing must strictly rely on the first item 'obtaining personal consent', and candidates must provide informed consent before any cross-border data transfer can occur.

#### 10.3.3.2 Information Disclosure

Before obtaining valid separate consent, enterprises must fulfill comprehensive information disclosure obligations to personal information subjects. Based on relevant regulations, enterprises should at least clearly disclose five categories of information to personal information subjects: (1) the purpose of cross-border transfer, explaining data export business scenarios; (2) the types and scope of data, listing transferred data items and whether sensitive information is involved; (3) information about data recipients, including name, address, etc.; (4) storage duration and processing methods; (5) security risk information. The disclosure should be clear, prominent, and easy to understand, and should be adapted to different scenarios and user characteristics. For the elderly, minors, or individuals with cognitive impairments, enterprises should provide auxiliary prompting mechanisms to ensure informed consent decisions.

This disclosure framework reflects a regulatory commitment to ensuring that consent is both substantively meaningful and procedurally fair. By requiring enterprises to articulate the purpose, scope, recipients, retention period, and risks associated with cross-border transfers, the regime shifts consent away from a formalistic checkbox exercise toward a genuinely informed decision-making process. At the same time, the obligation to adapt disclosures to vulnerable groups underscores a rights-based orientation. However, the prescriptive nature of these requirements also increases compliance complexity for enterprises, raising questions about whether the high level of granularity may inadvertently lead to information fatigue or reduce user comprehension.

#### 10.3.3.3 Consent Withdrawal Mechanism

During the process of cross-border data handling, personal information subjects should continuously retain the right to withdraw their authorization. Enterprises must establish a convenient and efficient withdrawal mechanism to ensure that data subjects can revoke their consent at any time without affecting their fundamental usage rights. The withdrawal mechanism should include the following elements: clear channels, a convenient process, response handling, and subsequent obligations.

However, the practical implementation of these obligations, especially the requirement that foreign recipients promptly halt processing and permanently delete data, poses significant challenges in jurisdictions with weaker enforcement or divergent data protection standards.

## 10.4 Contextual Adjustments for Cross-Border Data Transfers

Based on the general rules for cross-border data transfer, China has established more stringent or flexible regulatory mechanisms for specific entities, specific types of data, and specific regions, in order to achieve the governance goal of 'orderly flow and classified measures'. This section conducts an in-depth analysis of the restrictions on the outbound transfer of data by CIIOs and key data, as well as the innovative explorations of the data outbound transfer mechanism within free trade zones.

### *10.4.1 Data Transfer Involving CIIOs, Key Data, or Other Special Types*

#### 10.4.1.1 Burden of Proof for Meeting the 'Necessity for Outbound Data Transfer' Requirement

In China's data export regulatory framework, CIIOs and processing activities involving key data or other special types of data are subject to differentiated and hierarchical regulatory requirements. According to Article 40 of the PIPL, the Assessment Measures, and the Network Data Security Regulations, CIIOs must first meet the prerequisite condition of 'necessity of cross-border transfer' and pass the data export security assessment organized by the CAC before transferring key data or personal information overseas. This requirement reflects the state's highly prudent regulatory stance toward activities that may endanger national security or public interests, or infringe upon citizens' personal rights and interests, through cross-border data transfers involving special entities.

The 'necessity of cross-border transfer' is both a legal compliance threshold and a burden of proof that enterprises must bear. In scenarios where CIIOs transfer data abroad, enterprises are obligated to conduct a comprehensive evaluation of the necessity of cross-border data transfer and submit sufficient supporting evidence.

#### 10.4.1.2 Basis for Application of Industry/Region-Specific 'Key Data Catalogs'

Within China's data security management mechanism, the 'key data catalogs' issued by industry and regional authorities generally follow an overarching approach of 'national guidance plus local refinement'. At the national level, the DSL and supporting standards such as GB/T 43697-2024 Data Security Technology—Rules for Data Classification and Grading (Data Classification and Grading Rules) clearly specify the judgment criteria, offering a unified top-level framework for local and industry regulators to develop their specific catalogs. In practice, local or industry authorities typically combine regional characteristics or industry attributes with national standards to further refine these catalogs, progressively forming targeted lists through a process of 'top-level design followed by grassroots feedback'.

Regarding data classification and grading, regions and industries commonly adhere to principles such as 'being scientific and practical, clear boundaries, the strictest standards prevailing, combination of focused and broad scopes, and dynamic updating'. Classification is usually based on industry attributes (such as energy, telecommunications, transportation, etc.) and the type and processing stage of the data itself; the grading work mainly depends on the potential harm that data leakage, tampering, and abuse may cause to national security, economic operations, social order, and public interests. Data are divided into multiple levels such as general data and key data, which are subject to different regulatory measures over the flow of data.

At the local level, governments formulate 'key data catalogs' tailored to local economic structures, industrial foundations, and social governance needs. For example, some free trade zones, high-tech parks, and high-risk industry clusters designate specific business data as 'key data' to ensure that data security progresses in tandem with regional governance.

To ensure the scientific validity and timeliness of these catalogs, industries and localities have established dynamic adjustment mechanisms. On one hand, continuous monitoring of changes in data attributes is conducted via enterprise reporting and regulatory inspections; on the other hand, guidelines and catalogs are periodically revised, especially when significant policy, technological, or business changes occur. Industry regulators have also implemented mechanisms such as 'routine notifications', 'catalog consultation' and 'key data review', integrating key data catalogs into the full lifecycle of risk assessment and outbound data management.

#### 10.4.1.3 Post-outbound Data Processing Restrictions and Regulatory Traceability

China is building a comprehensive regulatory mechanism for cross-border data transfer, which includes three stages: pre-assessment, mid-process control, and post-tracing, to ensure the security and compliance of cross-border data transfer, reflecting the nation's strong emphasis on data sovereignty and controllability.[32]

[32] This content is provided for by the Data Security Law, and the Cybersecurity Law, the 2024 Cross-border Provisions, and the Assessment Measures.

Before data is exported, key data and large amounts of personal information (including sensitive personal information) need to pass through security assessments or personal information protection certifications to obtain compliance approval. However, what is more noteworthy is that after data is exported, Chinese regulatory authorities are increasingly strengthening control over the entire data usage process.

To ensure that outbound data is not misused or circulated illegally, overseas data recipients are required to cooperate by retaining auditable materials such as server access logs and system audit records, ensuring technical traceability throughout data processing. At the end of the data lifecycle, some industry regulations (such as those for human genetic resources, finance, and telecommunications) also require the recipient to provide a 'data destruction certificate' or 'irreversible proof' to achieve closed-loop data management and prevent secondary use or illegal retention.

In terms of post-event supervision, related enterprises may be required to regularly submit semi-annual or annual reports to regulatory authorities detailing data usage, permission changes, incidents, and risk management measures.[33] Furthermore, based on enforcement powers granted under the DSL, the CSL, the PIPL, and other relevant laws and regulations, regulators may conduct on-site inspections,[34] remote evidence collection,[35] and cross-border investigations[36] to ensure effective supervision and deterrence.

Overall, this regulatory framework not only strengthens the data security safeguards but also encourages enterprises to build more transparent, compliant, and resilient cross-border data governance capabilities, adapting to the global trend of data compliance and governance.

### *10.4.2 Innovative Measures in Pilot Projects and Free Trade Zones*

#### 10.4.2.1 Institutional Differentiation Explored in Pilot Free Trade Zones

To promote institutional optimization and pilot reforms in cross-border data governance, China has established multiple Free Trade Pilot Zones (FTZs) in cities such as Beijing, Shanghai, Shenzhen, and Hainan, exploring differentiated management mechanisms for cross-border data transfer. These zones are piloting different

[33] Data Security Law, Article 29 & Article 30.

The Measures for the Reporting of National Cybersecurity Incidents, Article 8 (国家网络安全事件报告管理办法) <https://www.cac.gov.cn/2025-09/15/c_1759583017563621.htm> accessed 30 November 2025.

[34] Personal Information Protection Law, Article 63; Cyberspace Data Security Management Regulation, Article 50.

[35] The Measures for the Administrative Law Enforcement Procedures of Cyberspace Administration Departments, Article 30 (网信部门行政执法程序规定) <https://www.gov.cn/gongbao/2023/issue_10506/202306/content_6885255.html> accessed 30 November 2025.

[36] Personal Information Protection Law, Article 41.

management methods and innovating regulatory frameworks, standards, and compliance procedures.

In February 2024, the Shanghai Lingang New Area piloted the Measures for Classified and Graded Management of Cross-Border Data Fransfers (Trial), categorizing cross-border data into three levels: core data, key data, and general data. The regulation explicitly prohibits the export of core data, requires security assessments for key data, and allows general data to be freely transmitted after filing. The Lingang Area also enhanced compliance convenience by establishing a Cross-Border Data Service Center and compiling positive lists, such as data field catalogs for key industries like intelligent connected vehicles and biomedicine.

Following the practice of Shanghai, the Tianjin FTZ also took similar measures during the same period, dividing data into 13 major categories and 40 subcategories, with the three-level security grading system: core, key, and general.[37] Based on the above classification, Tianjin enacted its first negative list for data export in May 2024, clearly specifying data items subject to outbound data management procedures, while exempting data outside the list for streamlined handling.

Specifically targeting the automotive industry, the Negative Lists for Data Export in Beijing FTZ entail the categories and subcategories of data that require a data outbound security assessment, such as geographic information, personnel flow, and vehicle flow related to military management areas, defense science and technology industrial units, and county-level or above Party and government organs and other important sensitive areas. These measures aim to precisely identify critical data and ensure the security and compliance of data outbound through cross-departmental collaborative supervision.

While all FTZs in China operate under a unified legal framework, each pilot zone implements differentiated practices based on local needs. Shanghai Lingang Area emphasizes a 'positive list, filing facilitation, and service center' model; Tianjin focuses on 'standards and negative list' management; Beijing highlights industry-specific 'sector list' administration. These institutional explorations contribute to building a more scientific and flexible compliance ecosystem for cross-border data transfer and advance China's systemic opening-up. As of August 2025, seven regions including Tianjin, Beijing, etc. have released negative lists for cross-border data transfer in their pilot free trade zones,[38] covering various sectors, thereby

[37] The Enterprise Data Classification and Grading Standards and Specifications of China (Tianjin) Free Trade Pilot Zone issued by the Tianjin FTZ Authority in February 2024.

[38] Tianjin Issued the First Cross-Border Data Transfer Negative List in China (Tianjin CAC, 9 May 2024); Beijing Issued a Negative List for Data Export (Beijing CAC, 30 August 2024); Hainan Released the Negative List for Cross-Border Data Transfer in the Free Trade Port (Hainan CAC, 20 February 2025); Shanghai Lingang New Area Issued the First Negative List for Data Cross-Border Transfer (Shanghai CAC, 8 February 2025); Zhejiang Issued the First Provincial Negative List for Cross-Border Data Transfer (Zhejiang CAC, 10 April 2025); Guangxi Released the Negative List for Cross-Border Data Transfer in the Pilot Free Trade Zone (Guangxi FTZ, 8 August 2025); Jiangsu Issued the Negative List for Cross-Border Data Transfer in the Pilot Free Trade Zone (Jiangsu CAC, 13 August 2025).

promoting the lawful, orderly, and free flow of data within the free trade zones as per regional regulatory frameworks.

#### 10.4.2.2 Simplified Governance Through the 'Negative List and Exemption Registration' Model

By adopting a 'negative list and exemption registration' model and implementing a risk-oriented hierarchical, and classified management system, data on the list must go through security assessment as required. Meanwhile, for data not included in the sensitive data catalog or key data catalog, enterprises may obtain exemption from filing requirements by submitting a brief declaration covering data categories, transfer purposes, and technical control measures. By reducing redundant approval procedures and alleviating compliance burdens on businesses, both security and efficiency in cross-border data transfers are expected to be realized.

In pilot zones, the negative list primarily encompasses sensitive categories such as financial transaction data, medical imaging and treatment records, government information project data, and population biometric data, which are restricted to transfer. On the contrary, data in emerging industries, including artificial intelligence, cloud computing, and cross-border e-commerce, are considered low risk. To transfer data such as AI training models, user browsing behavior logs, and supply chain monitoring data, enterprises need only submit a standardized Export Activity Description form to the local regulatory platform for exemption from additional approval procedures.

The practice of 'negative list and exemption registration' in FTZs has not only provided a realistic method for cross-border data transfer for most enterprises in China, enhancing transparency and adaptability, and also is expected to accumulate experience for the national legislation in the future.

### *10.4.3 International Cooperation for Cross-Border Data Transfer in China*

#### 10.4.3.1 Progress in Adequacy Recognition with the EU, Japan, and South Korea

The 'adequacy decision' concept, originating from the European Union, refers to the assessment by the European Commission under Article 45 of the General Data Protection Regulation. It evaluates the legislative frameworks, enforcement mechanisms, institutional capacities of data protection authorities, and participation in international or multilateral agreements on personal data protection in third countries. Due to differences in legal and regulatory mechanisms and concerns about data sovereignty and security, China and the EU have not yet aligned on the sufficient level of data protection necessary for an adequacy decision, despite high-level meetings held in recent years. Meanwhile, as Japan and South Korea have both received adequacy decisions from the EU, dialogues and meetings between China and Japan and South Korea on data governance collaboration have become increasingly frequent and substantive.

Although there are institutional differences and security concerns, ongoing policy communication and regulatory alignment demonstrate positive signs for international data governance, which also help establish legal frameworks for cross-border data transfers and contribute to the development of the digital economy.

#### 10.4.3.2 Alignment with Regional Collaborative Frameworks

As one of the important players in international trade and investment, China has been a member of the Asia-Pacific Economic Cooperation (APEC) and the Regional Comprehensive Economic Partnership (RCEP).

In advancing the institutional framework for cross-border data transfers, China has progressively enhanced its alignment with regional data governance mechanisms under APEC and RCEP.

The APEC Cross-Border Privacy Rules (CBPR) and the Cross-Border Privacy Enforcement Arrangement (CPEA) have set out a framework for international data governance within the region, in which China plays an important role in contributing to and promoting the harmonization of data transfer. Under the RCEP, China strongly supports the implementation of the E-Commerce chapter, particularly the provisions on ensuring the free flow of data while maintaining robust privacy protections. Through harmonization with CBPR and RCEP standards, China's cross-border data governance has demonstrated progressive improvements across multiple dimensions, including privacy protection, mutual recognition of regulatory standards, and cross-border regulatory cooperation. This alignment not only reduces corporate compliance burdens but also enhances the predictability and regulatory certainty of international data transfer.

#### 10.4.3.3 Strategic Outlook on China's Cross-Border Data Transfer and Its Role in Global Digital Governance

From a national strategic perspective, China's cross-border data transfer policies are progressively advancing toward higher-level openness and deeper integration into the global digital ecosystem.[39] These policies are characterized by three distinctive features: (1) prioritization of data security; (2) coordination between domestic and international institutional frameworks; and (3) the proactive export of digital governance norms.

[39] Yanqing 2024, pp. 201–212.

First and foremost, data security constitutes the primary concern in the design of the legal framework for cross-border data transfer in China, and all mechanisms governing cross-border data transfers are established upon the essential principle of safeguarding national information assets and personal privacy. Under this doctrine, continuous efforts are being made to refine risk assessment frameworks, strengthen dynamic oversight, and enhance early-warning mechanisms for data-related risks.

Secondly, China is progressively aligning the domestic legal architecture with the needs of international data transfer, centering its framework on the PIPL wile engaging with international regulatory systems. By promoting technical standards, sharing regulatory experiences, and fostering trust through collaborative platforms, China has actively advanced multilateral cooperation in data governance. Initiatives such as the Global Data Security Initiative exemplify China's commitment to fostering a fair and balanced global digital governance mechanism.

Lastly, under the Belt and Road Initiative's digital economy component, China is accelerating the "Digital Silk Road" development. By signing bilateral memoranda of understanding (MOUs) and establishing e-commerce cooperation frameworks with multiple countries, China is exploring cross-border data corridors and specialized data zones. These efforts aim to make China a key regulatory hub with regional influence in the Asia-Pacific.[40] In multilateral settings, China has proposed the Global Data Security Initiative and the Global AI Governance Initiative, advocating a multipolar governance model respecting national sovereignty and technological neutrality. Through these efforts, China aims to strengthen its digital economy, contribute to international rule-making, and shape a balanced model integrating security, openness, and sustainable development.

## References

Zhao, Jingwu, 'The Construction Basis and Regulatory Transformation of Standardised Contracts in Cross-Border Data Transmission' (数据跨境传输中标准化合同的构建基础与监管转型) (2022) 40 Faxue Kexue (Journal of Northwest University of Political Science and Law) (法律科学(西北政法大学学报)) 148.

Guo, Shuai and Li, Xiang, 'Cross-border data transfer in China: Shifting from restriction to relaxation?' (2025) 56 Computer Law & Security Review 1.

Chen, Si, 'Research on Data Sovereignty Rules in Cross-border Data Transfer and Chinese Solution' (2021) 18 US-China Law Review 261.

Wei, Guangxi, 'Standard Contract for the Outbound Transfer of Personal Information from the Perspective of Integration of Public and Private Law' (迈向公私法融合的个人信息出境标准合同) (2025) 43 Hebei Law Science (河北法学) 108.

Liu, Quan, 'Impact Assessment of Personal Information Protection: Focusing on Articles 55 and 56 of Personal Information Protection Act' (论个人信息保护影响评估——以《个人信息保护法》第55、56条为中心) (2022) 30 Journal of SJTU (Philosophy and Social Sciences) (上海交通大学学报(哲学社会科学版)) 39.

[40] Erie and Streinz 2021, pp. 3–92.

Zhao, Jingwu, 'On the Systematization of Data Cross-border Assessment, Contracts and Authentication Rules' (论数据出境评估、合同与认证规则的体系化) (2023) Administrative Law Review (行政法学研究) 78.

Hong, Yanqing, 'The "Rebalancing" of China's Data Export Security Management System: From the Perspective of International Data Competition Strategy' (中国数据出境安全管理制度的"再平衡"——基于国家间数据竞争战略的视角) (2024) China Law Review (中国法律评论) 201–212.

Erie, Matthew S and Streinz, Thomas, 'The Beijing Effect: China's Digital Silk Road as Transnational Data Governance' (2021) 54(1) New York University Journal of International Law and Politics 3–92.

# Chapter 11
# The Transfer of Personal Data Between EU and Japan: Protection of Taxpayers' Rights Concerns

**Satoe Takahashi**

## 11.1 Introduction

States and international organizations have combat cross-border tax avoidance and evasion in various ways. The tax information exchange system has played a role in these responses. The EU also works beyond the framework of a single country to tackle tax avoidance and evasion. The EU has repeatedly amended its Directive as regards mandatory automatic exchange of information in the field of taxation, particularly since 2014, which led to the OECD Action plan on Base Erosion and Profit Shifting (BEPS).[1]

In 2018, the EU enacted the General Data Protection Regulation (GDPR),[2] which stipulates the right to the protection of personal data. As stated in the EU Treaty, fundamental rights must be respected. Fundamental rights, including the protection

An earlier version of this article was published in Japanese as: 髙橋里枝, "租税に関するデータ移転とデータ保護　－EU　における税務執行共助指令とデータ保護法制を素材として－　," Hogaku Kenkyu, Vol.98, No. 1 (2025), pp. 301–317. This English version has been revised and is published with permission of the publisher. This chapter was supported by the Zengin Foundation for Studies on Economics and Finance (2128). The author gratefully acknowledges the Foundation's generous support, which made this research possible. The author declares that there are no conflicts of interest relevant to this study.

[1] OECD 2013.

[2] Regulation (EU) 2016/679 of the European Parliament and of the Council of 27 April 2016 on the protection of natural persons with regard to the processing of personal data and on the free movement of such data, and repealing Directive 95/46/EC (General Data Protection Regulation), [2016] OJ L 119, pp. 1–88.

S. Takahashi (✉)
Musashino University, Tokyo, Japan
e-mail: s-taka@musashino-u.ac.jp



H. Miyashita et al. (eds.), *The Evolution of Data Protection Laws in China, Japan, and Korea*, https://doi.org/10.1007/978-981-95-8609-7_11

of personal data, are provided for in Article 16 of the Treaty on the Functioning of the European Union (TFEU) and Article 8 of the Charter of Fundamental Rights of the European Union (Charter). The GDPR is a set of EU legislation that embodies the right to personal data protection set forth in TFEU and Charter. The Court of Justice of the European Union has demonstrated a high level of protection for personal data in cases.[3] While EU data protection norms must be consistently applied, the GDPR appears insufficient for tax-related data protection.[4] This is because the reservation clause in Article 23 of the GDPR is believed to limit the protection of date subjects, namely taxpayers' rights set forth in the GDPR for the purpose of preventing tax evasion and avoidance.

Personal data collected around the world is actively exchanged under tax treaties. Automatic information exchange systems have led to the collection and transfer of large amounts of data indiscriminately. On the one hand, this may be infringing on taxpayers' right to the protection of their personal data, on the other hand, this can be useful in identifying cases where there is a high risk of tax evasion and avoidance. The Data Protection Working Party,[5] established under Article 29 of the Data Protection Directive,[6] which was repealed by the enactment of the GDPR, has expressed concerns in its document[7] that the rights to data protection may be undermined in the case of automatic information exchange.

This article discusses the relationship between data transfer under the tax information exchange system and data protection norms.

## 11.2 EU Data Protection Legislation in Taxation

### *11.2.1 Primary Law*

Article 6 of the EU Treaty, which guarantees fundamental rights, provides that the Charter has the same legal standing as the EU Treaty and TFEU. Article 6 of the EU Treaty provides recognizing the rights, freedoms, and principles set forth therein (paragraph 1); the EU has acceded to the European Convention on Human Rights (paragraph 2); the fundamental rights guaranteed by the European Convention on Human Rights and those derived from the common constitutional traditions of

[3] See e.g. Joined Cases C-293/12 and C-594/12 Digital Rights Ireland and Seitlinger and Others, EU:C:2014:238; Case C-203/15 Tele2 Sverige AB, ECLI:EU:C:2016:970.

[4] See also, Kokot and Pistone 2022, pp. 393–395.

[5] It was abolished in May 2018 upon the entry into force of the GDPR. Its successor, the European Data Protection Board, was subsequently established.

[6] Directive 95/46/EC of the European Parliament and of the Council of 24 October 1995 on the protection of individuals with regard to the processing of personal data and on the free movement of such data, [1995] OJ L 281, pp. 31–50.

[7] Article 29 Data Protection Working Party, Statement of the WP29 on automatic inter-state exchanges of personal data for tax purposes, WP230 (2015).

Member States constitute general principles of EU law (paragraph 3). According to the precedents of the Court of Justice of the European Union, the European Convention on Human Rights is only respected as a general principle of law when considering the scope of fundamental rights.[8] Furthermore, respect for fundamental rights derived from the constitutions of Member States also constitutes a general principle of law.[9] Article 8 of the Charter provides for the protection of personal data.[10] Article 52 provides that any restrictions on the protection of rights must be in accordance with the principle of proportionality.

### *11.2.2 Secondary Law*

The GDPR is EU legislation related to data protection. When the GDPR was enacted, its predecessor, the Data Protection Directive (issued in 1995), was repealed. In 2012, the EU Commission proposed the GDPR, stating that 'technological advances and globalization have significantly changed the way data is collected, accessed, and used. Furthermore, member states have implemented the Data Protection Directive in different ways, resulting in variations in legal systems and their implementation among member states'.[11]

The provisions related to the tax field are as follows:

| | |
|---|---|
| Article 5 | Principles relating to processing of personal data |
| Article 12–22 (Chapter III) | Rights of the data subject |
| Article 23 | Restrictions |
| Article 34 | Communication of a personal data breach to the data subject |

Article 5, paragraph 1 of the GDPR sets out principles (a)–(f) regarding the processing of personal data.

(a) lawfulness, fairness and transparency
(b) purpose limitation
(c) data minimisation
(d) accuracy
(e) storage limitation
(f) integrity and confidentiality

---

[8] Case C-465/07 Elgafaji [2009] ECR I-921, para. 28; Case C-571/10 Servet Kamberaj [2012] ECLI:EU:C:2012:233, paras, 62, 63.

[9] Case C-11/70 Internationale Handelsgesellschaft, ECLI:EU:C:1970:114, para. 4.

[10] Article 8 of the Charter; Protection of personal data

1. Everyone has the right to the protection of personal data concerning him or her.

2. Such data must be processed fairly for specified purposes and on the basis of the consent of the person concerned or some other legitimate basis laid down by law. Everyone has the right of access to data which has been collected concerning him or her, and the right to have it rectified.

3. Compliance with these rules shall be subject to control by an independent authority.

[11] European Commission, Commission proposes a comprehensive reform of data protection rules to increase users' control of their data and to cut costs for businesses, Press Release (2012).

Article 23, paragraph 1 of the GDPR provides the circumstances in which the rights of data subjects guaranteed by the GDPR are reserved and the requirements for such reservation.

Union or Member State law to which the data controller or processor is subject may restrict by way of a legislative measure the scope of the obligations and rights provided for in Articles 12–22 and Article 34, as well as Article 5 in so far as its provisions correspond to the rights and obligations provided for in Articles 12–22, when such a restriction respects the essence of the fundamental rights and freedoms and is a *necessary and proportionate* measure in a democratic society to safeguard (emphasis added by the author):

> (e) other important objectives of general public interest of the Union or of a Member State, in particular an important economic or financial interest of the Union or of a Member State, including monetary, budgetary and taxation a matters, public health and social security;

According to Article 23, paragraph 1 of the GDPR, the rights granted to data subjects are limited when 'necessity and proportionality' are met and there are 'tax issues.'

## 11.3 The Conflict Between Automatic Information Directive (DAC) and Data Protection Legislation (GDPR)

### *11.3.1 Relationship Between DAC and GDPR*

The first EU legislation providing for the exchange of information regarding direct taxes, the Council Directive on Mutual Assistance by the Competent Authorities of the Member States in the Field of Direct Taxation, was enacted in 1977.[12] This Directive was repealed in 2011, and the Directive (commonly known as DAC 1),[13] which is the basis for the current Exchange of Information Directive, was enacted. DAC 1 has since been amended seven times, with the latest being DAC 8,[14] which was enacted in 2023. In 2021, a Directive was enacted making it mandatory for multinational corporations to disclose tax-related information.[15]

---

[12] Council Directive 77/799/EEC of 19 Dec. 1977 concerning mutual assistance by the competent authorities of the Member States in the field of direct taxation, OJ L 336, 27.12.1977, pp. 15–20.

[13] Council Directive 2011/16/EU of 15 February 2011 on administrative cooperation in the field of taxation and repealing Directive 77/799/EEC, [2011] OJ L 64, pp. 1–12.

[14] Council Directive (EU) 2023/2226 of 17 October 2023 amending Directive 2011/16/EU on administrative cooperation in the field of taxation, [2023] OJ L, 2023/2226.

[15] Directive (EU) 2021/2101 of the European Parliament and of the Council of 24 November 2021 amending Directive 2013/34/EU as regards disclosure of income tax information by certain undertakings and branches, [2021] OJ L 429, pp. 1–14.

Any of directives include in their preambles a commitment to respecting the fundamental rights and principles set out in the Charter and also state that the DAC must comply with the Data Protection Directive or the GDPR. For example, preamble 36 of DAC 7[16] states that 'Any processing of personal data carried out within the framework of Directive 2011/16/EU should continue to comply with Regulation (EU) 2016/679 of the European Parliament and of the Council and Regulation (EU) 2018/1725. Data processing is set out in Directive 2011/16/EU solely with the objective of serving a general public interest, namely the matters of taxation and the purposes of combating tax fraud, tax evasion and tax avoidance, safeguarding tax revenues and promoting fair taxation, which strengthen opportunities for social, political and economic inclusion in Member States. Therefore, in Directive 2011/16/EU, the references to the relevant Union law on data protection should be updated and extended to the rules introduced by this Directive. This is in particular important for the purpose of ensuring legal certainty for data controllers and data processors within the meaning of Regulations (EU) 2016/679 and (EU) No 2018/1725 while ensuring the protection of the rights of data subjects.'

DAC 7, which was issued after the GDPR came into effect, also includes provisions in its text that reflect the GDPR. Article 25, paragraph 1 of DAC 7 states, 'All exchange of information pursuant to this Directive shall be subject to Regulation (EU) 2016/679 of the European Parliament and of the Council. However, Member States shall, for the purposes of the correct application of this Directive, restrict the scope of the obligations and rights provided for in Article 13, Article 14(1) and Article 15, of Regulation (EU) 2016/679, to the extent required in order to safeguard the interests referred to in point (e) of Article 23(1) of that Regulation.'

### *11.3.2 Conflict Between DAC and GDPR*

Information exchange based on tax treaties, can be classified into requested information exchange, spontaneous information exchange, and automatic information exchange. As mentioned above, automatic information exchange is most likely to infringe on the right to personal data protection.[17]

[16] Council Directive (EU) 2021/514 of 22 March 2021 amending Directive 2011/16/EU on administrative cooperation in the field of taxation, [2021] OJ L 104, pp. 1–26.

[17] See also, Kokot and Pistone 2022, p. 407.

The Expert Group on Automatic Exchange of Financial Information[18] established by the European Commission pointed out the following problems with the DAC 2[19] in light of the right to data protection in a report published in 2015;[20]

(a) Principle of proportionality

On many aspects, DAC 2 may be compared with the Data Retention Directive which has recently been declared illegal by the CJEU. DAC 2 must respect the principle of proportionality according to which any data transfer is only allowed in case it is appropriate and not redundant. In its letter of 4 February 2015, the Article 29 Working Party considers that in order not to violate the proportionality principle, it is necessary to demonstrably prove the necessity of the foreseen processing and that the required data are the minimum necessary for attaining the stated purpose and thus avoid an indiscriminate, massive collection and transfer of the data. A legal challenge might arise from the current version of DAC 2 mainly because of the magnitude of the data to be collected and reported and the fact that it does not guarantee taxpayers a permanent access to their data and a mandatory notification in case of breach. DAC 2 must respect the principle of sufficient cause, i.e. the verification of indicia for a non-compliant behavior of taxpayers. In its current version, DAC 2 might be challenged because it does not request the existence of such sufficient cause or indicia of unlawful behavior.

(b) Standards for the protection of data in third countries

There is a risk that the data of account holders transferred to countries outside the EU, where data protection provisions comparable to those in the EU may not exist, may not be properly protected in these countries where the data could be used for purposes other than combating tax evasion. Data protection and confidentiality arrangements may be inadequate in some countries, although there is a provision which provides for non-transfer if countries security does not meet OECD standards.

(c) Not always be relevant

Automatic exchange of information may not always be relevant: for instance, nationals of certain countries may be residents of other countries for political reasons and it may not be reasonable that exchange of information occurs with respect to their data, for safety reasons.

To the best of my knowledge, there have been no court decisions in which the conflict between tax-related information exchange systems or mandatory disclosure systems and data protection systems has been disputed. However, there have

[18] https://taxation-customs.ec.europa.eu/taxation/tax-transparency-cooperation/administrative-co-operation-and-mutual-assistance/commission-expert-group-automatic-exchange-financial-account-information_en last visited 9 August 2025.

[19] Council Directive 2014/107/EU amending Directive 2011/16/EU as regards mandatory automatic exchange of information in the field of taxation, [2014] OJ L 359, pp. 1–29.

[20] European Commission (2015), First Report of the Commission AEFI expert group on the implementation of Directive 2014/107/EU for automatic exchange of financial account information.

been several cases in which the Exchange of Information Directive (DAC 6[21]) and Article 7 of the Charter have been disputed, and in which the question of whether the provision of tax information violates the GDPR has been disputed. I will analyze and consider these cases and attempt to examine the issues raised above.

Furthermore, DAC 6 provides for the introduction of an obligation to report cross-border tax arrangements that qualify as aggressive tax planning to the competent authorities. The recitals to DAC 6 state that, in order to prevent the erosion of the tax base, it is of paramount importance to obtain comprehensive and relevant information on aggressive tax planning arrangements. In particular, recital (8) explains as follows:

> To ensure the proper functioning of the internal market and to prevent loopholes in the proposed framework of rules, the reporting obligation should be placed upon all actors that are usually involved in designing, marketing, organising or managing the implementation of a reportable cross-border transaction or a series of such transactions, as well as those who provide assistance or advice. It should not be ignored either that, in certain cases, the reporting obligation would not be enforceable upon an intermediary due to a legal professional privilege or where there is no intermediary because, for instance, the taxpayer designs and implements a scheme in-house. It would thus be crucial that, in such circumstances, tax authorities do not lose the opportunity to receive information about tax-related arrangements that are potentially linked to aggressive tax planning. It would therefore be necessary to shift the reporting obligation to the taxpayer who benefits from the arrangement in such cases.

Pursuant to Article 1(2) of DAC 6, Article 8ab of the amended DAC 1, entitled "Scope and conditions of mandatory automatic exchange of information on reportable cross-border arrangements," provides as follows:

> 5. Each Member State may take the necessary measures to give intermediaries the right to a waiver from filing information on a reportable cross-border arrangement where the reporting obligation would breach the legal professional privilege under the national law of that Member State. In such circumstances, each Member State shall take the necessary measures to require intermediaries to notify, without delay, any other intermediary or, if there is no such intermediary, the relevant taxpayer of their reporting obligations under paragraph 6.
>
> Intermediaries may only be entitled to a waiver under the first subparagraph to the extent that they operate within the limits of the relevant national laws that define their professions.
>
> 6. Each Member State shall take the necessary measures to require that, where there is no intermediary or the intermediary notifies the relevant taxpayer or another intermediary of the application of a waiver under paragraph 5, the obligation to file information on a reportable cross-border arrangement lie with the other notified intermediary, or, if there is no such intermediary, with the relevant taxpayer.
>
> 9. Each Member State shall take the necessary measures to require that, where there is more than one intermediary, the obligation to file information on the reportable cross-border arrangement lie with all intermediaries involved in the same reportable cross-border arrangement.

[21] Council Directive 2018/822/EU of 25 May 2018 amending Directive 2011/16/EU as regards mandatory automatic exchange of information in the field of taxation in relation to reportable cross-border arrangements, [2018] OJ L 139, pp. 1–13.

> An intermediary shall be exempt from filing the information only to the extent that it has proof, in accordance with national law, that the same information referred to in paragraph 14 has already been filed by another intermediary.

## 11.4 Decisions of the Court of Justice of the European Union

### *11.4.1 Orde van Vlaamse Balies and Others Case*[22]

(a) Facts

Belgium enacted, on 21 June 2013, the Decree on administrative cooperation in the field of taxation in the Flemish Region in order to transpose DAC 1 into domestic law (Belgisch Staatsblad of 26 June 2013, p. 40587; 'the Decree of 21 June 2013'). Following the adoption of DAC 6, the Decree of 21 June 2013 was amended by the Decree of 26 June 2020 amending the Decree of 21 June 2013 with regard to the mandatory automatic exchange of information in the field of taxation on reportable cross-border arrangements (Belgisch Staatsblad of 3 July 2020, p. 49170; 'the Decree of 26 June 2020'). The Decree of 26 June 2020 transposes DAC 6 into domestic law.

Article 11/6 of the Decree of 21 June 2013, as amended, was inserted into that Decree by Article 14 of the Decree of 26 June 2020 and governs the relationship between the legal professional privilege borne by certain intermediaries and the reporting obligation. That provision transposes paragraphs 5 and 6 of Article 8ab of Directive 2011/16, as amended, into domestic law.

Paragraph 1 of Article 11/6 provides as follows:

> When an intermediary is bound by legal professional privilege, he or she is required:
>
> 1° to notify any other intermediary or intermediaries in writing, giving reasons, that he or she is unable to comply with the reporting obligation, as a result of which that reporting obligation automatically rests with the other intermediary or intermediaries;
>
> 2° in the absence of any other intermediary, to notify the relevant taxpayer or taxpayers of their reporting obligation, in writing, giving reasons.
>
> The waiver from the reporting obligation shall take effect only when an intermediary has fulfilled the obligation referred to in paragraph 1.

According to the first subparagraph of Article 11/6(1) of the Decree of 21 June 2013, as amended, where a lawyer is subject to legal professional privilege, the lawyer is required to notify, in writing, the other intermediaries concerned of the reasons why he or she is unable to comply with that obligation. The applicant lawyers brought an action, arguing that it is impossible for lawyers to fulfil the

[22] Case C-694/20, Orde van Vlaamse Balies and Others, ECLI:EU:C:2022:963.

obligation to provide information without infringing the legal professional privilege to which they are subject.

The Belgian Constitutional Court referred the following question to the Court of Justice of the European Union for a preliminary ruling:

> Does Article 1(2) of [Directive 2018/822] infringe the right to a fair trial as guaranteed by Article 47 of the [Charter] and the right to respect for private life as guaranteed by Article 7 of the [Charter], in that the new Article 8ab(5) which it inserted in [Directive 2011/16], provides that, where a Member State takes the necessary measures to give intermediaries the right to waiver from filing information on a reportable cross-border arrangement where the reporting obligation would breach the legal professional privilege under the national law of that Member State, that Member State is obliged to require the intermediaries to notify, without delay, any other intermediary or, if there is no such intermediary, the relevant taxpayer, of their reporting obligations, in so far as the effect of that obligation is to oblige a lawyer acting as an intermediary to share with another intermediary, not being his [or her] client, information which he [or she] obtains in the course of the essential activities of his [or her] profession, namely, representing or defending clients in legal proceedings and giving legal advice, even in the absence of pending legal proceedings?

(b) Decision

> As regards the validity of Article 8ab(5) of amended Directive 2011/16 in the light of Article 7 of the Charter, it is apparent from the case-law of the ECtHR that Article 8(1) ECHR protects the confidentiality of all correspondence between individuals and affords strengthened protection to exchanges between lawyers and their clients (see, to that effect, ECtHR, judgment of 6 December 2012, Michaud v. France, CE:ECHR:2012:1206JUD001232311, §§ 117 and 118). Like that provision, the protection of which covers not only the activity of defence but also legal advice, Article 7 of the Charter necessarily guarantees the secrecy of that legal consultation, both with regard to its content and to its existence. As the ECtHR has pointed out, individuals who consult a lawyer can reasonably expect that their communication is private and confidential (ECtHR, judgment of 9 April 2019, Altay v. Turkey (No 2), CE:ECHR:2019:0409JUD001123609, § 49). Therefore, other than in exceptional situations, those persons must have a legitimate expectation that their lawyer will not disclose to anyone, without their consent, that they are consulting him or her. (para 27)

> The obligation laid down by Article 8ab(5) of amended Directive 2011/16 for a lawyer-intermediary where he or she is, on account of the legal professional privilege by which he or she is bound by national law, exempt from the reporting obligation laid down in Article 8ab(1) to notify without delay other intermediaries who are not his or her clients of their reporting obligations under Article 8ab(6) of that directive, necessarily entails the consequence that those other intermediaries become aware of the identity of the notifying lawyer-intermediary, of his or her assessment that the arrangement at issue is reportable and of his or her having been consulted in connection with the arrangement.
>
> In those circumstances and in so far as those other intermediaries do not necessarily have knowledge of the identity of the lawyer-intermediary and of his or her having been consulted on the reportable cross-border arrangement, the obligation to notify, laid down in Article 8ab(5) of amended Directive 2011/16, entails an interference with the right to respect for communications between lawyers and their clients, guaranteed in Article 7 of the Charter. (paras 29–30)

The Court of Justice of the European Union then examined whether the notifications could be justified.

Paragraph 51 is 'that disclosure also does not appear to be strictly necessary for the pursuit of the objectives of amended Directive 2011/16 of combating aggressive tax planning and preventing the risk of tax avoidance and evasion.'

The Court concluded that 'Article 8ab(5) of amended Directive 2011/16 is invalid in the light of Article 7 of the Charter.'

## 11.4.2 *Peter Puškár Case*[23]

(a) Facts

Peter Puškár filed a lawsuit seeking to prevent his name from appearing on certain tax lists and to have his data removed from those lists and from the Treasury's electronic systems. The Supreme Court of the Slovak Republic referred the case to the Court of Justice of the European Union for a preliminary ruling on the question:

> Whether the right to the protection of personal data under Articles 7 and 8 of the Charter is limited by the fact that personal data are provided to public authorities for the purpose of combating tax evasion, given that the right to the protection of personal data is primarily implemented in the EU through the Data Protection Directive and does not permit Member States to compile lists of personal data for tax administration purposes without the consent of the individuals concerned.

(b) Decision

> In that regard, it must be observed that Article 6(1)(b) of Directive 95/46 requires that personal data be collected for specific, explicit and legitimate purposes. As the Advocate General stated in point 106 of her Opinion, the objective of the processing of personal data is inextricably linked, within the scope of Article 7(e) of Directive 95/46, to the task of the controller. Consequently, the transfer of the task to the latter must clearly include the purpose of the processing. It is also for the referring court to determine whether the establishment of the contested list is necessary for the performance of the tasks carried out in the public interest at issue in the case in the main proceedings, taking account, in particular, of the precise purpose of the establishment of the contested list, the legal effects to which the persons appearing on it and the public nature of that list are subject and whether or not that list is of a public nature. (paras 110–111)

> It appears that an infringement of this kind can be proportionate only if there are sufficient grounds to suspect the person concerned of purportedly acting as a company director of the legal persons associated with him and accordingly undermines the public interest in the collection of taxes and combating tax fraud. (para 114)

> In the light of the foregoing considerations, the answer to the second question is that Article 7(e) Directive 95/46 must be interpreted as not precluding the processing of personal data by the authorities of a Member State for the purpose of collecting tax and combating tax fraud such as that effected by drawing up the contested list in the main proceedings, without the consent of the data subjects, provided that, first, those authorities were invested by the national legislation with tasks carried out in the public interest within

[23] Case C-73/16 Peter Puškár, ECLI:EU:C:2017:725.

> the meaning of that article, that the drawing-up of that list and the inclusion on it of the names of the data subjects in fact be appropriate and necessary for the purpose of attaining the objectives pursued and that there be sufficient indications to assume that the data subjects are rightly included in that list and, second, that all of the conditions for the lawfulness of that processing of personal data imposed by Directive 95/46 be satisfied. (para 117)

### *11.4.3 SIA 'SS' case*[24]

(a) Facts

SIA 'SS' is a Latvian company specializing in online advertising services. SIA 'SS''s website advertisements included vehicles, such as used cars and motorcycles. Pursuant to Article 15(6) of the Latvian Tax and Customs Law,[25] the Latvian tax authorities requested SIA 'SS' to provide advertisers' telephone numbers, vehicle registration numbers published on the advertising website, and information about advertisements published in the car section over a certain period of time in an electronic format that allows for data filtering. SIA 'SS' filed a lawsuit alleging that the request violated the proportionality or data minimization principle set forth in Article 5(1) of the GDPR.

The Latvian National Court of Justice referred the case to the Court of Justice of the European Union for preliminary ruling on whether requests for information by tax authorities seeking disclosure of information containing a significant amount of personal data must comply with the GDPR, particularly Article 5(1).

(b) Decision

> Consequently, any measure adopted under Article 23 of Regulation 2016/679 must, as the EU legislature, moreover, emphasised in recital 41 of that regulation, be clear and precise and its application be foreseeable to persons subject to it. In particular, those persons must be able to identify the circumstances and conditions under which the scope of the rights which that regulation confers on them may be the subject of a restriction. It follows from the foregoing considerations that the tax authorities of a Member State cannot derogate from the provisions of Article 5 of Regulation 2016/679 in the absence of a clear and precise legal basis under EU or national law, whose application is foreseeable to persons subject to it, laying down the circumstances and conditions under which the scope of the obligations and rights provided for in that Article 5 may be restricted. (paras 56–57)

> In that regard, it should be emphasised, in the first place, that Article 5(1)(b) of Regulation 2016/679 provides that personal data are to be collected, inter alia, for specified, explicit and legitimate purposes. First of all, the requirement that the purposes of the processing be specified implies, as can be seen from recital 39 of that regulation, that those purposes must be identified, at the latest, at the time of the collection of the personal data. Next, the purposes of the processing must be explicit, which means that they must be clearly stated. Lastly, those purposes must be legitimate. It is important, consequently, that they ensure lawful processing within the meaning of Article 6(1) of that regulation. (paras 63–66)

[24] Case C-175/20 SIA 'SS', ECLI:EU:C:2022:124.

[25] Article 15(6) of the Likums 'Par nodokļiem un nodevām'.

> …in accordance with Article 5(1)(c) of Regulation 2016/679, personal data are to be adequate, relevant and limited to what is necessary in relation to the purposes for which they are processed. In that regard, it should be recalled that, according to settled case-law, derogations and limitations in relation to the principle of protection of such data must apply only in so far as is strictly necessary. It follows that the controller, including where it acts in connection with a task which it has been charged with carrying out in the public interest, may not proceed, in a general and undifferentiated manner, with the collection of personal data and it must refrain from collecting data which are not strictly necessary in relation to the purposes of the processing. (paras 72–74)

### *11.4.4 Implications from Decisions*

The Court of Justice of the European Union ruled in favor of data subjects (taxpayers) in both determining whether their data protection rights are guaranteed and whether they are limited. It stated that personal data must be collected for 'specified, explicit and legitimate purposes' and that the purpose of processing must be 'identified, clearly and lawful'. In other words, data subjects must be able to foreseeable the purpose. Even when collecting data to combat tax evasion or tax avoidance, the Court required that the precise purpose, its public nature, and the legal consequences for data subjects be taken into consideration, and the principle of proportionality must be respected. An infringement of a data subject's data protection rights will only be considered proportionate if there are sufficient grounds to suspect that the individual is engaging in tax evasion or tax avoidance, thereby prejudicing the public interest in collecting and combating tax evasion. The Court also noted that the recipient of the data must be able to provide sufficient guarantees to effectively eliminate the risk of misuse of the data. Furthermore, consistent with the principle of proportionality, personal data must be adequate, relevant, and limited to what is necessary in light of the purposes for which it is processed. In the SIA 'SS' case, the court ruled that, with regard to big data, 'personal data may not be collected in a general and indiscriminate manner.'

This decision took into account the principles of purpose limitation and data minimization set out in Article 5 of the GDPR (Article 6 of the Data Protection Directive). The three case law cases discussed above provide a positive view that a consistent interpretation of the GDPR can ensure that tax data, as well as non-tax data, can be subject to the right to data protection.[26] Furthermore, the Orde van Vlaamse Balies and Others case made clear that the provision of data may be restricted if it is not strictly necessary to pursue the objectives of the DAC 1 Directive. Under the exchange of information regime and mandatory disclosure regime, only data processing that is clear, legitimate, and proportionate to the purpose will not violate data protection norms. In other words, 'personal data may not be collected in a general and indiscriminate manner.'

---

[26] See also, Tomo 2023, p. 152, p. 162.

## 11.5 Data Transfer and Protection in Tax Matters: Implications for Japan

I now examine the aforementioned issues under the DAC, namely the problem of the principle of proportionality, the adequacy of data protection in third countries outside the EU Member States, and the issue that the exchanged information may be unrelated to cases of tax evasion or tax avoidance.

Regarding the principle of proportionality, as indicated in the earlier case law and Article 5 of the GDPR, data transfers are not permitted unless appropriate measures are taken. The data must pursue a specific, explicit, and legitimate purpose and must be 'adequate, relevant and limited to what is necessary in relation to the purposes for which they are processed.'

With respect to the issue of data protection in third countries, the court has held that 'the recipient of the data must also be able to sufficiently guarantee the effective elimination of risks of data misuse.' In the case of Japan, the Japanese Act on the Protection of Personal Information has been regarded as providing an 'adequate' level of protection under the GDPR framework. As a result, transfers of information from within the EU to Japan are permitted without the need for burdensome additional procedures.

Where the exchanged information is unrelated to cases of tax evasion or tax avoidance—in other words, where it concerns the processing of indiscriminate big data—the court has held that 'the collection of personal data in a general and indiscriminate manner is not permissible.' This issue is also relevant in the context of automatic exchange of information, and if the circumstances of data processing were to be disclosed and challenged, it is conceivable that a decision could be rendered in favor of protecting taxpayers' data-protection rights.

In the case of Japan, the *Administrative Guidelines on Procedures for Information Exchange and Mutual Assistance in Service of Documents under Tax Treaties, etc.* provide that data obtained through information exchange under tax treaties is subject to confidentiality obligations. When responding to disclosure requests, not only must the permissibility of lifting confidentiality under the General Rules for National Taxes and other relevant laws be examined, but the specific provisions of each applicable tax treaty must also be verified.

European political and legal DNA. It is supported by the Treaty on the Functioning of the European Union and the Charter of Fundamental Rights, both of which serve as constitutional foundations within the EU. The case law of the Court of Justice of the EU has likewise consistently acted as a guardian of the fundamental right to the protection of personal data. In the field of taxation as well, it is considered that—save for specific reservations—the data-protection rights of data subjects must be respected in the same manner and at the same level as in other policy areas.[27]

---

[27] For example, the same applies to the transfer of Passenger Name Record (PNR) data for airline passengers.

This paper has clarified the relationship between tax-related information-exchange mechanisms, mandatory disclosure regimes, and the EU data-protection framework through an analysis of the relevant legislative provisions and case law. To the best of the author's knowledge, there has been no case to date in which the DAC and the GDPR have directly come into conflict; however, it has been possible to examine the issue on the basis of cases involving conflicts between the DAC and the right to privacy, as well as cases in which the processing of tax data and the GDPR (or the former Data Protection Directive) constituted the central points of dispute. For the time being, the conclusion reached is that if data processing in the context of automatic exchange of information were to be carried out in a general and indiscriminate manner, such processing would likely be incompatible with the GDPR in order to ensure the protection of taxpayers' data-protection rights. In this regard, except in cases involving tax evasion or tax avoidance, disclosure of information exchanged under these regimes is not easily obtained, and therefore a case that brings this issue before the Court of Justice of the European Union is anticipated.

## References

Kokot, Juliane, and Pistone, Pasquale, Taxpayers in International Law – International Minimum Standards for the Protection of Taxpayers Rights – Oxford 2022, pp. 393-395

OECD (2013), Action Plan on Base Erosion and Profit Shifting, OECD Publishing

Tomo, Alessia, Tax Information, Third Parties and GDPR: Legal Challenges and Hints from the Court of Justice, 32 EC TAX REVIEW 4 (2023), p. 152, p. 162

# Chapter 12
# Cross-Border Transfers of Personal Data Under the Personal Information Protection Act of the Republic of Korea

**Eung Jun Jeon**

## 12.1 Introduction: A Paradigm Shift in Korea's Regulation of Cross-Border Personal Data Transfers

### *12.1.1 From a Consent-Centric Model to a Risk-Based Framework*

The Personal Information Protection Act of the Republic of Korea (hereinafter 'PIPA') has traditionally been regarded as one of the world's most prominent 'consent-centric' regulatory models, establishing the data subject's 'consent' as the core principle for processing personal data. This approach was consistently applied to 'cross-border transfers', where moving personal information across national borders made obtaining explicit and separate consent from the data subject the only viable legal means of transfer. However, the rapid globalisation of the digital economy and the widespread adoption of cloud computing services have necessitated a fundamental reassessment of this rigid regulatory framework.

In response to these contemporary demands, the amended PIPA, which took effect on 15 September 2023, has brought about a significant paradigm shift in the regulation of cross-border transfers. Whilst maintaining the existing consent-based approach, the amended Act introduces a variety of legal bases, such as the performance of a contract with the data subject (only where data processing is outsourced), recognised certifications, and adequacy decisions by the supervisory authority. This marks a transition toward a more flexible and multifaceted 'risk-based' framework. This change reflects a legislative intent to provide predictability and flexibility for

E. J. Jeon (✉)
LIN LLC, Seoul, Korea
e-mail: ejjeon@law-lin.com



H. Miyashita et al. (eds.), *The Evolution of Data Protection Laws in China, Japan, and Korea*, https://doi.org/10.1007/978-981-95-8609-7_12

global business activities whilst effectively controlling the risks of infringing on data subjects' rights that may arise from cross-border transfers.

### *12.1.2 The Amended PIPA in the Global Data Governance Landscape*

This amendment holds significant meaning not only for domestic regulation but also for the global data governance landscape. As one of the few countries to have received an adequacy decision from the European Union (EU) for its level of personal data protection, Korea plays a substantial role in data protection on the international stage. In this context, the attempt to enhance the alignment of PIPA's cross-border transfer framework with global standards like the EU's General Data Protection Regulation (GDPR) is expected to promote the free and secure flow of data between nations and vitalise digital trade. Furthermore, newly introduced powerful enforcement tools, such as the authority to order the suspension of cross-border transfers and the imposition of substantial administrative fines, will function as a substantial safeguard to strengthen the protection of data subjects' rights.

### *12.1.3 Purpose and Structure of This Article*

The primary purpose of this chapter is to examine in depth the new regulatory framework governing cross-border transfers of personal data under the 2023 amendments to the PIPA, with particular attention to its doctrinal structure, practical operation and prospective challenges.

To that end, the article first delineates the scope of the cross-border transfer regime by situating it within the PIPA's rules on extraterritorial application and by identifying its legal foundations in relevant Supreme Court decisions. It then offers a systematic analysis of the five legal bases for cross-border transfers introduced by the amended Act and explores the extent to which the distinction between 'third-party provision' and 'outsourcing of processing' constrains or guides the choice of transfer mechanism.

The article further considers a range of post-transfer control tools aimed at safeguarding data subjects, including obligations to implement appropriate security measures, restrictions on onward transfers and the power of the competent authority to order the suspension of transfers. On that basis, it proceeds to a comparative assessment with the GDPR, with a view to bringing into relief the structural characteristics and limitations of the current PIPA framework.

Finally, drawing on recent enforcement actions involving AliExpress, Kakaopay (& Apple) and Temu, the article analyses how the amended provisions are being applied in practice and offers some reflections on how the emerging geopolitical emphasis on 'data security' in the context of US–China tensions may shape the future direction of Korea's cross-border transfer policy.

## 12.2 Content of the Provisions on Cross-Border Transfer Under PIPA

### *12.2.1 Clarifying the Boundary Between Extraterritorial Application and Cross-Border Transfers*

#### 12.2.1.1 The Core Distinction: Direct Application vs. Cross-Border Transfer Rules

The first step in understanding the legal framework governing the cross-border movement of personal data is to clearly distinguish between PIPA's 'extraterritorial application' and its 'cross-border transfer' rules. Although often used interchangeably, these two concepts are fundamentally different in their legal nature and application requirements.

'Extraterritorial application' concerns whether PIPA directly applies to the personal data processing activities of a business operator located outside the country (hereinafter 'foreign business operator'). In contrast, the 'cross-border transfer' rules (Article 28-8 of the PIPA) are procedural control mechanisms that regulate the act of a data controller in Korea, who is already subject to PIPA, transferring collected and held personal data to a location outside the country.

This distinction is confirmed by the official interpretation of the Personal Information Protection Commission (hereinafter 'PIPC'). The PIPC has clarified that when a foreign business operator 'directly collects' personal data from a data subject in Korea, this act does not constitute a 'cross-border transfer' under PIPA.[1] This is because the foreign business operator becomes subject to the extraterritorial application of PIPA and is thus obligated to directly comply with the general principles of personal data collection and use (e.g., Article 15 of the PIPA), rather than undergoing a separate cross-border transfer procedure. This interpretation follows the same legal structure as the GDPR, which clearly distinguishes between extraterritorial application (Article 3(2) of the GDPR) and cross-border transfers (Chapter V of the GDPR).

For example, if Samsung Electronics, from its headquarters in Korea rather than a local EU subsidiary, directly offers services to and collects personal data from EU users, it becomes subject to the GDPR's extraterritorial application (Article 3(2)).

---

[1] Personal Information Protection Commission (PIPC), 'Guidelines on Applying the Personal Information Protection Act to Foreign Business Operators' (April 2024) 5. "In principle, the PIPA may be applicable where a foreign business operator provides goods or services globally, or processes personal information of Korean Data Subjects or Korean nationals overseas, or processes personal information within the Korean territory."

However, this is not considered a ‘cross-border transfer’ from the EU to Korea. Similarly, when foreign business operators such as AliExpress and Google directly collect personal data from Korean users during membership registration, this act itself is a matter of PIPA’s extraterritorial application, and the cross-border transfer regulations do not apply at this stage. However, if AliExpress then forwards this data to a third-party seller in China, that action constitutes a ‘cross-border transfer’ and is subject to the regulations of Article 28-8. As such, within a single business process, extraterritorial application and cross-border transfer can be relevant at different stages, making it crucial to analyse each step separately for compliance purposes.

#### 12.2.1.2 The Scope of PIPA’s Extraterritorial Application

Under what circumstances, then, does a foreign business operator become subject to the extraterritorial application of PIPA? Unlike Article 3 of the GDPR, PIPA does not have an explicit provision on extraterritorial application. In response, the PIPC, in its ‘ Guidelines on Applying the Personal Information Protection Act to Foreign business operators’ published in April 2024, presented the following three criteria:[2]

(1) Where goods or services are provided to data subjects in the Republic of Korea.
(2) Where data processing activities affect data subjects in the Republic of Korea.
(3) Where the operator has a place of business within the territory of the Republic of Korea.

These criteria appear to be based on widely recognised principles of international law, such as territoriality, and particularly the ‘effects doctrine’, which asserts jurisdiction based on the effects of an extraterritorial act within the domestic territory. However, some academics have criticised the regulation of such a significant jurisdictional issue through a non-binding ‘guideline’ from an administrative agency, rather than through explicit legislation.[3] The argument is that exceptional and critical matters like extraterritorial application should be clearly defined by law to ensure legal stability and predictability.

Despite this debate, the Supreme Court of Korea has already established through precedent the possibility of applying domestic law to foreign business operators. Notably, in the Google case (Supreme Court Decision 2017Da219232, decided on 13 April 2023), the Court ruled that even if a contract between a foreign business operator and a domestic user specifies a foreign law as the governing law and a foreign court as the exclusive jurisdiction, if the contract qualifies as a ‘consumer contract’, the court of the consumer’s habitual residence (the Republic of Korea) has jurisdiction. Furthermore, the application of mandatory provisions of domestic law,

---

[2] Ibid 11.

[3] Nohyoung Park, ‘Concerns Regarding Guidelines on Applying the Personal Information Protection Act to Foreign Business Operators’ (in Korean) (*The Law Times*, 18 May 2024) <https://www.lawtimes.co.kr/opinion/198334> accessed 30 November 2025.

such as the right to access personal data, cannot be excluded. This ruling provides strong judicial legitimacy to the PIPC's criteria for extraterritorial application and clearly demonstrates that foreign business operators substantially targeting the Korean market are obligated to comply with PIPA.

#### 12.2.1.3 Definition of 'Cross-Border Transfer' Under PIPA

Article 28-8(1) of the PIPA defines 'cross-border transfer' as an act by a data controller of providing personal data overseas (including cases where such data is accessed from overseas), outsourcing the processing of personal data overseas, or storing personal data overseas. Key points to note from this definition include:

(a) **Comprehensive Scope**
A cross-border transfer includes not only the physical movement of data to an overseas server but also entrusting processing tasks to a third party abroad (outsourcing of processing) and simply storing data on an overseas cloud server (storage).

(b) **Inclusion of 'Access'**
The phrase 'including cases of being accessed' significantly broadens the scope of cross-border transfers. This means that even if data is stored on a domestic server, the act of an employee of an overseas branch or a foreign partner remotely accessing or viewing that data also constitutes a 'cross-border transfer' subject to regulation. This interpretation is consistent with the approach under the GDPR, where remote access is considered a 'transfer'.

(c) **Transfer by a data controller**
A cross-border transfer must be an act of a data controller. Where it is the data subject who provides personal data directly to a foreign business operator, this does not constitute a cross-border transfer. This interpretation is consistent with the relevant interpretation under the GDPR.[4]

In conclusion, to determine whether PIPA's cross-border transfer regulations apply, one must first confirm whether the data controller is subject to PIPA (including through extraterritorial application) and then sequentially examine whether the processing activity falls under the definition of a 'cross-border transfer' as defined in Article 28-8.

[4] European Data Protection Board (EDPB), 'Guidelines 05/2021 on the Interplay between the Application of Article 3 and the Provisions on International Transfers as per Chapter V of the GDPR' (Version 2.0, 14 February 2023) para 18, example 1. "In addition, this second criterion cannot be considered as fulfilled when there is no controller or processor sending or making the data available (i.e. no 'exporter') to another controller or processor, such as when data are disclosed directly by the data subject to the recipient."

### 12.2.2 The Legal Structure of PIPA Article 28-8: A Multi-Pillar System

The core of the 2023 amended PIPA is the diversified legal bases for cross-border transfers newly established in Article 28-8. Moving away from the previous single-pillar system based on consent, it now offers five legitimate pathways for transfers, which can be chosen according to the diverse situations faced by businesses and the nature of the data processing.

#### 12.2.2.1 Explicit and Separate Consent from the Data Subject (Article 28-8(1)(1))

Consent remains a crucial legal basis for cross-border transfers, but its requirements have been strengthened.

(a) **Principle of 'Separate Consent'**

Consent for a cross-border transfer must be obtained 'separately' and distinctly from the general consent for the collection and use of personal data. This is to ensure that data subjects are clearly aware of the fact that their data is being transferred across borders and the associated risks, allowing them to exercise their right to control. This aims to address the issue of 'consent fatigue' caused by past practices of blanket consent and to restore the substantive value of consent.[5]

(b) **Strengthened Notification Obligations**

Before obtaining consent, the data controller must clearly and easily inform the data subject of the following:

(1) The items of personal information being transferred.
(2) The country to which the personal data is being transferred, and the timing and method of the transfer.
(3) The name of the recipient (in the case of a legal entity, its name and contact information).
(4) The recipient's purpose for using the personal data and the period of retention and use.
(5) The method and procedure for refusing the transfer of personal information, and the effects of such refusal.

The recent enforcement action by the PIPC against AliExpress clearly illustrates the importance of these requirements. AliExpress obtained a blanket 'consent for overseas transfer of personal data' at the membership registration stage. However, this was deemed unlawful because it did not involve providing specific information and

[5] 'Consent fatigue' is used to denote a state in which data subjects, having become habituated to purely formal requests for consent, grow desensitised to the very act of consenting, so that consent effectively loses its substantive meaning.

obtaining consent at the time of purchase, when the information is actually transferred to a specific overseas (China) seller, about who that seller is and to which country the information is being transferred. This case sets an important precedent, establishing that for consent for a cross-border transfer to be valid, it must be obtained at the time the transfer occurs and be based on specific information related to the transfer.

#### 12.2.2.2 Transfer Pursuant to Law or Treaty (Article 28-8(1)(2))

This basis allows for transfers when there are special provisions regarding the cross-border transfer of personal data in Korean law or in a treaty or international agreement to which Korea is a party. Whilst its scope of application is clear, it can only be utilised in very limited cases, such as the exchange of investigative information under the 'Korea-U.S. Agreement on Enhancing Cooperation in Preventing and Combating Crime'. This Agreement provides for automated searches of personal information, including fingerprint data, between Korea and the United States for the prevention and investigation of crimes such as terrorism, and therefore constitutes a 'cross-border transfer of personal information' pursuant to an international treaty.

#### 12.2.2.3 Outsourcing or Storage Necessary for the Conclusion and Performance of a Contract (Article 28-8(1)(3))

This is one of the most noteworthy and practically significant provisions in the amendment. It permits cross-border transfers without consent when 'the outsourcing of processing or storage of personal data is necessary for the conclusion and performance of a contract with the data subject', provided that the relevant information is disclosed in the privacy policy or separately notified to the data subject. It may be inferred that the rationale for exempting cross-border outsourcing of processing and storage of personal data from the requirement to obtain user consent is that such outsourcing or storage is not expected to give rise to any processing of personal data that departs from, or is incompatible with, the original purposes for which the data were collected.[6] Under the GDPR, in the absence of an adequacy decision by the European Commission and appropriate safeguards, a transfer to a third country or an international organisation is permitted, by way of a derogation for specific situations, where the transfer is necessary for the performance of a contract between the data subject and the controller or for the implementation of pre-contractual measures taken at the request of the data subject. In this respect, the PIPA and the GDPR may be said to reflect a markedly different understanding of this provision.

---

[6] Park 2023, pp. 169, 179, n 40.

The biggest issue with this provision is the scope of interpretation for 'necessary for the performance of a contract'. For instance, using a cloud service provider (CSP) with overseas servers to provide the core functions of a service is likely to be recognised as 'necessary'. However, there is considerable room for interpretation regarding whether activities such as backing up data to an overseas data centre for service stability, using overseas SaaS solutions for customer relationship management (CRM) or data analysis, or disaster recovery are 'indispensable' for contract performance. This uncertainty presents a significant compliance risk for businesses. Companies face a difficult choice between interpreting 'necessity' broadly to enjoy the convenience of omitting the consent process or taking a conservative approach and maintaining the cumbersome consent procedures.

#### 12.2.2.4 Certification Recognised by the PIPC (Article 28-8(1)(4))

If the recipient of the personal data has obtained a certification designated and announced by the PIPC, a cross-border transfer is permitted, subject to certain protective measures. Should the PIPC conclude that certifications such as Global CBPR, Europrivacy, and ISO 27001 afford a level of personal data protection substantially equivalent to Korean law, it may issue a public notice designating them as lawful bases for cross-border transfers.[7]

(a) **Domestic Certification**

A representative certification currently recognised under this provision is the domestic 'Information Security Management System-Personal Information (ISMS-P)' certification. However, there appears to be insufficient practical incentive for foreign business operators to obtain Korea's ISMS-P certification.

(b) **Contradiction of Global CBPR**

The Korean government is a founding member of the 'Global Cross-Border Privacy Rules (Global CBPR)' Forum, which originated from APEC and has expanded worldwide. It actively promotes this system to support the overseas expansion of domestic companies. The Global CBPR certification is recognised as a means for cross-border transfers in some countries, such as Japan and Singapore. However, the PIPC has maintained a negative stance on recognising this Global CBPR certification as a means for cross-border transfers under PIPA Article 28-8(1)(4), leading to criticism for a lack of policy consistency.

[7] Choi et al. 2024, p. 432.

#### 12.2.2.5 Adequacy Decision by the PIPC (Article 28-8(1)(5))

This is a system similar to the GDPR's Adequacy Decision, where if the PIPC recognises that the level of personal information protection in a specific country or international organisation is 'substantially equivalent' to that of PIPA, it allows for the free transfer of personal data to that country or international organisation.

Until recently, the PIPC had not yet issued an adequacy decision for any country. Conversely, Korea has received an adequacy decision from the EU. During this process, to reflect the EU's requirements, Korea had to enact 'Supplementary Rules' in the form of a public notice to clarify the interpretation of certain provisions of PIPA. Nonetheless, Korea has not been recognised by the EU as providing an adequate level of protection in the area of credit information.

As of 16 September 2025, the PIPC adopted an adequacy decision in respect of the European Union, recognising that the level of protection of personal data in the EU is essentially equivalent to that under Korean law. As a result, personal data may now be transferred reciprocally between Korea and the EU without the need for additional transfer mechanisms.

### *12.2.3 Key Distinction: Third-Party Provision vs. Outsourcing of Processing*

One of the most critical criteria in selecting a legal basis for a cross-border transfer is whether the transfer constitutes a 'third-party provision' or an 'outsourcing of processing'.

(a) **Third-Party Provision**

This refers to cases where the recipient processes the personal data for its own business and purposes. For example, when AliExpress, acting in its capacity as a sales intermediary, provides a buyer's shipping information to a local seller in China, it is a 'third-party provision' because the seller uses the information for their own delivery operations.[8] In this case, 'separate consent' from the data subject is, in principle, almost the only legitimate pathway for transfer.

(b) **Outsourcing of Processing**

This refers to cases where the recipient (the processor) processes personal data only for the business purposes of the data controller (the entrusting party) and under their direction and supervision. A typical example is a domestic company using a global cloud service like Amazon Web Services (AWS) for data storage and management. In this case, in addition to 'separate consent', a cross-border transfer is also possible based on the 'necessity for the performance of a contract' simply by disclosing it in the privacy policy, which offers greater flexibility to businesses. The PIPC took the view that Temu, a Chinese online

[8] PIPC, Case No 2024-013-192 (24 July 2024).

marketplace, was outsourcing the processing of personal data of data subjects in Korea to foreign business operators for the purpose of delivering to buyers the sellers' goods stored in intermediary warehouses.[9]

As the distinction between these two concepts is a key factor in determining the range of permissible legal bases, businesses should begin their compliance analysis by clearly classifying all cross-border data flows based on this distinction.

### *12.2.4 Ensuring Continuous Protection: Safeguards, Onward Transfers, and Enforcement*

The amended PIPA not only diversifies the legal bases for cross-border transfers but also establishes robust post-transfer control mechanisms to ensure that transferred personal data is protected to a level equivalent to that in Korea.

#### 12.2.4.1 Mandatory Safeguards and Contractual Requirements (Article 28-8(4), (5))

Regardless of the legal basis for a cross-border transfer, data controllers are obligated to implement protective measures as prescribed by the Presidential Decree. According to the enforcement decree, these measures include (1) ensuring the security of personal data, and (2) measures for handling grievances and resolving disputes related to personal data infringements. Data controllers must consult with the recipient on these matters in advance and reflect them in the contract.[10]

Furthermore, Article 28-8(5) prohibits the conclusion of contracts for cross-border transfers that contain provisions violating PIPA. This regulation is intended to preemptively block any attempts to circumvent the application of PIPA through contractual agreements.

Recent enforcement cases against AliExpress and Temu suggest that the PIPC views these provisions as highly important. Both companies were cited for violations for neglecting their duty to manage and supervise overseas sellers or processors and for failing to establish sufficient contractual and technical measures for personal data protection. This implies that the responsibility of the data controller does not end with the lawful transfer of data but extends to continuously managing and supervising the recipient to ensure the secure processing of the data.

However, it has been pointed out that the wording of Article 28-8(4) is somewhat problematic from a legislative technique perspective. The provision requires compliance with the domestic third-party provision regulation (Article 17), which is no

[9] PIPC, Case No 2024-013-193 (14 May 2025).

[10] Enforcement Decree of the PIPA, art 29-10(2).

longer directly applicable to cross-border transfers, potentially causing confusion in the legal framework.[11]

#### 12.2.4.2 Chain of Responsibility: Onward Transfer Regulation (Article 28-11)

The amended PIPA explicitly regulates 'onward transfers', where personal data transferred overseas is subsequently transferred to a third country. According to Article 28-11, when a recipient of personal data transfers that information to a third country, the provisions of Article 28-8 (Cross-Border Transfer) and Article 28-9 (Suspension Order) are applied mutatis mutandis. In this case, the initial 'recipient' assumes the status of a 'data controller' for the onward transfer and must again satisfy the legality requirements for the transfer.

This provision is known to have been one of the key requirements from the EU side during the adequacy decision negotiations and is an important mechanism to ensure that the level of protection for the original data subject is not weakened even if the data moves through multiple countries. The 'Supplementary Rules' enacted by the PIPC for the EU adequacy decision detail the procedures for notifying the original data subject before an onward transfer occurs.

#### 12.2.4.3 The PIPC's New Power: Order to Suspend Cross-Border Transfers (Article 28-9)

One of the most powerful enforcement tools introduced by the amended PIPA is the authority to order the suspension of cross-border transfers. The PIPC may order a data controller to suspend the cross-border transfer of personal data in any of the following cases:

(1) Where the transfer is carried out in violation of the provisions of the PIPA governing cross-border transfers.
(2) Where the recipient of the personal data, or the country to which it is transferred, fails to ensure a level of protection of personal data equivalent to that required under the PIPA, thereby causing, or creating a significant risk of harm to data subjects.

This power is significant in that it goes beyond merely imposing sanctions ex post; it provides the supervisory authority with a dynamic and powerful tool to pre-emptively block data flows where substantial harm to data subjects is anticipated. It thereby evidences a legislative commitment to the substantive protection of data subjects' rights through continuous post-transfer supervision, marking a departure from the previous model centred on prior authorisation.

[11] Park 2023, p. 187.

As will be discussed in more detail below, because the foregoing legal requirements involve an element of discretionary assessment, the PIPC's power to order the suspension of cross-border transfers may, in practice, be exercised in light of considerations of international politics or national security.

## 12.3 Comparative Perspectives and Recent Cases

### *12.3.1 Comparative Perspective: PIPA's Position in the Global Data Transfer Ecosystem*

Although the cross-border transfer framework of the amended PIPA has made significant progress, there are still structural differences and areas for improvement when compared to global standards like the GDPR.

#### 12.3.1.1 Comparison of PIPA and GDPR Frameworks

PIPA's five legal bases share some similarities with the GDPR's cross-border transfer mechanisms, but there are also clear fundamental differences.

(a) **Similarities**

PIPA's 'adequacy decision' (basis 5) is functionally equivalent to the GDPR's 'adequacy decision' (Article 45). Additionally, PIPA's 'consent' (basis 1) and 'necessity for contract performance' (basis 3) play roles similar to the consent and contract performance necessity provisions found in the GDPR's 'Derogations' (Article 49). PIPA's 'certification-based transfer' (basis 4) may be also understood as a certification-based mechanism for cross-border transfers corresponding to Article 46(2)(f) of the GDPR.

(b) **Differences**

While the GDPR takes transfers on the basis of an adequacy decision as the primary rule and, in their absence, regulates cross-border transfers in a hierarchical sequence of appropriate safeguards and, as a last resort, derogations for specific situations, the PIPA lacks an independent legal basis corresponding to 'appropriate safeguards' under Article 46 of the GDPR, which plays the central role in the GDPR's cross-border transfer framework.

Instead, the PIPA sets out five grounds for cross-border transfers in a purely parallel fashion, without any explicit normative hierarchy or value-based differentiation.

#### 12.3.1.2 The Missing Core Mechanisms: Standard Contractual Clauses (SCCs) and Binding Corporate Rules (BCRs)

The most significant structural limitation of PIPA's cross-border transfer framework is the absence of mechanisms like **Standard Contractual Clauses (SCCs)** and **Binding Corporate Rules (BCRs)**, which are based on GDPR Article 46.

(a) **Standard Contractual Clauses (SCCs)**: These are standardised contract clauses pre-approved by the regulatory authority. By entering into this contract, the personal data exporter and importer commit to ensuring a level of protection for the transferred data equivalent to that of the GDPR. SCCs are the most common and practical means of transferring data to most countries that do not have an adequacy decision, used globally.

(b) **Binding Corporate Rules (BCRs)**: These are internal data protection policies established by a multinational corporate group for transferring personal data within the group, which are approved by the supervisory authority. They provide an efficient solution for systematic and repetitive data transfers within the group.

Due to the absence of these mechanisms in PIPA, companies face difficulties when they need to systematically transfer data to countries without an adequacy decision. They must either rely on the ambiguous and rigid 'necessity for contract performance' provision or obtain 'consent', which is impractical for large-scale processing. Compared to the three-tiered structure provided by the GDPR (Tier 1: Adequacy Decision, Tier 2: Appropriate Safeguards like SCCs/BCRs, Tier 3: Derogations like consent/contract), PIPA is missing the most widely used 'middle ground' of Tier 2.

Fortunately, the PIPC is aware of this limitation and has indicated that it is considering the introduction of a Korean version of SCCs in the future. If Korean SCCs are introduced, it would be a significant step forward, filling the largest gap in the current system and dramatically improving global alignment (Table 12.1).

### *12.3.2 Regulatory Enforcement: Recent Enforcement Cases and Future Outlook*

The effectiveness of the amended PIPA ultimately depends on the enforcement will and capacity of the regulatory authority. Since the law's implementation, the PIPC has taken strong enforcement actions against global platform companies, clearly demonstrating that the new regulatory framework is not merely a declaration.

**Table 12.1** Comparison between the PIPA and the GDPR

| Transfer mechanism category | PIPA (Art. 28-8) | GDPR (Chapter V) | Key differences and analysis |
|---|---|---|---|
| Equivalency-based | **Adequacy Decision (Art. 28-8(5)):** PIPC recognises a country's protection level as equivalent. | **Adequacy Decision (Art. 45):** European Commission recognises a country's protection level as adequate. | Functionally identical. At present, Korea and the European Union have granted each other adequacy status. |
| Contractual safeguards | **(Not explicitly provided as a standalone basis)** | **Standard Contractual Clauses (SCCs) (Art. 46):** Model contracts approved by the Commission. | **Major gap in PIPA.** The most common transfer tool globally. The PIPC is considering its introduction. |
| Intra-group rules | **(Not specified)** | **Binding Corporate Rules (BCRs) (Art. 47):** Rules approved by a supervisory authority for transfers within a multinational corporate group. | **Major gap in PIPA.** An essential tool for multinational corporations. |
| Certification-based | **PIPC-Recognised Certification (Art. 28-8 (4)):** e.g., ISMS-P. The recipient must obtain the certification. | **Approved Certification Mechanisms (Art. 46):** Must be combined with binding commitments. | PIPA's approach is more direct. However, its reluctance to recognise international standards like Global CBPR limits its utility. |
| Situational exceptions | **Explicit Consent (Art. 28-8(1)):** Obtained after providing specific information on the cross-border transfer | **Explicit Consent (Art. 49):** A derogation for non-repetitive transfers. | PIPA treats consent as a primary basis, whereas GDPR considers it a last-resort derogation, showing a philosophical difference. |
| | **Necessity for Contract Performance (Art. 28-8(3)):** Limited to outsourcing of processing and storage for contract performance. | **Necessity for Contract Performance (Art. 49):** A derogation for transfers necessary for contract performance. | PIPA is limited to outsourcing/storage but allows systematic transfers via privacy policy disclosure. GDPR is broader but a limited derogation. The ambiguity of 'necessity' under the PIPA is a key issue. |

#### 12.3.2.1 Testing the New Regulations: Analysis of Enforcement Cases

The sanctions against major e-commerce and payment platforms have set important precedents for the interpretation and application of the amended law.

The case against AliExpress (run by Alibaba.com Singapore E-Commerce Private Limited), decided in July 2024, serves as a critical example.[12] The company was found to be in violation of PIPA for failing to properly notify users about the transfer of their personal data to overseas sellers and for not implementing adequate protective measures. The core of the violation was AliExpress's reliance on a blanket consent obtained during membership registration, rather than specifically notifying and obtaining consent at the point of purchase when data was actually transferred to sellers in China. As a result, the PIPC imposed a significant administrative fine of KRW 1.978 billion (approximately USD 1.43 million). This landmark decision established a crucial precedent: consent for cross-border transfers must be contemporaneous and specific to the actual transfer, rendering broad, prior consent invalid.

Similarly, the enforcement action against Temu in May 2025 highlighted violations related to the outsourcing of data processing.[13] Temu was found to have improperly handled its outsourcing practices and failed to implement protective measures and supervision as required by PIPA. The company did not properly disclose in its privacy policy the fact that personal data processing was being outsourced to and stored by overseas entities in countries like Japan, Singapore, and China. Consequently, the PIPC levied an administrative fine of KRW 1.369 billion (approximately USD 980,000).

Another landmark enforcement action involved a complex data transfer arrangement between Kakao Pay, Apple, and Alipay, resulting in significant sanctions in January 2025.[14] The PIPC found that Kakao Pay had unlawfully transferred the personal data of approximately 40 million users to Alipay without obtaining the necessary separate consent for a cross-border transfer, a violation of PIPA Article 28-8. This transfer, which occurred multiple times and involved 24 categories of data including sensitive financial information, was for the purpose of generating 'Non-Sufficient Funds' (NSF) scores for Apple's payment services. Critically, the data of all Kakao Pay users was transferred, not just those who used Apple's services. Apple was sanctioned for its role in this scheme, specifically for failing to notify users that it was entrusting their personal data processing to Alipay for the NSF score calculation. This lack of transparency in its privacy policy regarding the outsourcing arrangement and the subsequent cross-border transfer was also deemed a violation of PIPA. Consequently, the PIPC imposed a substantial fine of KRW 5.97 billion on Kakao Pay and KRW 2.4 billion on Apple, along with corrective orders. Alipay, as the recipient and processor of the unlawfully transferred data,

[12] PIPC, Case No 2024-013-192 (24 July 2024).

[13] PIPC, Case No 2024-013-193 (14 May 2025).

[14] PIPC, Case No 2025-001-002 (22 January 2025).

was ordered to destroy the NSF score model it had built. This case further solidifies the PIPC's stance on the necessity of explicit, granular consent for cross-border transfers and underscores the accountability of all parties involved in a data processing chain.

A representative case concerning AI development and services is the PIPC's investigation into DeepSeek.[15] PIPC conducted an ex ante inspection of Hangzhou DeepSeek Artificial Intelligence Co., Ltd. following privacy concerns raised immediately after the launch of its AI service in Korea in January 2025. The PIPC found that DeepSeek's original privacy policy was available only in Chinese and English, omitted core items required under the PIPA (such as destruction procedures, security measures and the CPO's contact details), and referred broadly to the collection of keystroke patterns, although the company later explained that such data were not in fact collected and submitted a revised Korean-language policy including a Korea-specific jurisdiction clause. The inspection further revealed that DeepSeek had transferred personal data, including user prompts entered into the AI service, to multiple entities in China and the United States (notably Beijing Volcano Engine Technology Co., Ltd., an affiliate of Bytedance), for purposes such as service improvement and security, without obtaining data subjects' consent to cross-border transfers or properly disclosing such transfers in its privacy policy. In response to the PIPC's findings, DeepSeek amended its Korean privacy policy to include the statutory elements on cross-border entrustment, and blocked any new transfers of user prompts to Volcano Engine as of 10 April 2025.

The PIPC also confirmed that user prompts were being used for AI development and training without a clear legal basis or an opt-out mechanism, and required DeepSeek to implement an opt-out function and to comply with the 'enhanced protective measures' for AI services previously recommended by the PIPC, including the exclusion of URLs containing Korean identification numbers from training data and clearer notice of the purposes and use of user-input data. Additional issues were identified regarding the absence of effective age-verification procedures despite a stated policy of not collecting the data of children under 14, and certain security vulnerabilities in development-server access and directory listing, which DeepSeek has since rectified.

On the basis of these findings, the PIPC issued corrective recommendations that DeepSeek (1) secure a lawful basis for any cross-border transfers and immediately destroy user prompts already transferred unnecessarily to Volcano Engine, (2) publish and maintain a compliant Korean-language privacy policy, and (3) enhance transparency and security across its processing systems, including verification and appropriate handling of any children's data and the designation of a domestic agent. In this case, it is noteworthy that, taking into account the nascent state of the AI governance framework, the PIPC refrained from imposing strong corrective measures such as administrative fines and instead issued corrective recommendations in the form of administrative guidance.

[15] PIPC, Case No 2025-009-026 (23 April 2025).

These cases provide several important insights into the PIPC's enforcement stance. First, the PIPC demands 'substantive consent', where the data subject can genuinely understand and exercise control, rather than a mere formal consent procedure. Second, the responsibility of the data controller extends across borders, emphasising the duty of active management and supervision over overseas processors and third parties. Third, it shows a shift in the enforcement paradigm from a focus on criminal penalties to economic sanctions, by actively utilising the powerful administrative fine system, which can impose fines of up to 3% of the relevant turnover for violations.

#### 12.3.2.2 Geopolitical Variable: The Rise of 'Data Security'

Another important axis in recent international data governance discussions is the shift in focus from traditional 'privacy' to 'data security'. This change has been particularly accelerated by the technological rivalry between the United States and China.

The United States has issued an executive order prohibiting the transfer of sensitive personal information to 'countries of concern' and has restricted the use of Chinese-affiliated platforms like TikTok, citing data breach risks. These measures, which control data flows under the pretext of national security, show that data is now recognised not just as an economic asset or an object of individual rights, but as a strategic asset directly linked to national security.

This geopolitical trend could significantly influence Korea's future cross-border transfer policies. Although the authority to order the suspension of cross-border transfers under PIPA (Article 28-9) is currently primarily triggered by the infringement of data subjects' rights, the possibility that it could be used to halt data transfers to a specific country based on national security concerns in the future cannot be ruled out. This could introduce a new layer of complexity for businesses, requiring them to consider not only the personal data protection laws of the recipient country but also geopolitical risks when reviewing their cross-border transfer compliance.

## 12.4 Conclusion

The 2023 amendments to the Personal Information Protection Act (PIPA) have reconfigured Korea's regime on cross-border transfers of personal data in a manner that is both structurally and normatively significant. What had long operated as a quintessentially consent-centric system has been transformed into a multi-pillar framework centred on Article 28-8, which recognises five distinct legal bases for transfers. This change is not exhausted by the mere multiplication of legal grounds. It reflects a broader movement away from a formalistic reliance on separate consent as a universal solution, toward a risk-oriented architecture that seeks to accommodate the complexity of contemporary data flows while upholding a high level of protection for data subjects' rights.

One of the most important achievements of this new framework lies in the conceptual clarification it brings to the relationship between PIPA's extraterritorial application and its cross-border transfer rules. By distinguishing between situations in which foreign business operators are directly subject to PIPA because they target or affect data subjects in Korea, and situations in which a Korean controller exports personal data abroad, the amended regime prevents the collapse of two distinct legal questions into a single, amorphous notion of 'overseas data handling'. The articulation of extraterritorial reach through the PIPC guidelines, read together with Supreme Court case law such as the Google decision, confirms that foreign operators substantially engaging with the Korean market cannot evade domestic obligations merely by relying on choice-of-law clauses or offshore infrastructure. At the same time, Article 28-8 is reserved for acts of transfer by controllers subject to PIPA, whether by provision, outsourcing or storage, including cases of remote access. This layered structure aligns PIPA more closely with the analytical model of the GDPR, which separates the territorial scope of application from the specific regime governing transfers to third countries.

The diversification of transfer bases in Article 28-8(1) is another central feature of the reform. Explicit and separate consent remains an indispensable element of the system, but it is now embedded within a broader set of options that include transfers pursuant to law or treaty, transfers necessary for the conclusion and performance of contracts in outsourcing and storage contexts, certification-based transfers, and transfers to jurisdictions benefiting from a PIPC adequacy decision. This multiplicity responds to the functional demands of a digital economy in which cloud computing, global logistics and cross-border service provision are the norm rather than the exception. It also mitigates, to some degree, the phenomenon of 'consent fatigue: the formalisation of consent' by reserving consent for situations in which data subjects can make a genuinely informed and contextual decision, rather than treating it as a catch-all justification for every form of international data movement.

The regulatory weight attached to the distinction between third-party provision and outsourcing of processing illustrates how the new framework seeks to connect legal categories with actual risk profiles. Where personal data are transferred to an independent foreign entity that determines its own purposes and means of processing, the law generally insists on explicit, transaction-specific consent; the AliExpress decision makes plain that blanket consent obtained at registration cannot substitute for informed consent given at the point of transfer to an identifiable foreign recipient. Where the recipient operates as a processor acting solely on behalf of the data controller, as in the Temu case, the regime allows reliance on the 'necessity for contract performance' ground, provided that the outsourcing is transparent and appropriately safeguarded. This differentiation reflects an underlying assumption that transfers outside the original controller's sphere of influence raise qualitatively different risks for data subjects than intra-ecosystem outsourcing, and that the allocation of legal bases should track this difference.

Post-transfer control mechanisms introduced or reinforced by the amendments ensure that the protection of personal data does not evaporate once the data have left Korean territory. Mandatory safeguards under Article 28-8(4), contractual requirements that prohibit attempts to contract out of PIPA, and an explicit chain-of-responsibility model for onward transfers under Article 28-11 all operate to extend the protective horizon of the statute beyond national borders. The insistence that an overseas recipient assuming the role of a further exporter must itself satisfy the conditions of Article 28-8, and remains subject to suspension orders under Article 28-9, is especially noteworthy. This approach was crucial for securing an EU adequacy decision for Korea and positions PIPA as a regime that aspires to maintain an equivalent level of protection along the entire trajectory of cross-border processing, rather than only at the initial point of export.

The empowerment of the Personal Information Protection Commission (PIPC) to order the suspension of cross-border transfers under Article 28-9 marks a decisive strengthening of supervisory capacity. The authority to halt data flows where there is a violation of the transfer provisions, or where the recipient or destination state fails to ensure an equivalent level of protection, enables the PIPC to act not merely as an ex post sanctioning body but as a forward-looking regulator capable of intervening before serious harm materialises. Combined with the enhanced administrative fine regime, which permits the imposition of significant turnover-based penalties, this power renders the amended PIPA a robust instrument of governance. The enforcement actions against AliExpress, Temu and Kakao Pay/Apple/Alipay demonstrate that the PIPC is prepared to deploy these tools assertively, demanding substantive consent, meaningful transparency and active oversight of overseas processors and partners.

From a comparative perspective, the amended PIPA exhibits clear elements of convergence with the GDPR, particularly through the introduction of an adequacy mechanism and a certification-based transfer ground that echoes Article 46(2)(f) of the GDPR. At the same time, structural differences remain pronounced. The GDPR's cross-border transfer regime is organised around a hierarchy: adequacy as the preferred route, appropriate safeguards such as Standard Contractual Clauses (SCCs) and Binding Corporate Rules (BCRs) as the general fallback, and derogations for exceptional situations. PIPA, by contrast, lists its five transfer bases in a formally parallel fashion and does not yet provide a fully developed safeguards tier analogous to SCCs and BCRs. This absence creates a notable gap in situations where adequacy is unavailable and consent or contract necessity are ill-suited to sustained, large-scale transfers. The PIPC's declared intention to introduce a Korean version of SCCs is therefore not merely a technical adjustment but a necessary step towards completing the architecture of the system and enhancing its compatibility with the dominant global model.

The broader geopolitical environment in which these legal developments unfold is also relevant. As cross-border data flows increasingly intersect with discourses of data security and national security, there is a growing risk that privacy law will be drawn into strategic competition and security confrontation. The possibility that suspension powers under Article 28-9 might, in the future, be invoked in contexts framed as security-sensitive, for example with respect to transfers to particular jurisdictions, cannot be dismissed. Such a trajectory would raise difficult questions about how to preserve the autonomy of data protection law as a rights-based discipline while responding to legitimate state interests in protecting critical information infrastructures and preventing misuse of personal data at scale.

Against this backdrop, the amended PIPA can be understood as both an accomplishment and a work in progress. It succeeds in moving Korean law beyond an over-reliance on consent, articulating a richer set of transfer bases, clarifying foundational concepts, and equipping the supervisory authority with meaningful tools to oversee and, where necessary, to interrupt risky data flows. At the same time, the remaining gaps—most notably the lack of codified SCC- or BCR-like mechanisms, the absence of an explicit normative hierarchy among transfer grounds, and the interpretive uncertainty surrounding 'necessity' for contract performance—point to the need for further legislative and regulatory refinement.

Future reform agendas would therefore benefit from focusing on three broad directions. One is the development of a comprehensive safeguards layer that can support routine transfers to non-adequate countries without resorting to consent or stretching contract-based necessity beyond its natural limits. Another is the provision of more detailed statutory or regulatory guidance on key distinctions, including the line between third-party provision and outsourcing, and on the scope of permissible reliance on privacy policies as vehicles for legitimising systematic outsourcing transfers. A further direction concerns the articulation of principled criteria for the use of suspension powers in an era where data protection and data security are increasingly intertwined.

## References

Kyungjin Choi and others, *Data Protection Law* (in Korean) (Pakyoungsa 2024) 432

Nohyoung Park, 'Analysis of the Provisions on Cross-Border Transfer of Personal Data under the Amended Personal Information Protection Act: With Reference to the GDPR' (in Korean) (2023) 109 Korea University Law Review 169, 179 n 40

The manufacturer's authorised representative in the EU is Springer Nature Customer Service Centre GmbH, Europaplatz 3, 69115 Heidelberg, Germany. If you have any concerns regarding our products, please contact ProductSafety@springernature.com

Printed and bound by CPI Group (UK) Ltd, Croydon, CR0 4YY
22/10/2026
02236369-0004